This book is dedicated to
my grandchildren:

Ellie and Anna.

Matthew and Amy.

Jacob and Martha.

In the hope that they may get as much pleasure
from the countryside as I have always done.

Published by Glendale Studio

First Printed in 2012

SET IN TIMES NEW ROMAN AND
PRINTED BY HART & CLOUGH
AT EZRA HOUSE, WEST 26 BUSINESS PARK,
CLECKHEATON, BRADFORD, BD19 4TQ

www.glendalestudio.co.uk

With A Pencil In My Rucksack.

BY

GEOFF COWTON

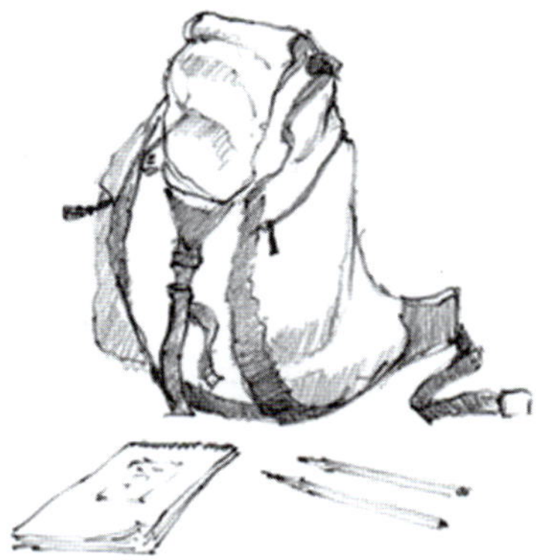

PUBLISHED BY

GLENDALE STUDIO

Introduction

Today, when many people find release and rejuvenation by taking to the hills for their holidays, numerous books have been written with advice for hill walkers. These usually detail all the things you should carry in your rucksack - compass, whistle, food, drinks, warm clothing, water-proof clothing, maps, plan of your route and first aid equipment. I often wonder, when does this become counter productive? When does all this weight you are carrying sap your energy to the point where it becomes dangerous? Much as all this equipment is useful, one thing is missing. No one mentions a pencil and a sketch book.

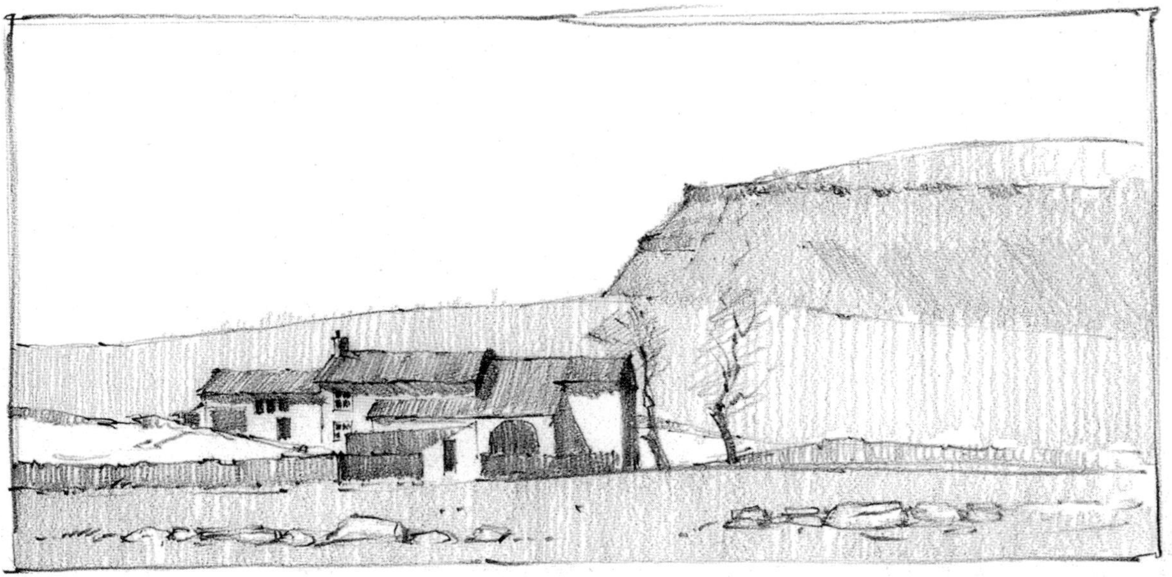

Dalehead, and Penyghent

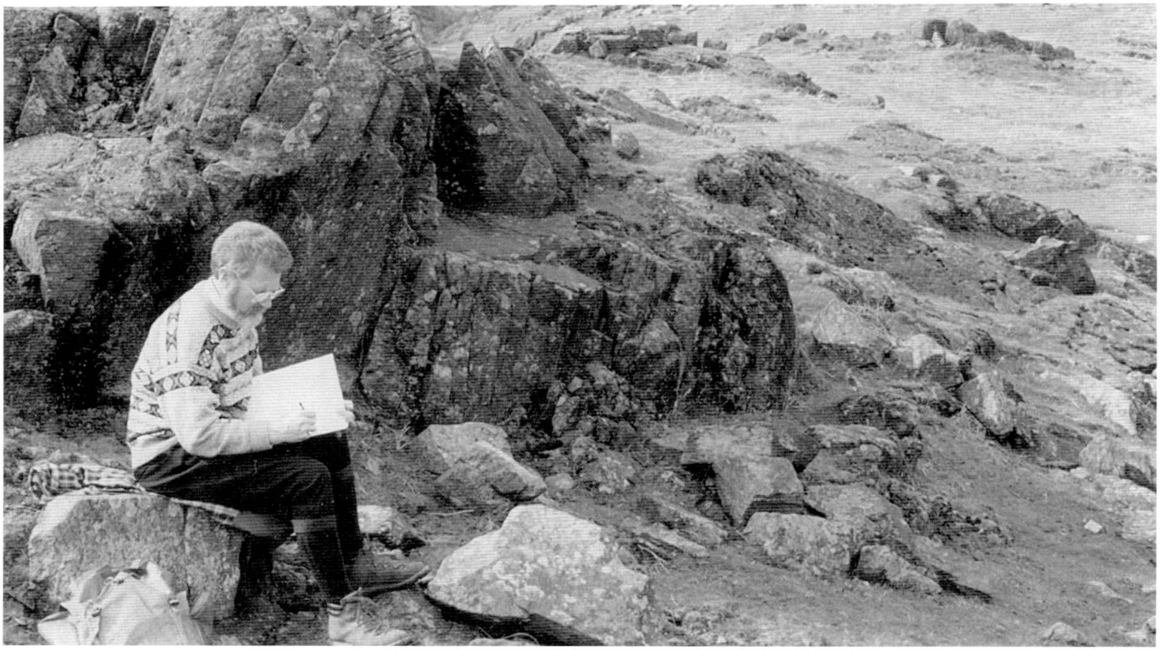

I began carrying a pencil and sketch book when I was a teenager and sixty years later I am still doing it. True, I also carry a camera (drawing on wet paper is not possible and it has been known to rain in the Lake District!) which is useful but can also be a stumbling block. The camera can record everything no matter what the weather is doing but it is essential to remember that what you have recorded must be regarded simply as information from which you are going to "make" a painting. It is not an end in itself. It is there to help you remember what it was like in the small instant of time when you pressed the shutter. The danger when you sit at the drawing board, is to find yourself making a faithful copy of the photograph. In the words of Ralph Thompson, "The camera must be kept as a valuable tool, but as a servant - never a master."

Whilst the camera is useful as a recorder of information, there is nothing quite so satisfying as using the simplest and most basic of equipment - the pencil and the sketch book. Making your drawing involves a degree of concentration not needed when taking a photograph. So many things need your attention - the relative size of things; the intricate shapes of landscape; the play of light and shade; the movement of clouds; wind in the trees and should the weather be bad, some indication of driving rain. All these things occupy your brain and give great satisfaction when all goes well and total despair when all goes badly. Although I draw very quickly (this is not boasting, it is simply a statement of fact) this is because I discovered long ago, how quickly the weather can change. It is best to get things down before the rain comes. If I should be walking with a companion I am also conscious that they must be getting cold and bored waiting for me to complete my sketch and notes. If the purpose of the walk was to spend much time making sketches, then I would prefer to walk alone.

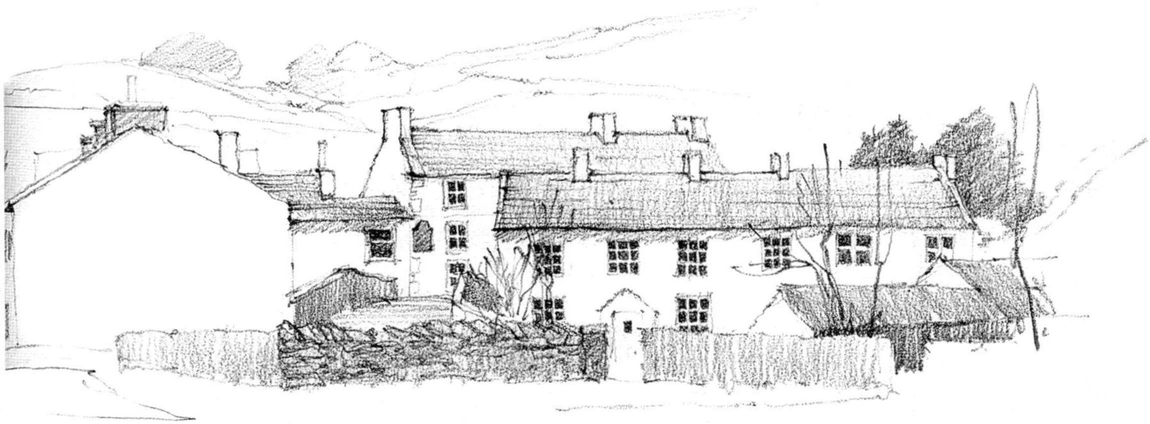

Horton-in-Ribblesdale

Many people regard those who walk the hills unaccompanied as being rather foolhardy. An accident waiting to happen. However, over the last sixty years, I have walked many miles solo and have found it very rewarding. It maybe that I am very cautious and do not take undue risks, but I have never felt the hills as being hostile or threatening.

When walking alone, nothing disturbs your thoughts. Nothing interrupts your quiet contemplation. No one gets bored whilst you watch wildlife, make a sketch or take a photograph. If you make a mistake in navigation you can blame nobody but yourself. There is also a great feeling of satisfaction in completing a new walk with only the map as your companion. It may appear to others that I am really antisocial! This is not the case. I have spent many happy days in the company of other walkers, especially my friend JD who at a time when I thought my walking days were over, came with me until my confidence was restored. Now many years later when, sadly the number of miles I can walk has decreased, my friend Rod is quite prepared to match my steady pace. Walking with friends or alone is really a matter of contrasts as is so much in life. You can only properly appreciate being warm if at some time you have experienced being cold. You can only really appreciate good health if at sometime you have been ill. You can really only appreciate how wonderful is the work of the great painters when you contrast it with your own efforts. Sometimes it is a blessing to have a friend to walk with and sometimes an equal blessing to walk alone.

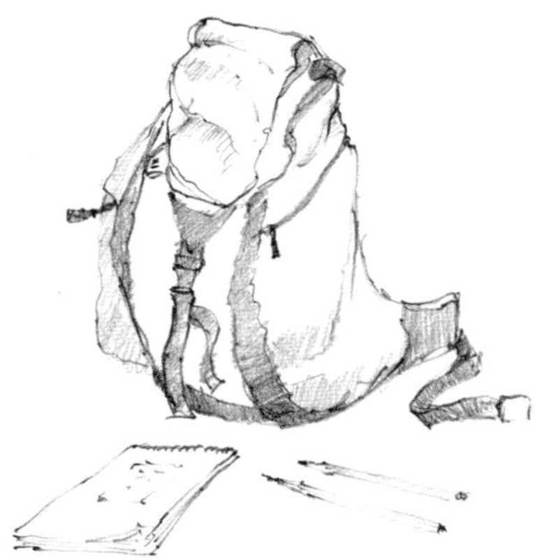

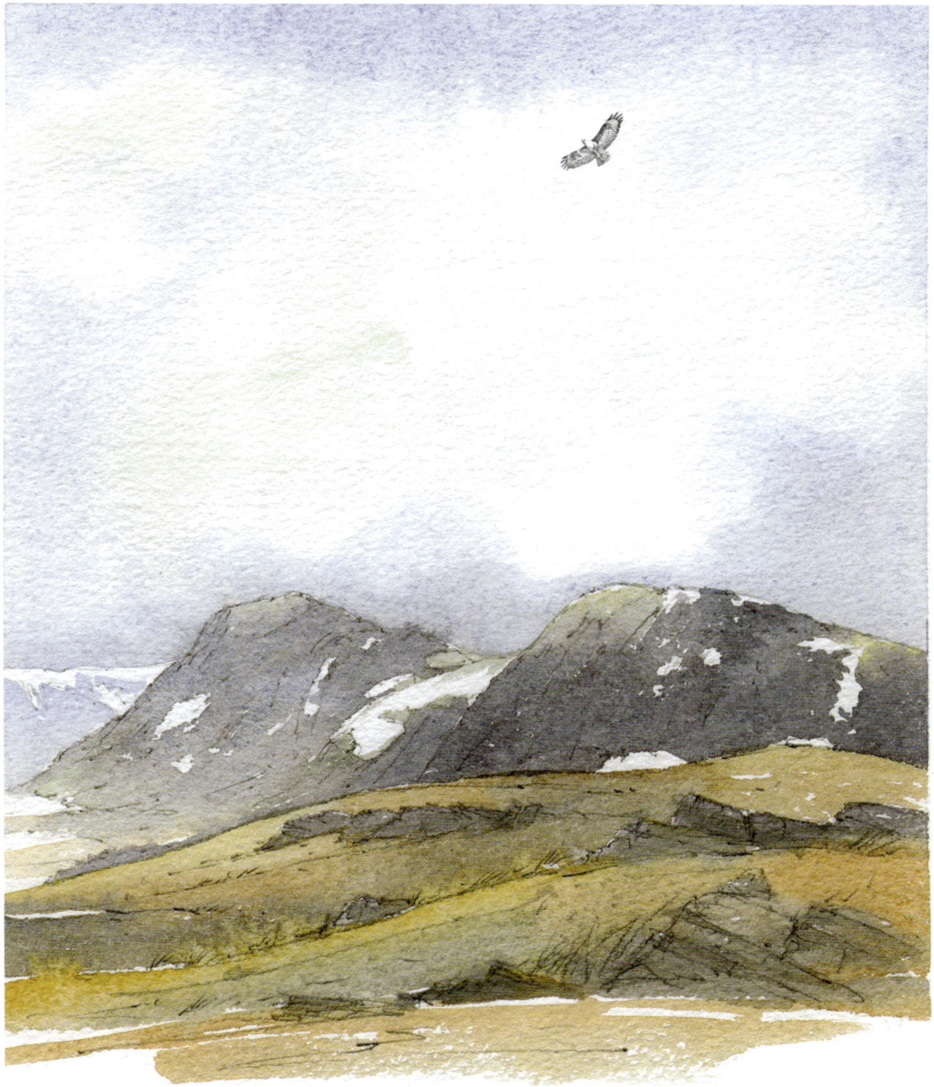

Only the mountain,
The mewing call of the circling Buzzard,
And me------.

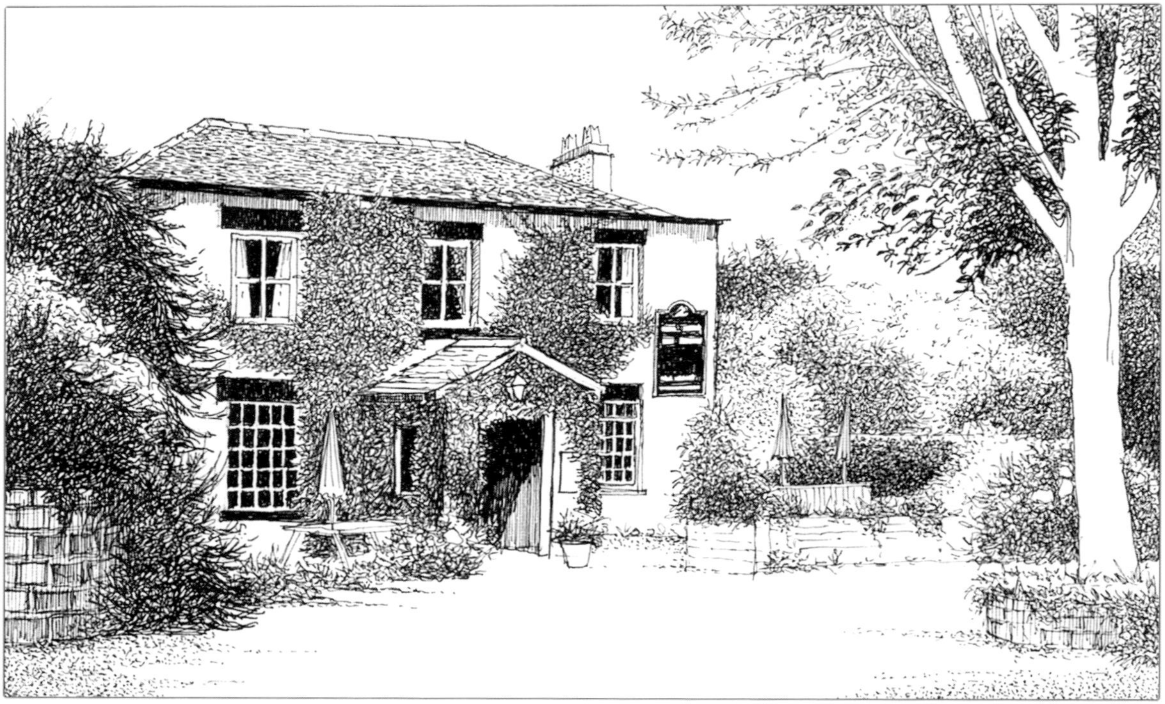

The Hambleton Inn

The majority of pencil drawings in this book were not done as an end in themselves, but as drawings which could later (sometimes much later) become paintings. However, when doing a commission, you have to do what the customer requires. In this case accurate black & white drawings which would reproduce easily. These were to be used by a publishing company to illustrate a series of books called "Pub Walks". The drawings were done from photographs supplied by the publisher, using a Staedtler technical drawing pen with a stylus of 0.13mm.

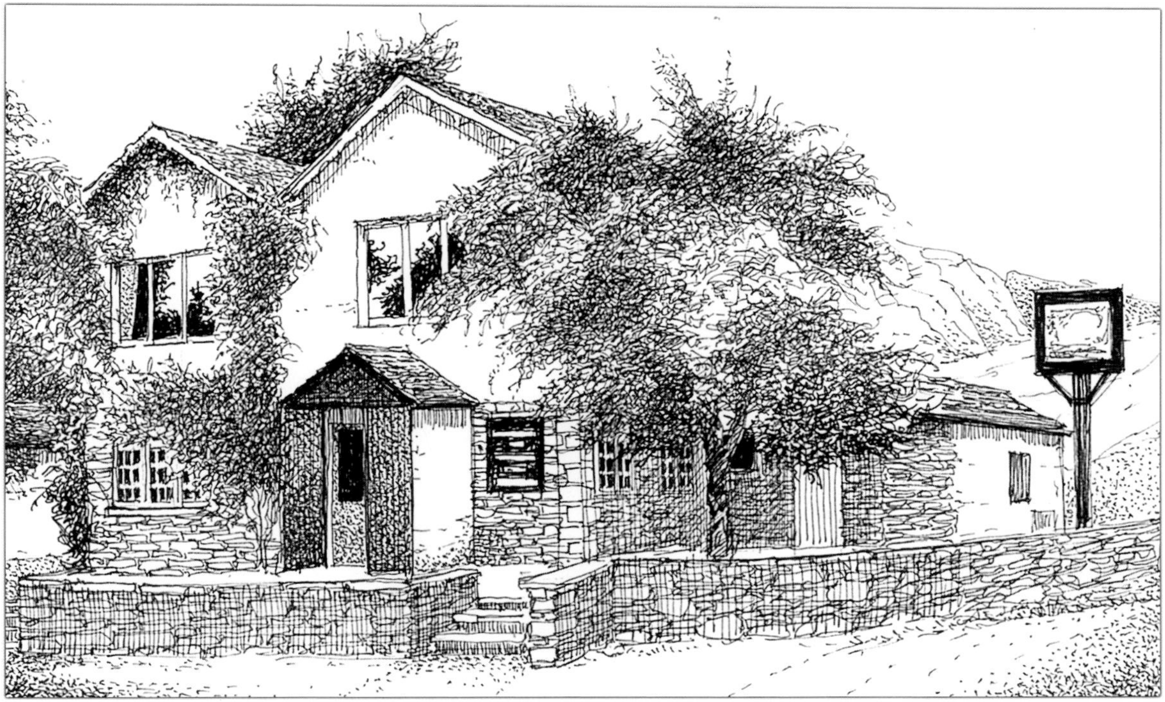

Wainright Inn

This fine detailed work was a great strain on eyes and fingers, I could only complete one drawing per day. After many hours of drawing, I suddenly realised what a ridiculous thing I had been asked to do. I phoned the girl at the publishers to make this point. She didn't understand, so I explained "All the pubs you have asked me to draw are white painted buildings and I am drawing them with a black pen".

Life is never easy!

When writing a book, it always pays to have some idea
of where you are going. As an old Yorkshireman once said :-

" Tha must allus av a plan - even if it's nobbut a bad un!"

(For those people not from Yorkshire you
may need the services of a translator)

So my plan for this book was quite simple.
Look at all the old sketch books, sort the drawings out
into seasons of the year and let that be the plan for the book.

Simple!

Spring

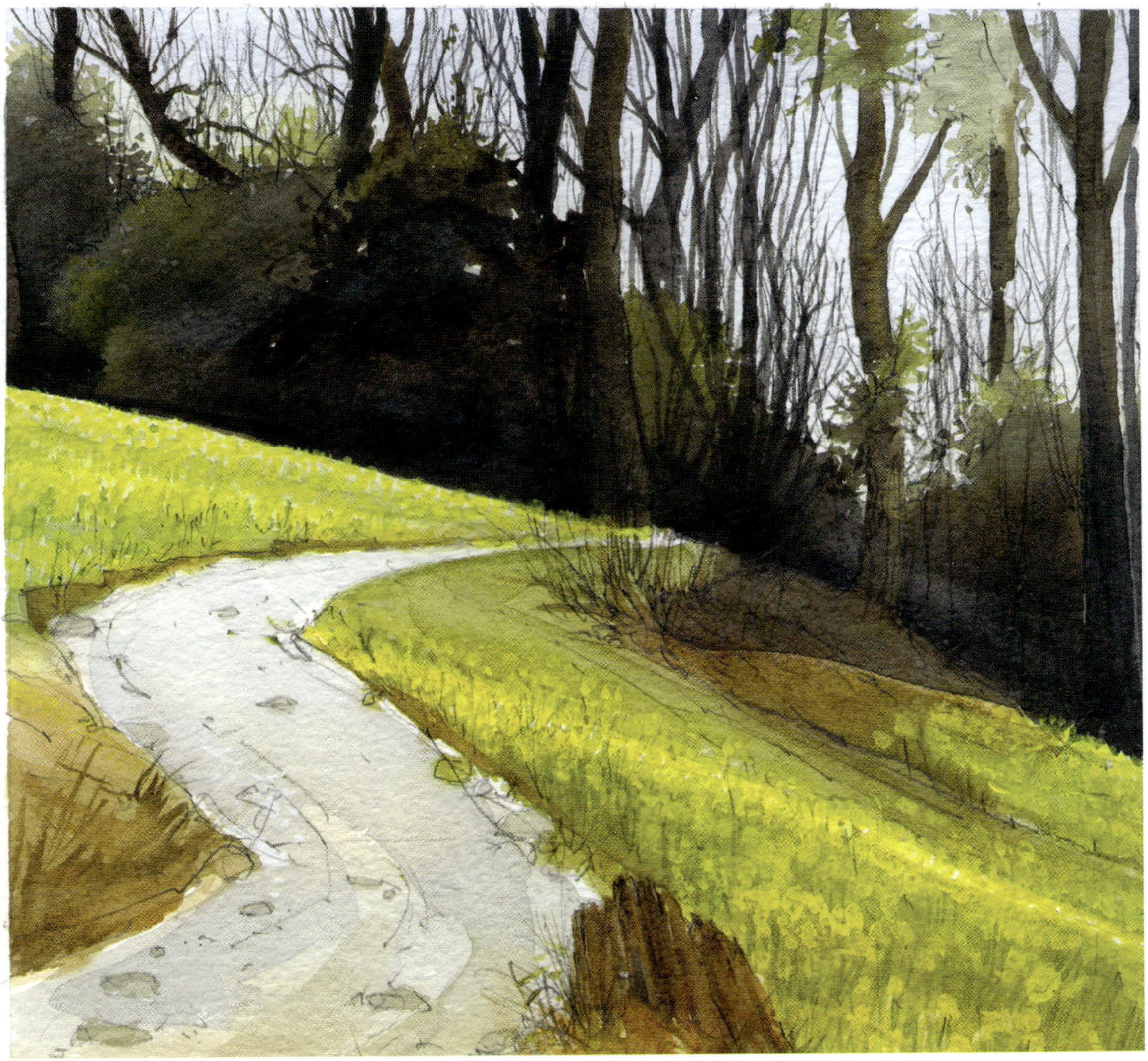

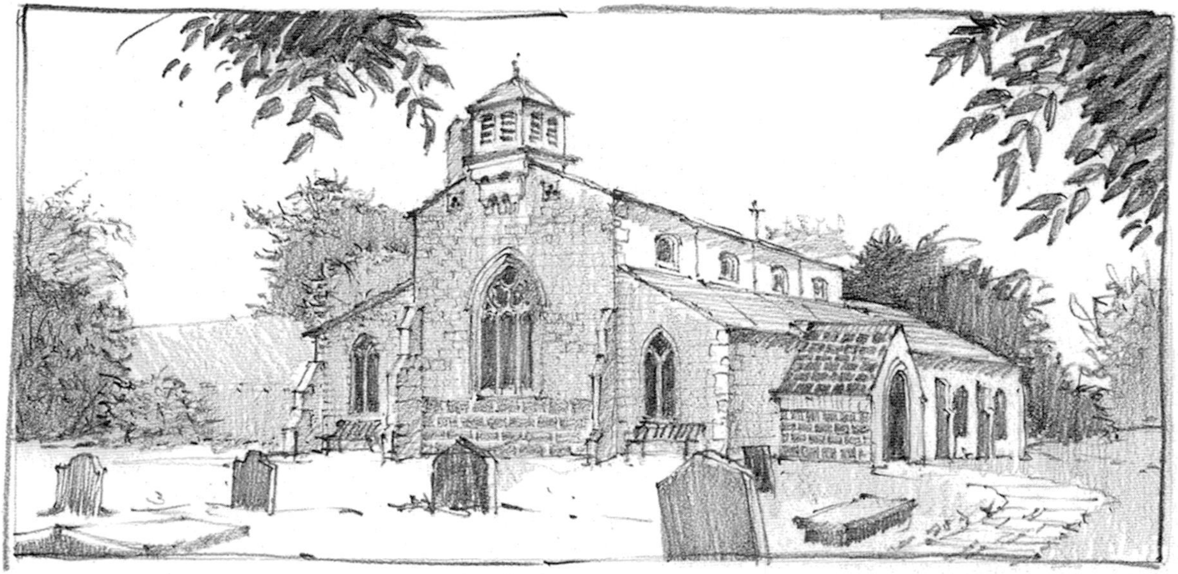

St. Michael and all Angels

Looking every bit it's 800 years of age, the Church of St. Michael and all Angels stands beside the River Wharfe at Linton Falls. It sits quietly in this spot surrounded by those who have worshipped there over all those years. If you enter the church you will find on the wall to the right, a list of all the incumbents from 1200 A.D.

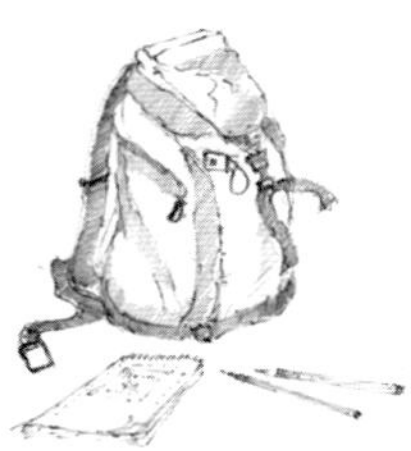

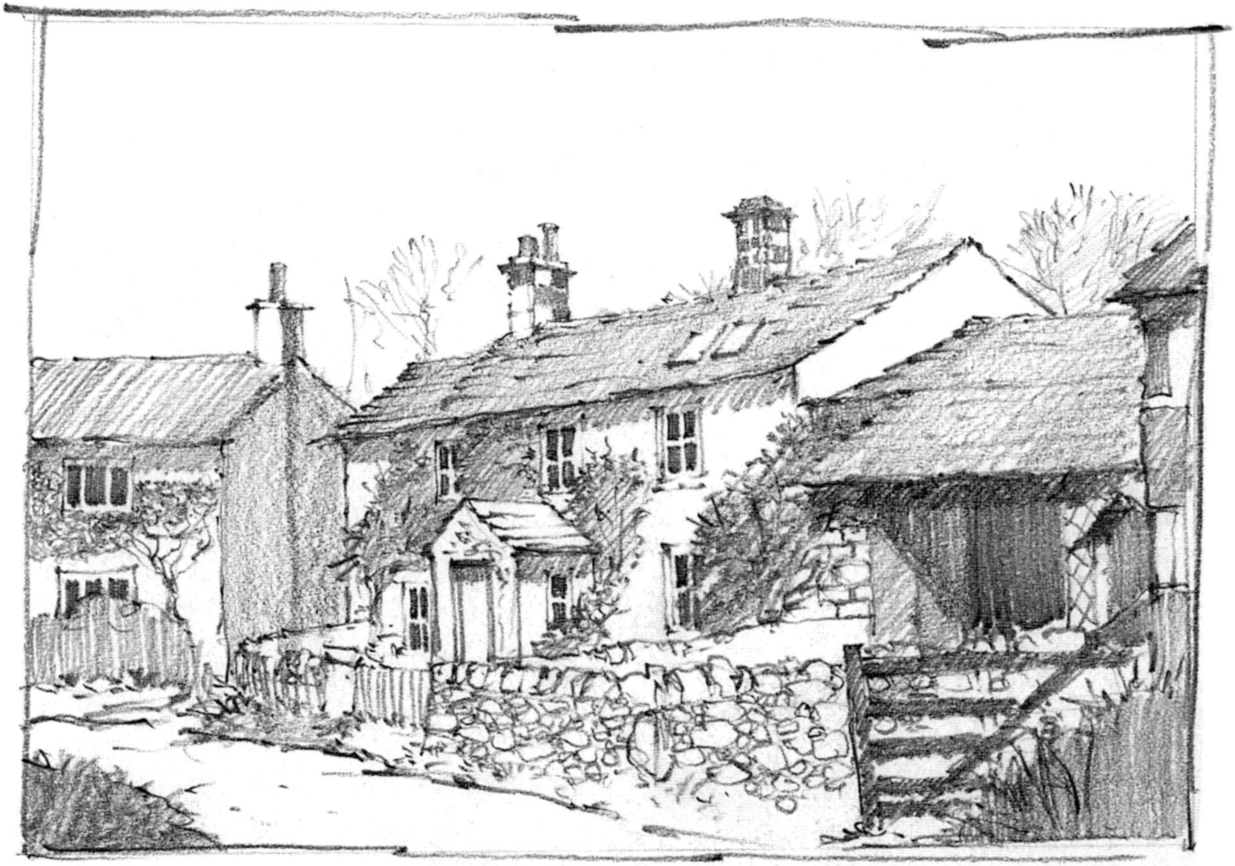

Bell Bank Cottages Nr Skyrethorns

Many years ago, the farmer from Bell Bank farm found me sitting, opposite his farm and making my drawing. He crossed the lane and stood quietly watching me draw. When I had finished, he said "*Aye lad, tha's getn it just reight*".

Praise indeed!

When Spring Begins

It's difficult to tell when spring actually begins. Often in the middle of winter, the shoots of snowdrops and daffodils can been seen pushing through the frozen ground. When the first snowdrops are in bloom in my garden, then I feel that spring is only just around the corner. The first time that I see primroses and celandines, it is then that I know that winter has gone and spring has arrived.

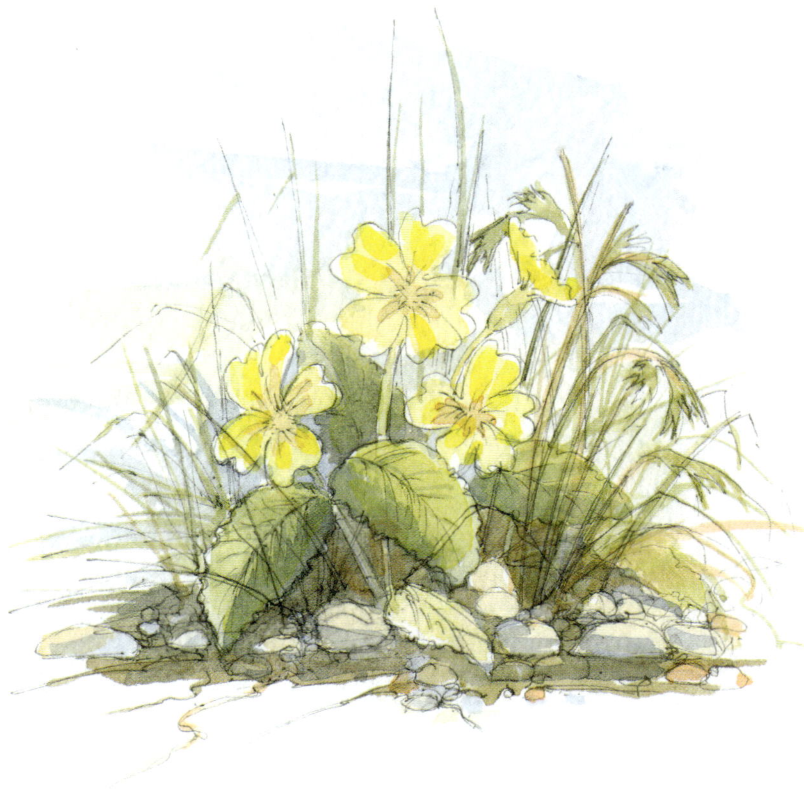

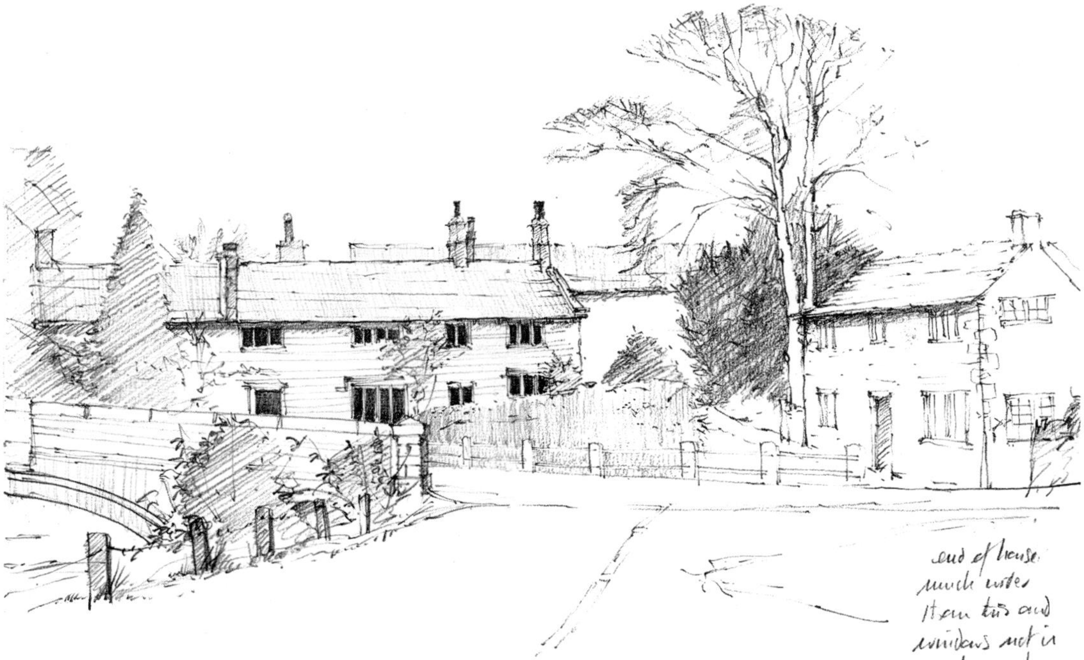

Linton

Linton is always good for a sketch. A really beautiful village which ever way you look at it. Did almost the same scene some time ago but did n't print it. Could have extended it much more to the left but too many trees and as we all know, I am not very good at trees. Much better than the last drawing – someone up there has smiled on me again.

One of those wonderful things happened when making this drawing – which you never forget. A robin came down and settled on the mirror beside Pauline's open window and me drawing for several minutes before another car appeared and frightened it away.

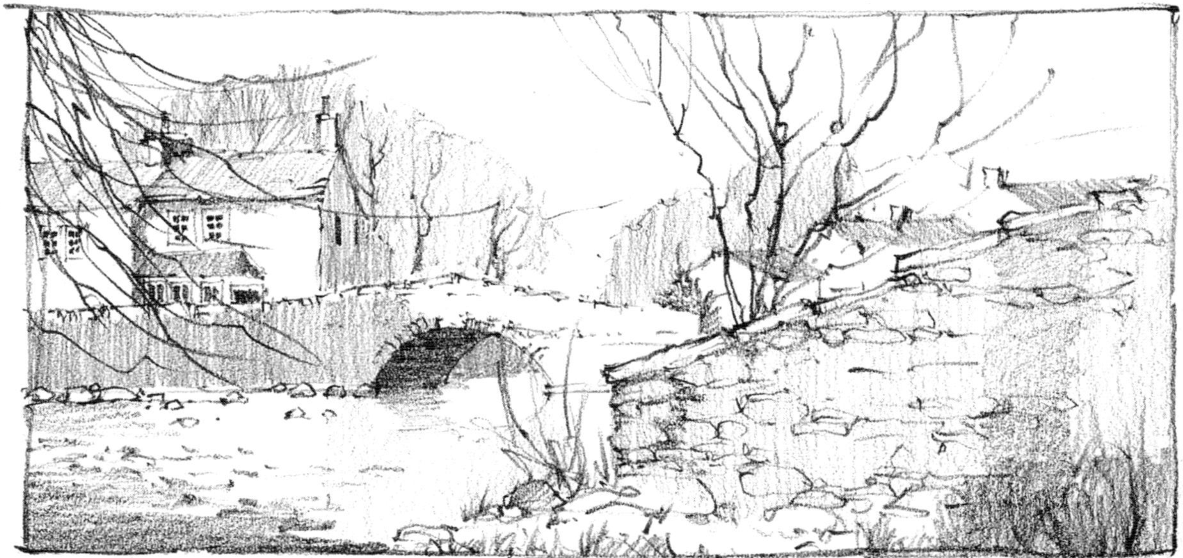

Bridge at Malham.

A very bright, cold day in April, even so there were many walkers about. It took a little while to find a spot where none of them was visable. (I also cheated and simply left them out of my drawing).

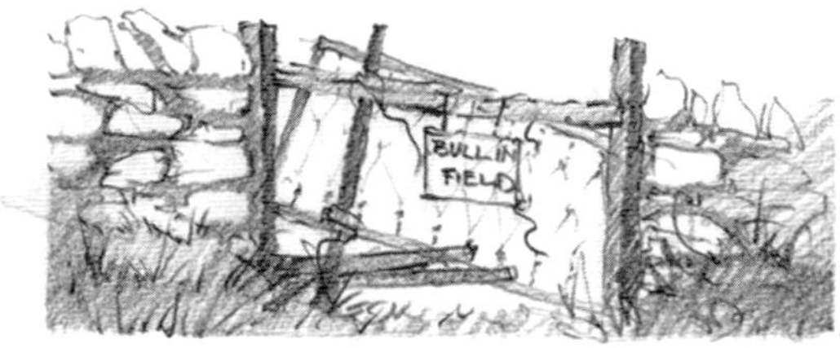

After the last drawing we walked through the village and stopped for morning coffee at Beck Hall. This made an attractive scene - the white house and the brightly lit trees casting dark shadows across the stream.

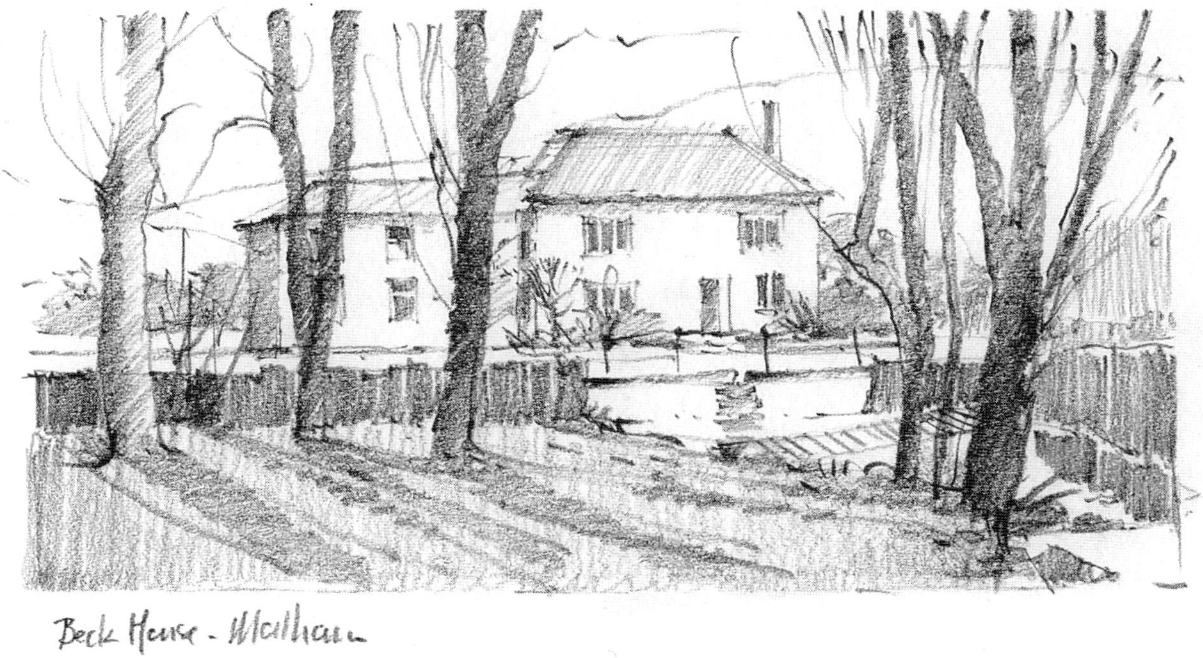

I visited Beck Hall many years ago with forty other boys on a Geography excursion. We had walked from Grassington via Kilnsey to Malham and we were all extremely hungry. Beck Hall did us proud. This was the days of rationing and eggs were scarce, but here we were treated to a boiled egg each. Luxury!

Yes I Am!

"You going again?"
"Yes."
"The same walk?"
"Yes."
"But you did it two weeks ago."
"Yes."
"And three times before that."
"Yes."
"Why?"
"Because it's there!"

It was no use explaining.
He went away with a satisfied smirk on his face.
"The man's a fool," he thought.
Little did he know. Little did he understand.
Nothing is the same.
No two days are the same.
I am not the same.
Each day, each walk, a new experience
Familiarity does not always breed contempt,
Familiarity brings about a deeper understanding
A deeper love
Like two people growing together.

"Are you going again?"

"YES! I AM!"

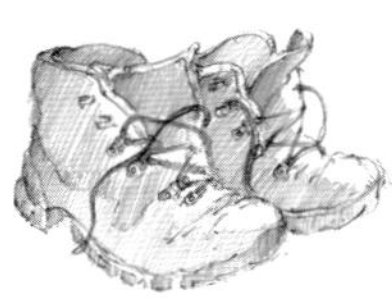

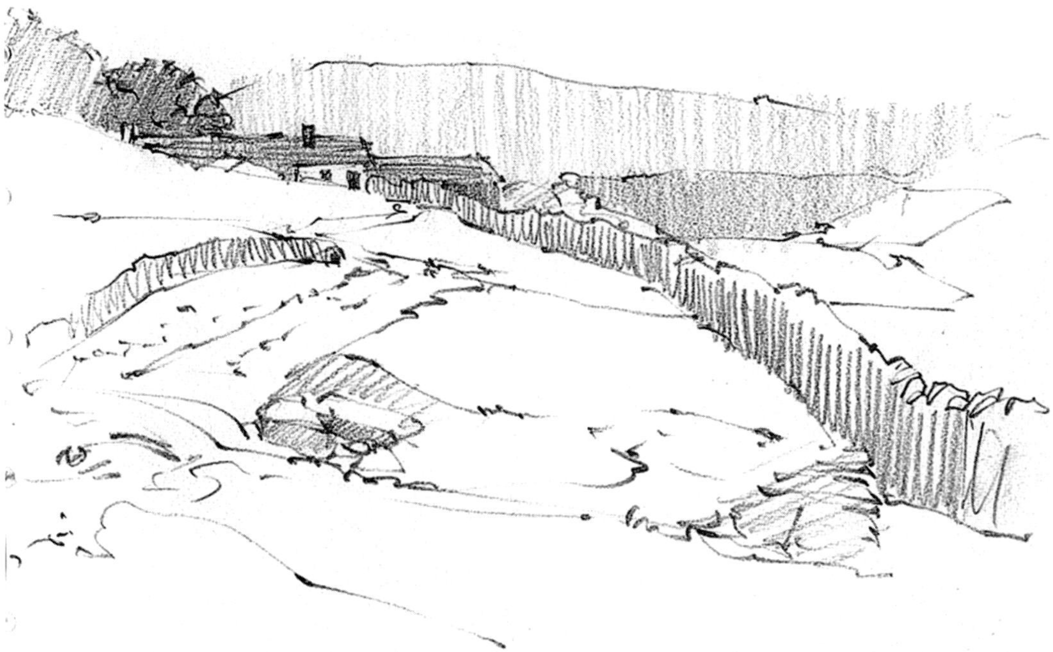

Moorend Farm.
Decided to do this walk again but the other way round! Kettlewell full - scarecrow week! Drove on and left the car at Starbotton. Walked back to Kettlewell and then the long drag up to Moorend. Arrived at this point without a stop.

(Just can't write in this book - too small)

Very dense dark green trees.

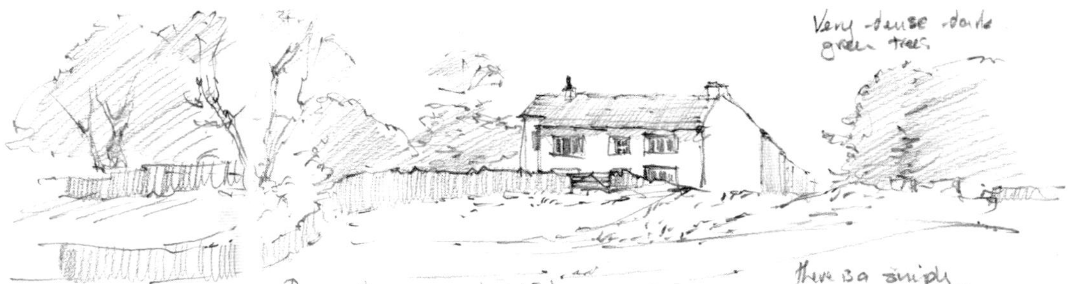

Heavy shade under trees at this side of path

Day rather mixed. Windy Grey clouds and a little blue sky. Quite good for walking. Heavy rain earlier but so far O.K.

There is a simple dignity about this farm. Nothing pretentious at all

Nice to be sketching again!!!

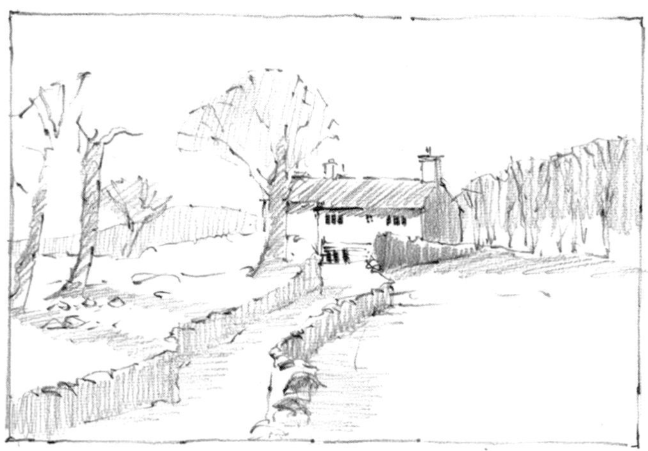

Spring Morning
Lower Winskill.

A long steep walk up from Langcliffe. Sitting to make my sketch a welcome rest. More trees than I have drawn. - shall have to consult my photograph.

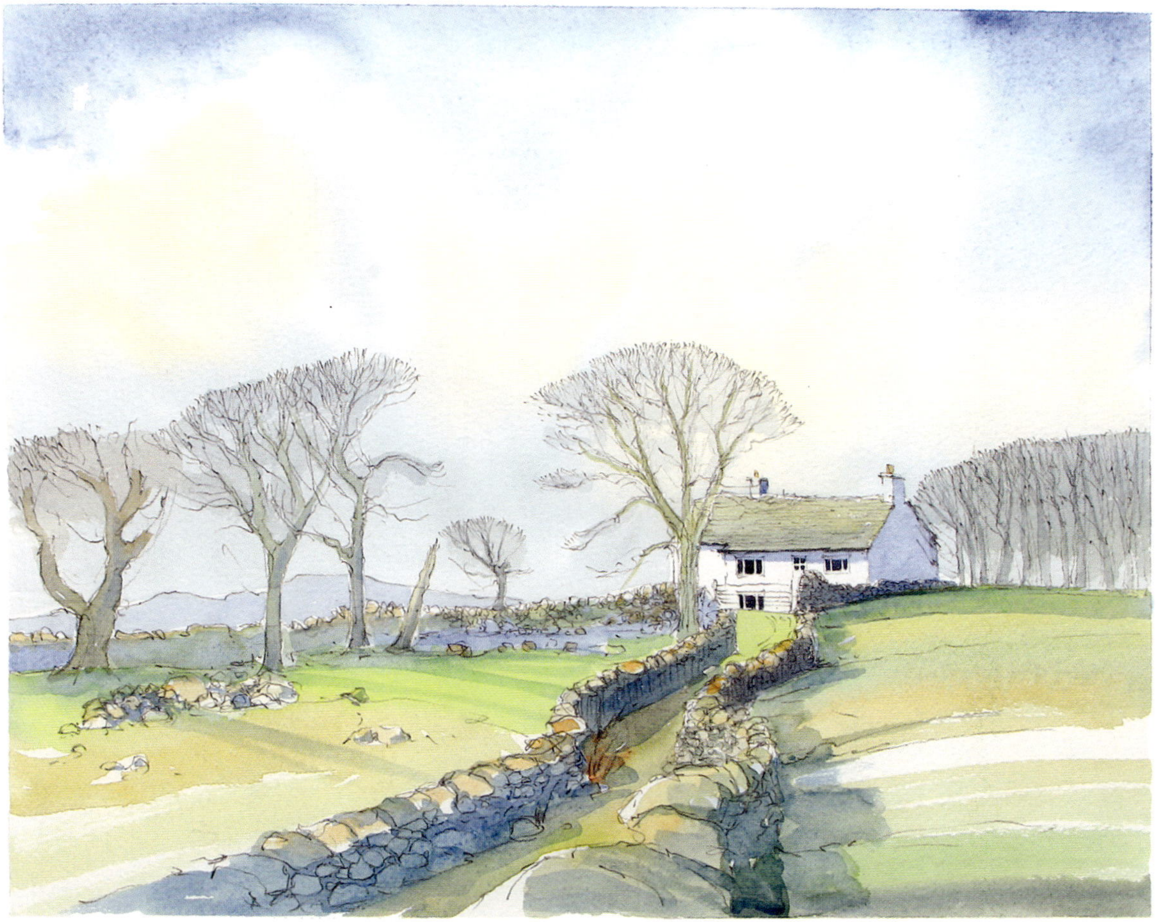

Spring Morning - Lower Winskill.

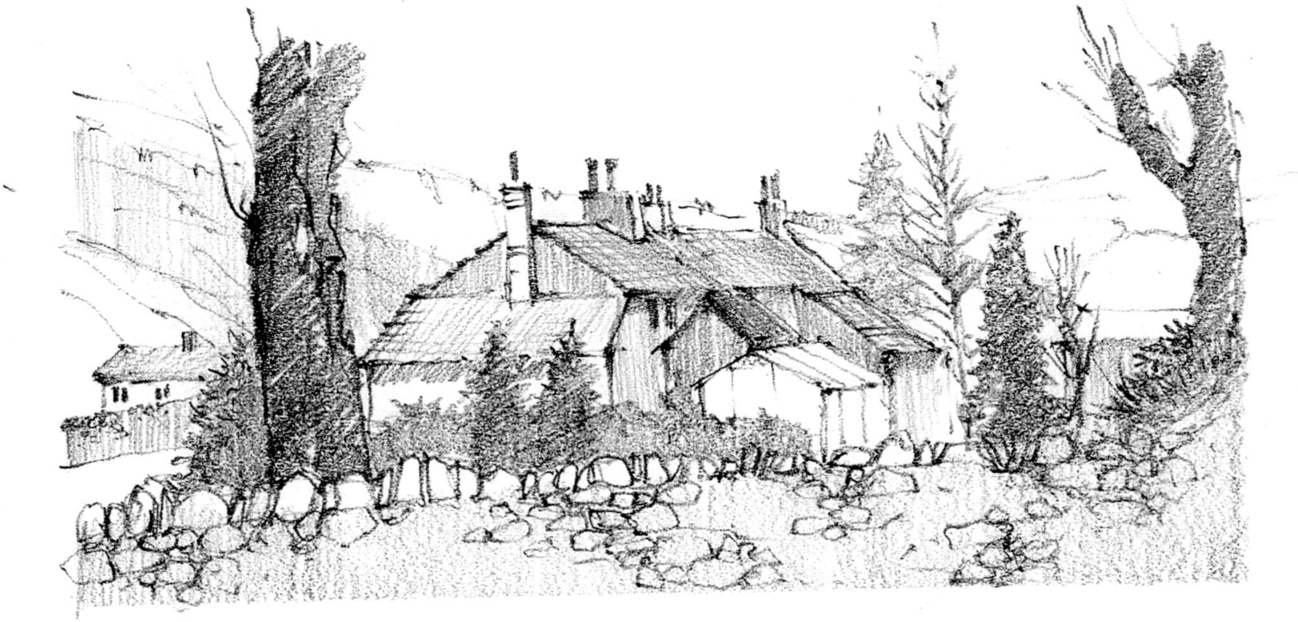

Starbotton - Upper Wharfedale

The walk along the hillside from Kettlewell is not difficult and the small village of Starbotton is certainly worth a visit. This view caught my eye as I walked downhill towards the village. Simply someone's back garden but it makes a very interesting composition.

Across the main road, a rather overgrown lane leads down to the River Wharfe and the footbridge on the opposite page.

Cross the river, turn right and have a delightlful walk to Burnsall.

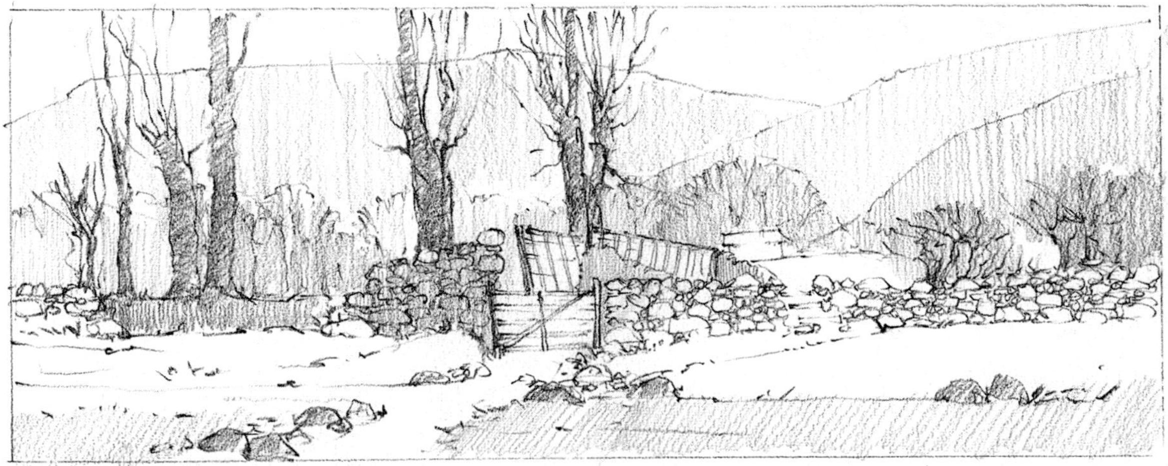

Footbridge to Starbotton.
14.4.02

Bright sun after days of rain. Motored with J.D to Buckden. Walked the Dales Way towards Kettlewell and then back up the otherside of the valley to Starbotton.

Until to-day I never thought that this bridge existed! You are never too old to learn new things about the Dales.

Not beautiful in the accepted sense of the word but quite interesting and a good start.

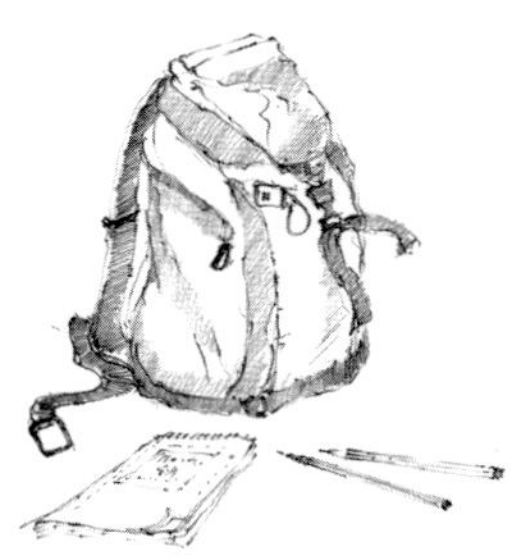

The Sins Of My Youth

It saddens me to think of it.
I carried the guilt for years
But in those days we did not know any better.

It was one of our favourite walks.
We had not long been married
And little thought that what we were doing was wrong.

Above us rose the limestone covered hill
And there, between the bleached rocks, they stood.
A small group of primroses.

"How wonderful they would look in our garden", we said.
Using fingers and a small piece of limestone,
I dug one up and carefully placed it in my rucksack.

That small plant grew and multiplied in our garden.
On moving house, the primroses went with us
Until attitudes changed and guilt began to trouble me.

And so, fifty years later and accompanied by J.D.
I returned to the limestone covered hill
And carefully replaced three young primroses from my garden.

Now the guilt has receded.
I have atoned for my sins
And the primroses live on to give pleasure to others.

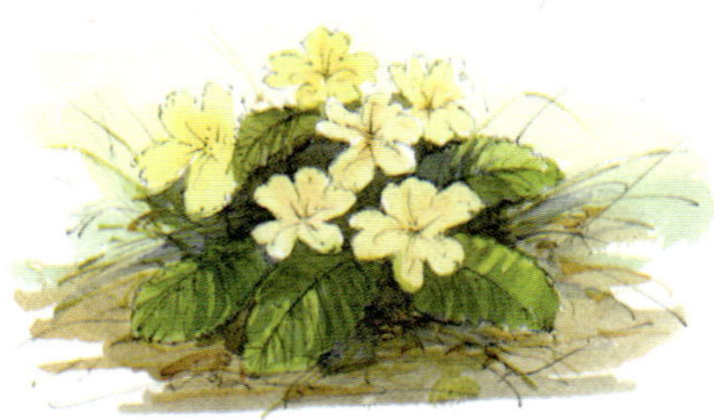

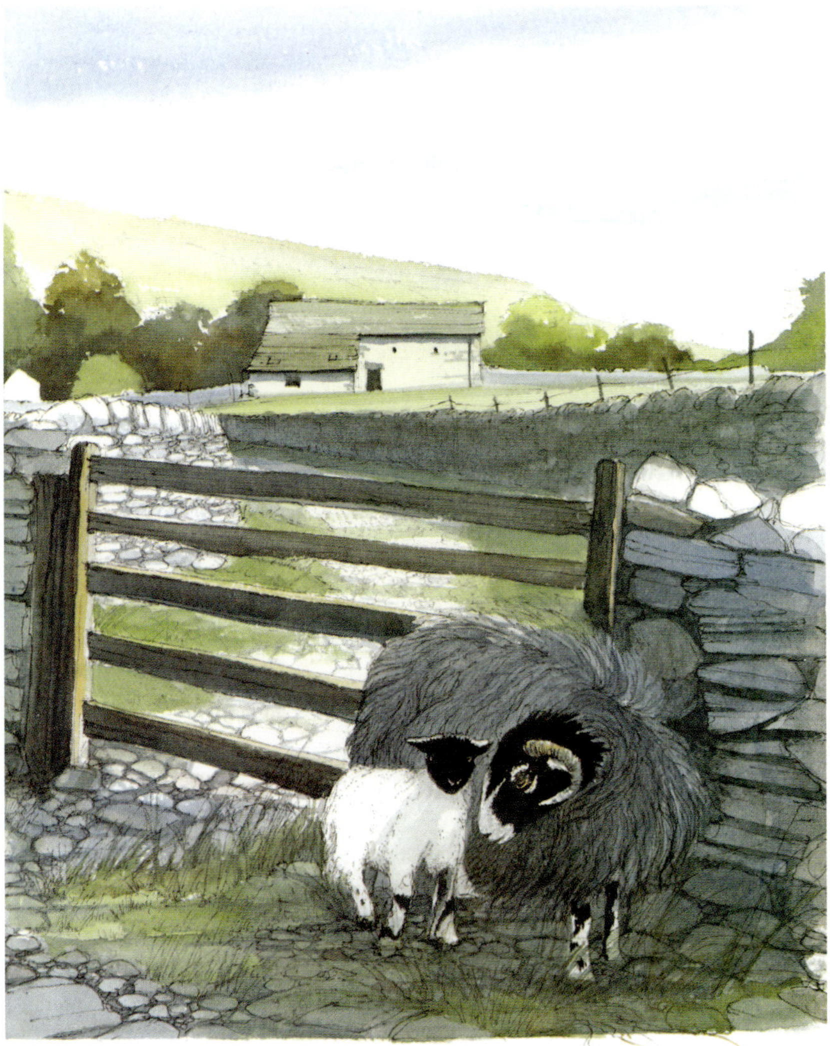

Lamb time in Littondale

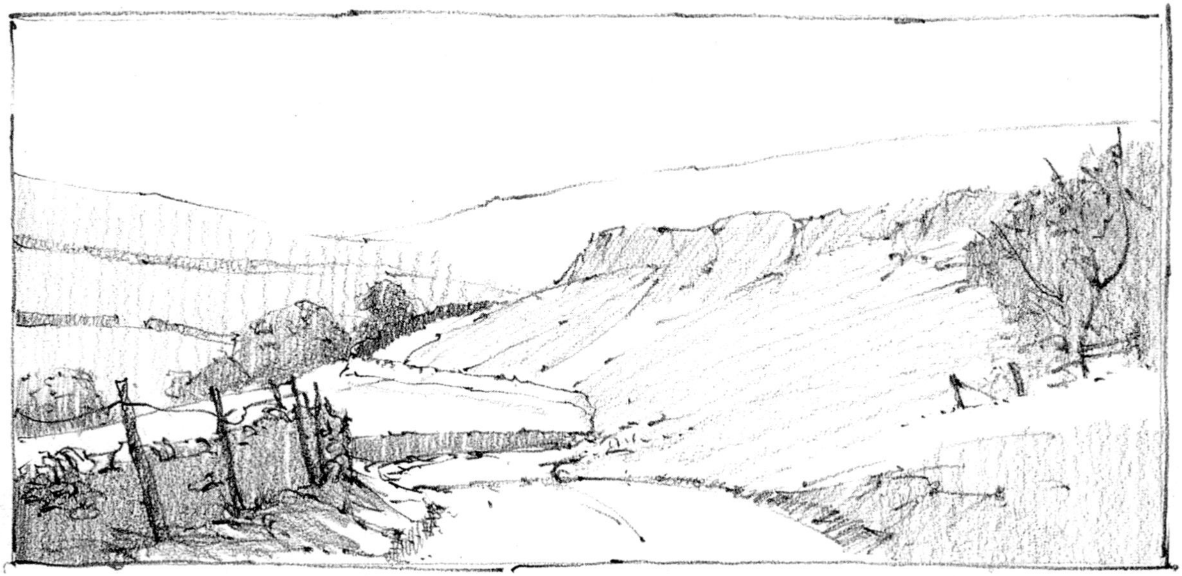

Mastiles Lane Near Kilnsey.

Mastiles Lane runs all the way from Kilnsey to Malham Tarn. I first did this walk with a school party on a geography ramble. I thought it was wonderful.
This drawing was done from the old quarry road. At this point the gradient eases only to start again just round the corner, where the long drag really begins.

The second part of the climb is a long steady ascent best undertaken using the *"Alpine plod"*. Once the top is reached, everything changes. Wide open moorland stretches all the way to Malham Tarn. You can stride out with Curlew, Lapwing and Dales sheep the only company.

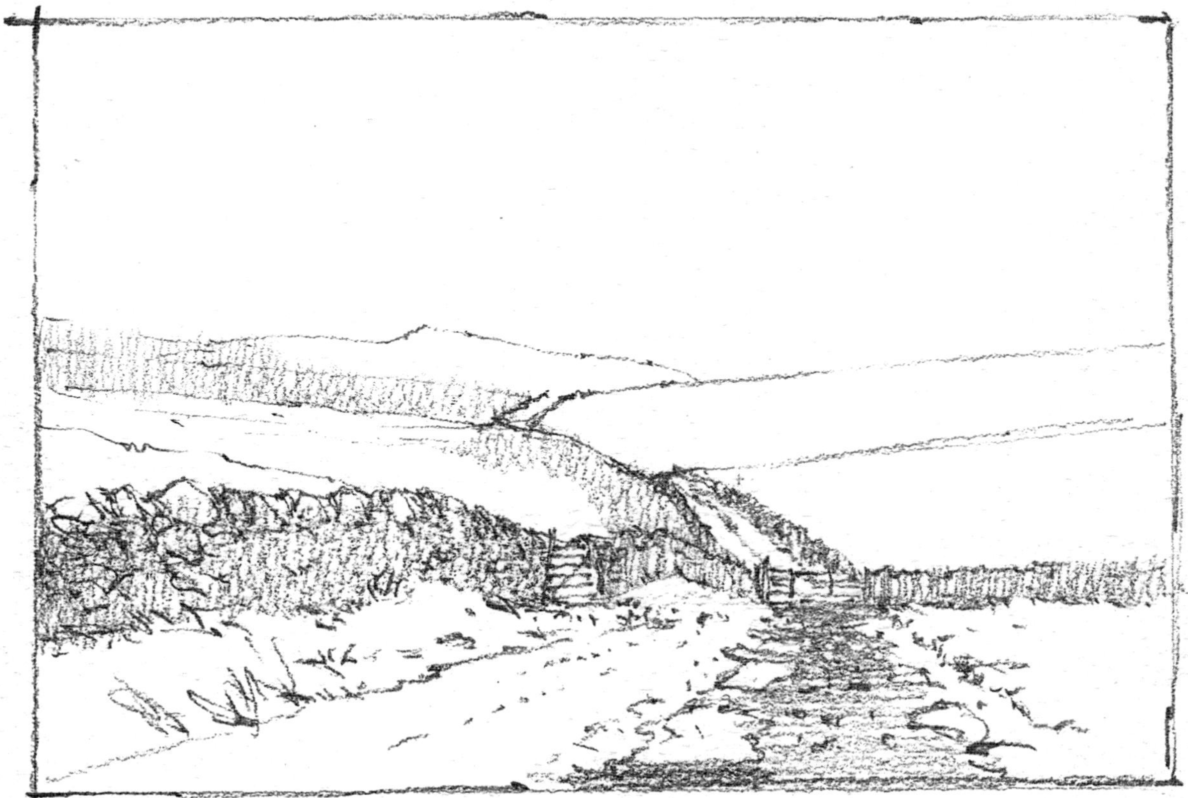

Mastiles Lane - Spring.

Having reached this spot, I paused to make a drawing and take a photograph.

A quick and simple sketch but it contains all the information I need. This will tell me how I want the painting to look - the photograph will supply any necessary detail.

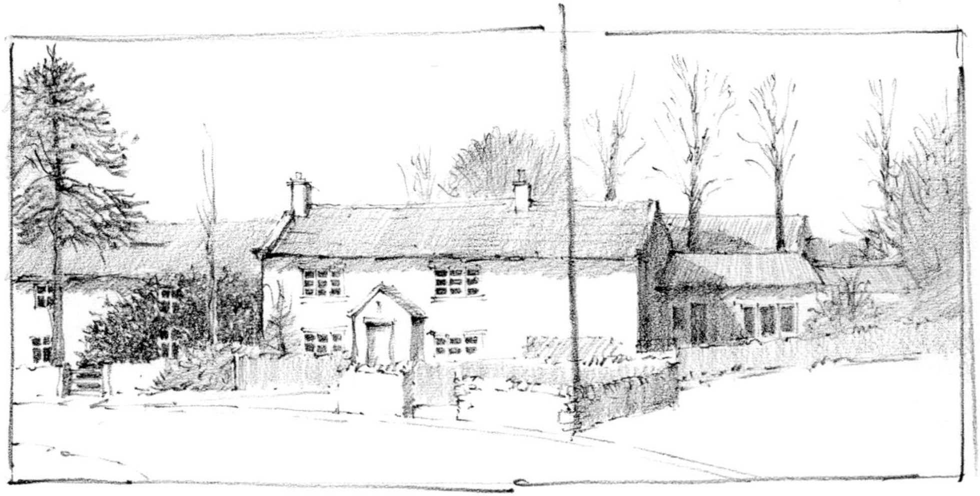

Monkey puzzle and Maypole - Cowstone

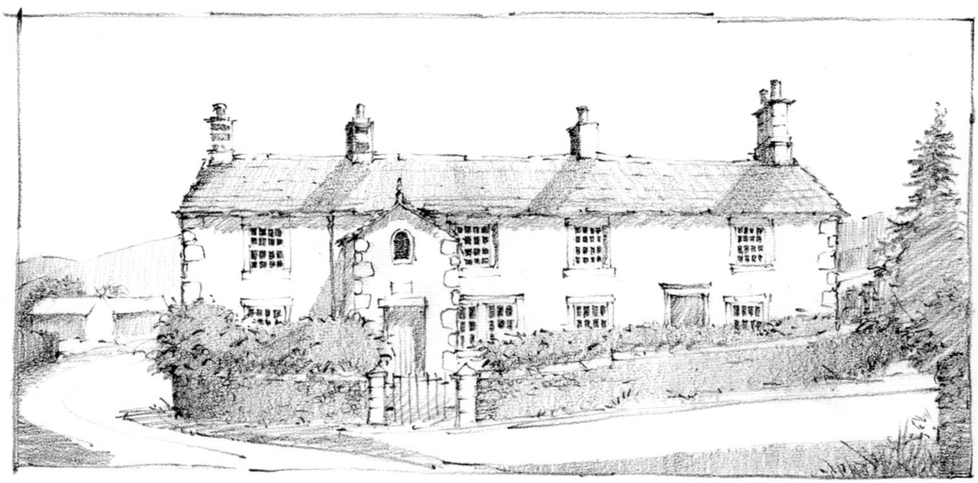

They don't build them like they did in 1657! Cowstone-

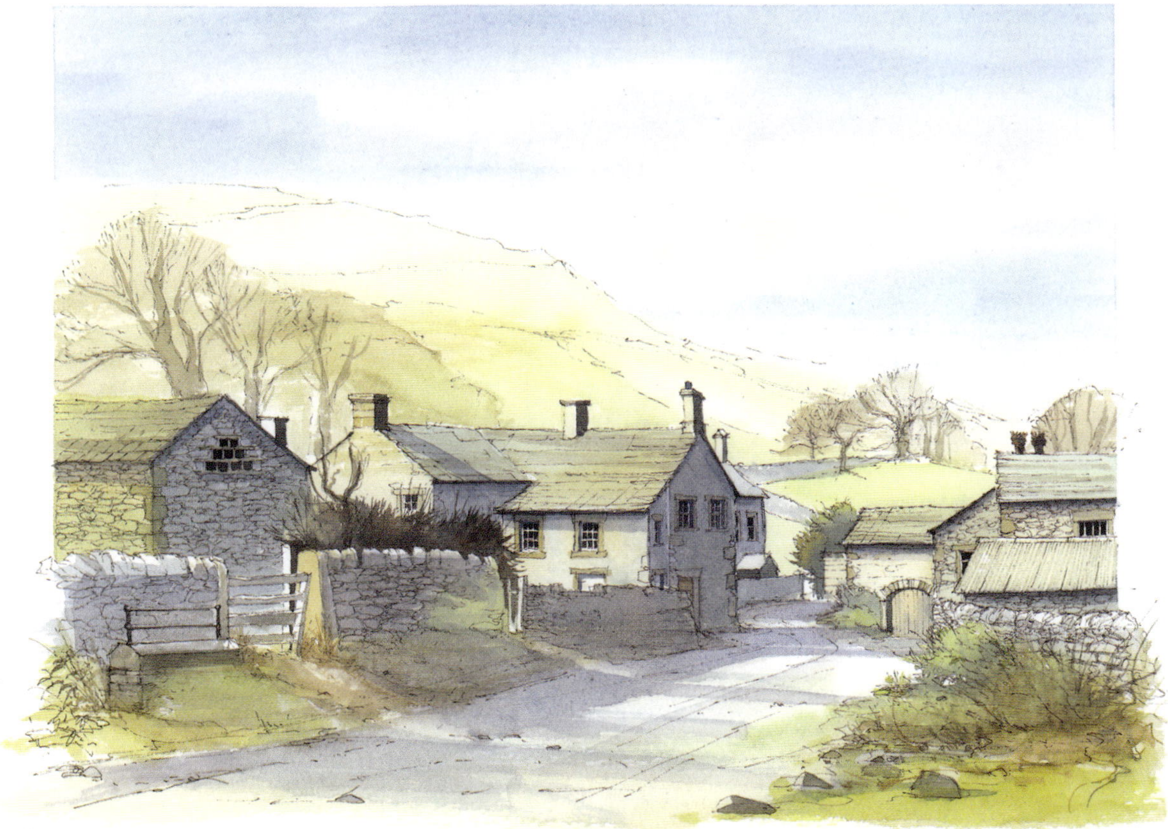

Limestone Village - Conistone

This delightful village sits just across the river from Kilnsey. It contains some beautiful old Dales houses and farms, just waiting for you to get to work with the pencil.

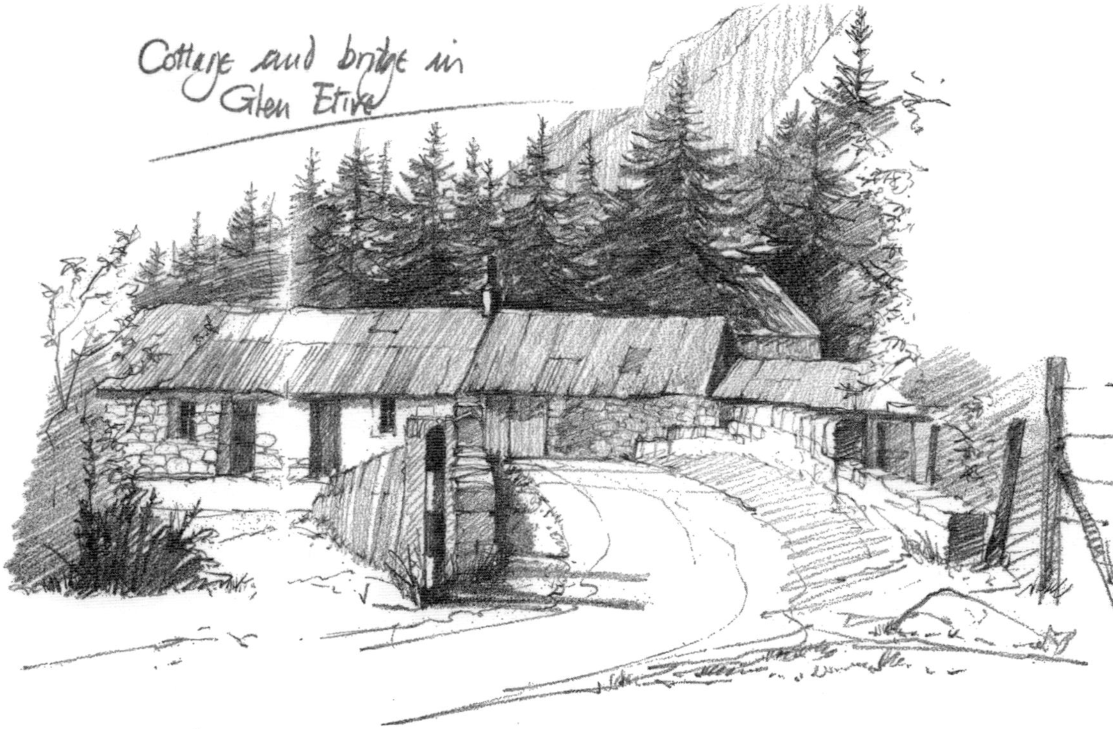

Another wonderful day. Blue sky and white clouds - 10 miles on a single track road down the valley from Glen Coe and worth every minute of it. Super little cottages - corrugated iron roofs - black tar and rust on the barn over the bridge. Blackbirds and willow warblers singing - lovely and warm - at last, a satisfactory drawing and the usual numb bum!

One drawing - one photograph - and back to the car for lunch

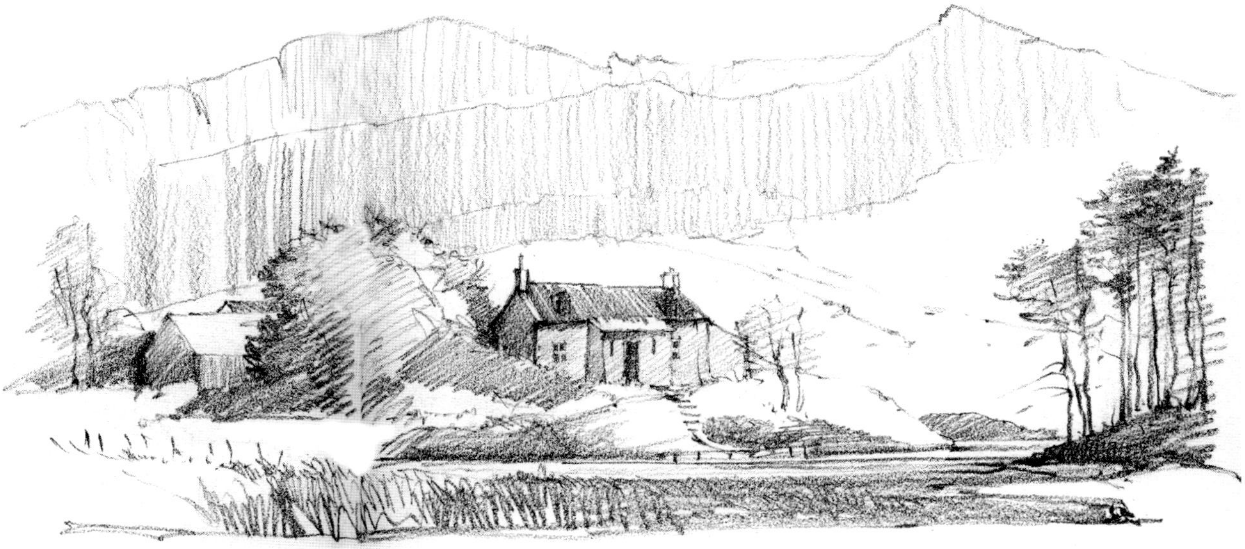

Game Keepers Cottage – Glen Finnan
(so the man said)

Beautiful day after all the bad weather. Went to Glen Finnan and had coffee. Motored a little further and came upon this. Another tourist said it was the game keepers cottage so perhaps it is. Just time for a photograph then on a little further

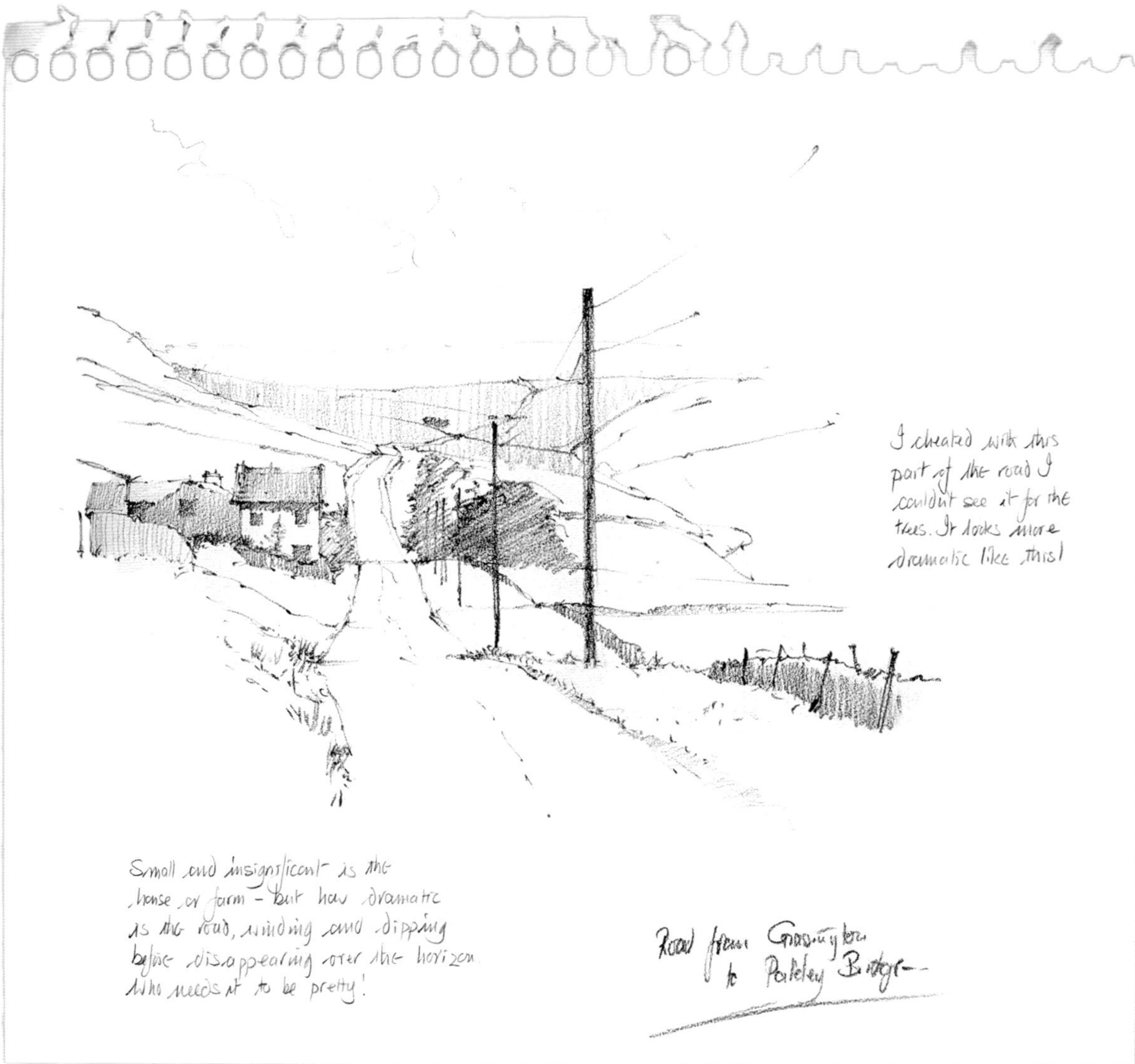
I cheated with this
part of the road I
couldn't see it for the
trees. It looks more
dramatic like this!
Small and insignificant is the
house or farm - but how dramatic
is the road, winding and dipping
before disappearing over the horizon
Who needs it to be pretty!
Road from Grassington
to Pateley Bridge

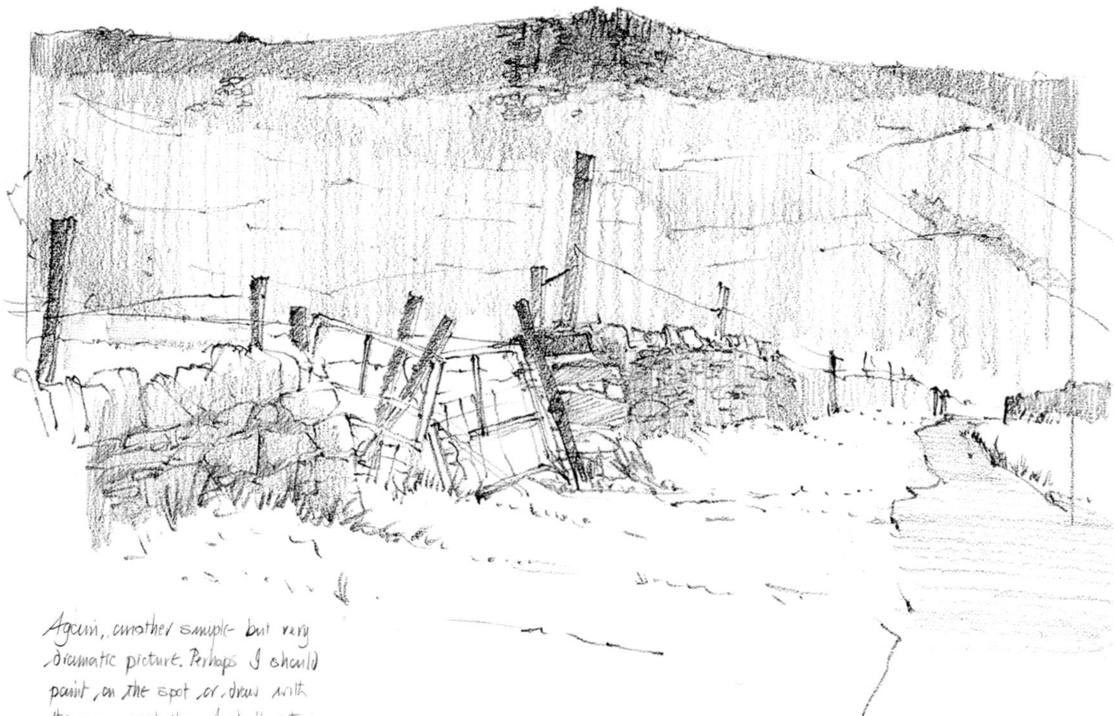

Again, another simple but very dramatic picture. Perhaps I should paint on the spot or draw with the pen and then I shall retain the spontaneity. Farmers are really mean – just look at the gate – bed ends held together with binder twine and barbed wire!!!

"Simon's Seat" above the road to Parceval Hall.

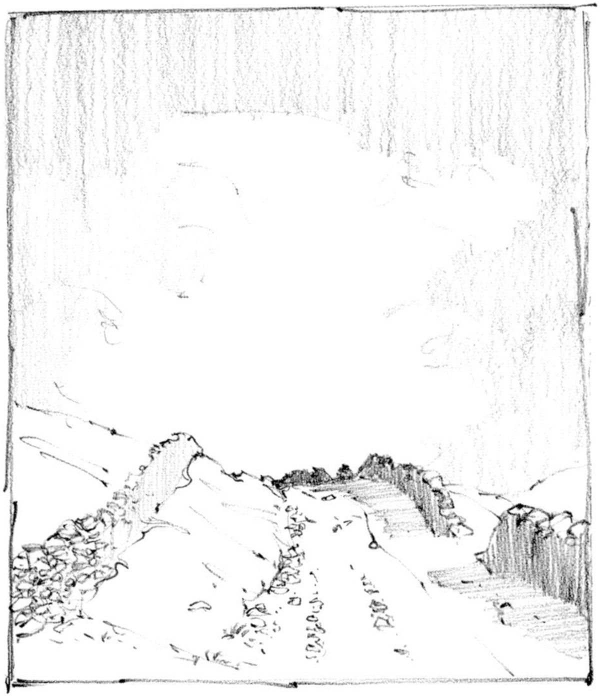

Road to Cam Head from Kettlewell.

I cannot think how many times I have driven into Kettlewell and seen this lane climbing out above the village. Some day I would have to walk up it to see where it went. Blue sky. White clouds and a super walk. A fine spring day

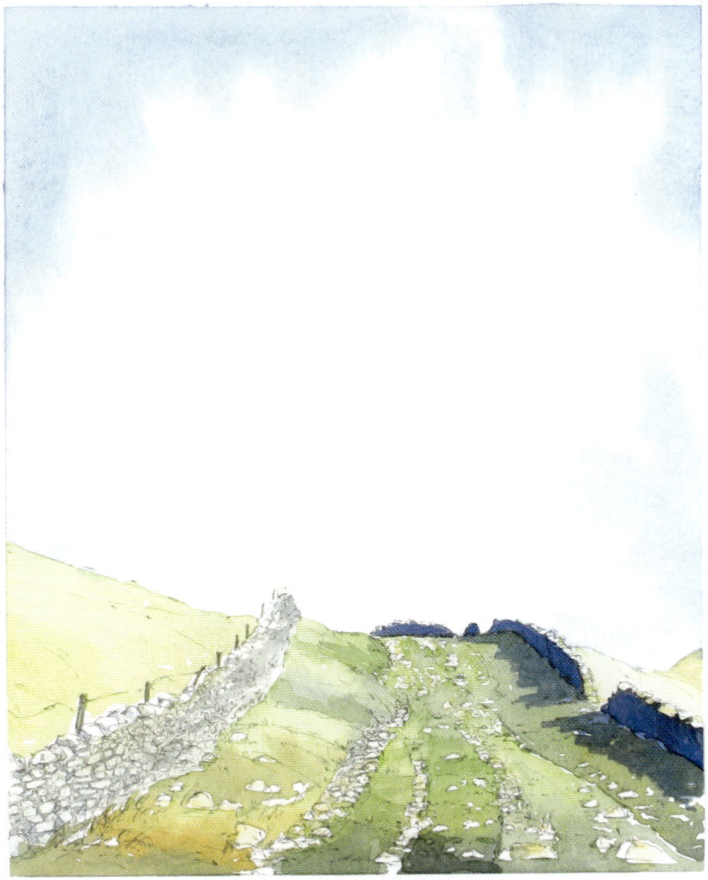

The road to Cam Head.

"Believe not those who say
The upward path is smooth."
Anne Brontë

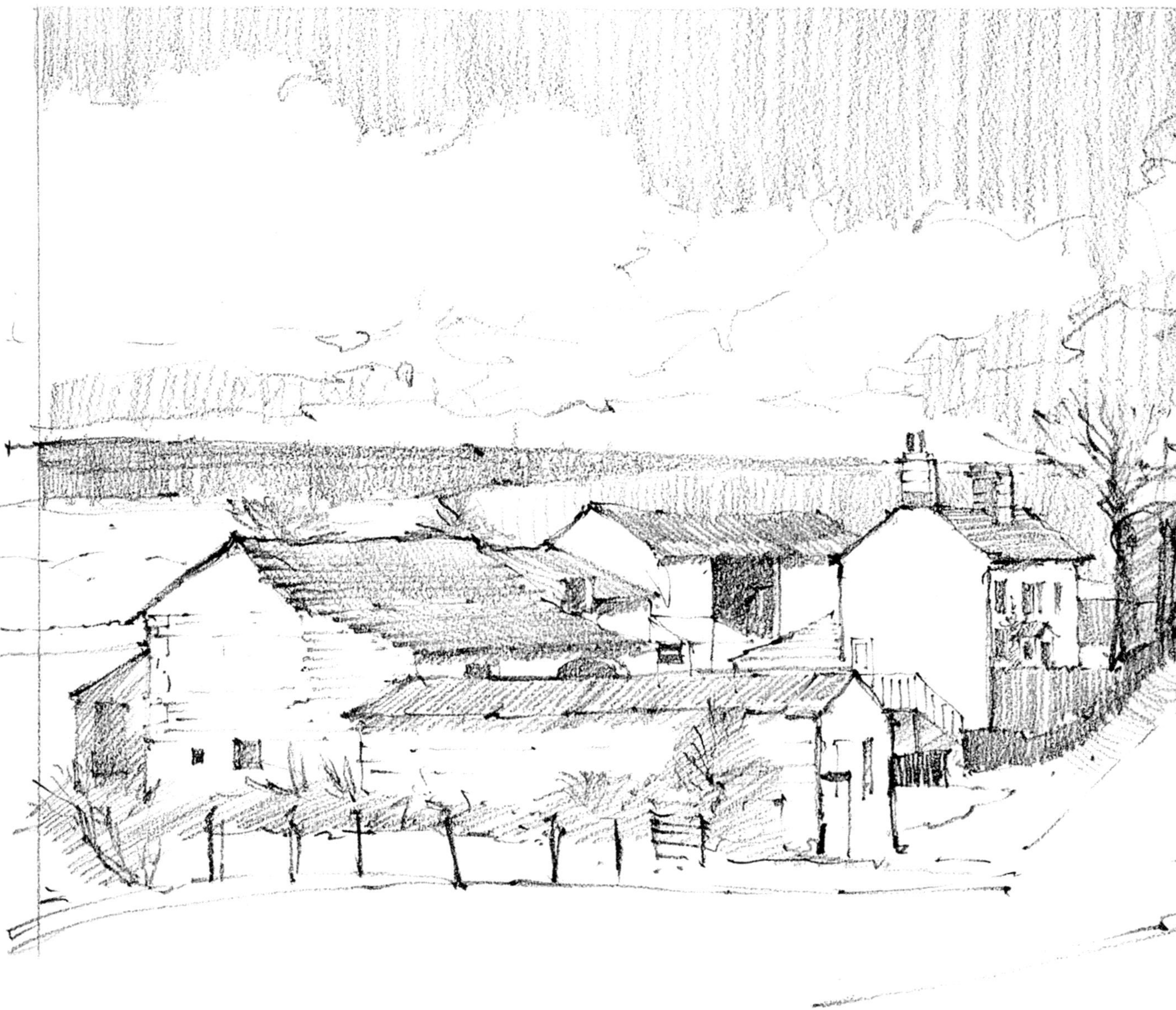

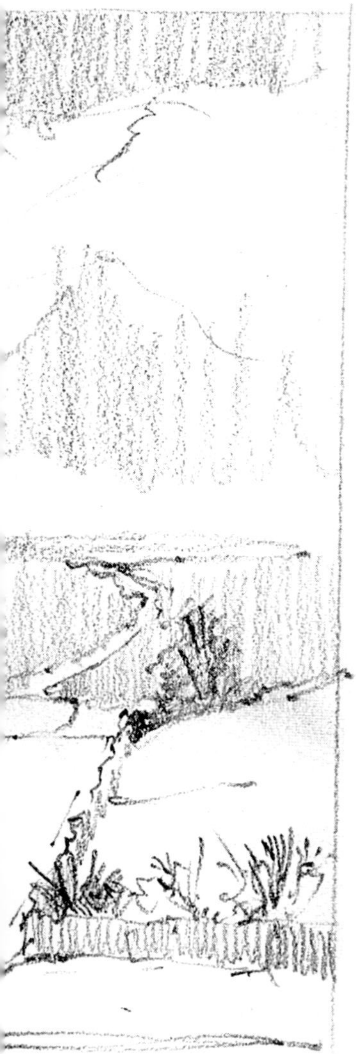

Gaping Goose Farm.

In the days before I had transport other than an old bike, the only way to get to Ilkley was by bus to Bingley or Baildon and then walk. the walk to Gaping Goose Farm was a long slog on the road before the walking really began. Rombald's Moor now stretched all the way to Ilkley and was soon to become a favourite walk.
On my last day at school, I had an examination in the morning and once it was over, this is where I came. All afternoon I sun-bathed near the old shooting-box, savouring the feeling of freedom, before walking back to Bingley and the bus home.

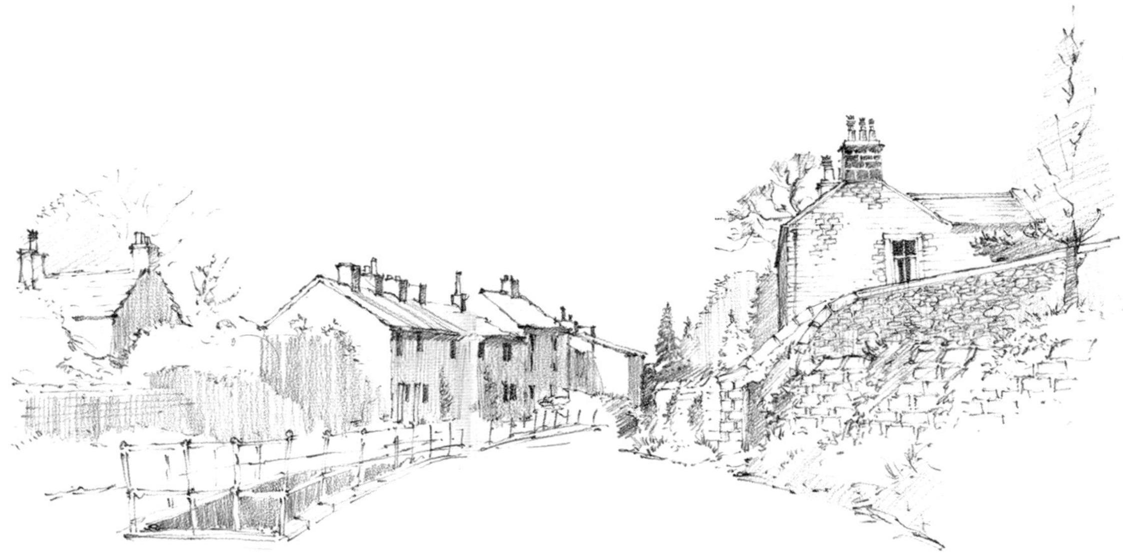

First visit in Pendleton
We had a good day – sun
and white clouds. No people!
the stream wasn't very deep.
Perhaps after rain it really floods –
it was certainly in a deep
enough channel. Nice houses, which looked
as if they had grown out of the
ground along with the plants and
not been made by man. Just
the way I like them.

Pendleton

Another visit to the Pendle country.
A nice quiet village – pity about the
railings which go along the stream side.
I have tried to minimise their appearance
in the drawing. They were white once
upon a time but now are streaked with rust.
Blue sky, white clouds – a super day!

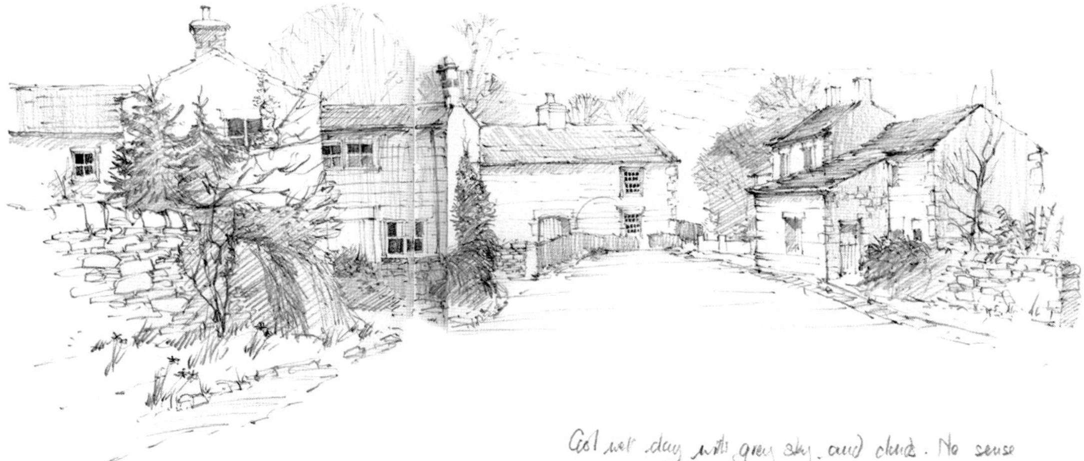

West Scrafton

Cool wet day with grey sky and cloud. No sense of direction for the light so may have got it wrong. Must check on map when I have time. Enjoyed this subject although I appear to have stretched it a little too much in an east/west direction. Now to take a photograph to back up the drawing. Very lush vegetation for so early in the year. Had a pleasant chat with a farmer who kept passing the car on his way muck-spreading to one of the fields. Walked through the village and took more photographs – an old red phone box (but now every-one seems to be doing it!)

Warm coloured stone with only a little smoke blackening on the chimneys. Walls dry stone on left – mortar on the right – both with vegetation from the gardens hanging over and hiding long stretches of the wall. White painted woodwork round the windows.

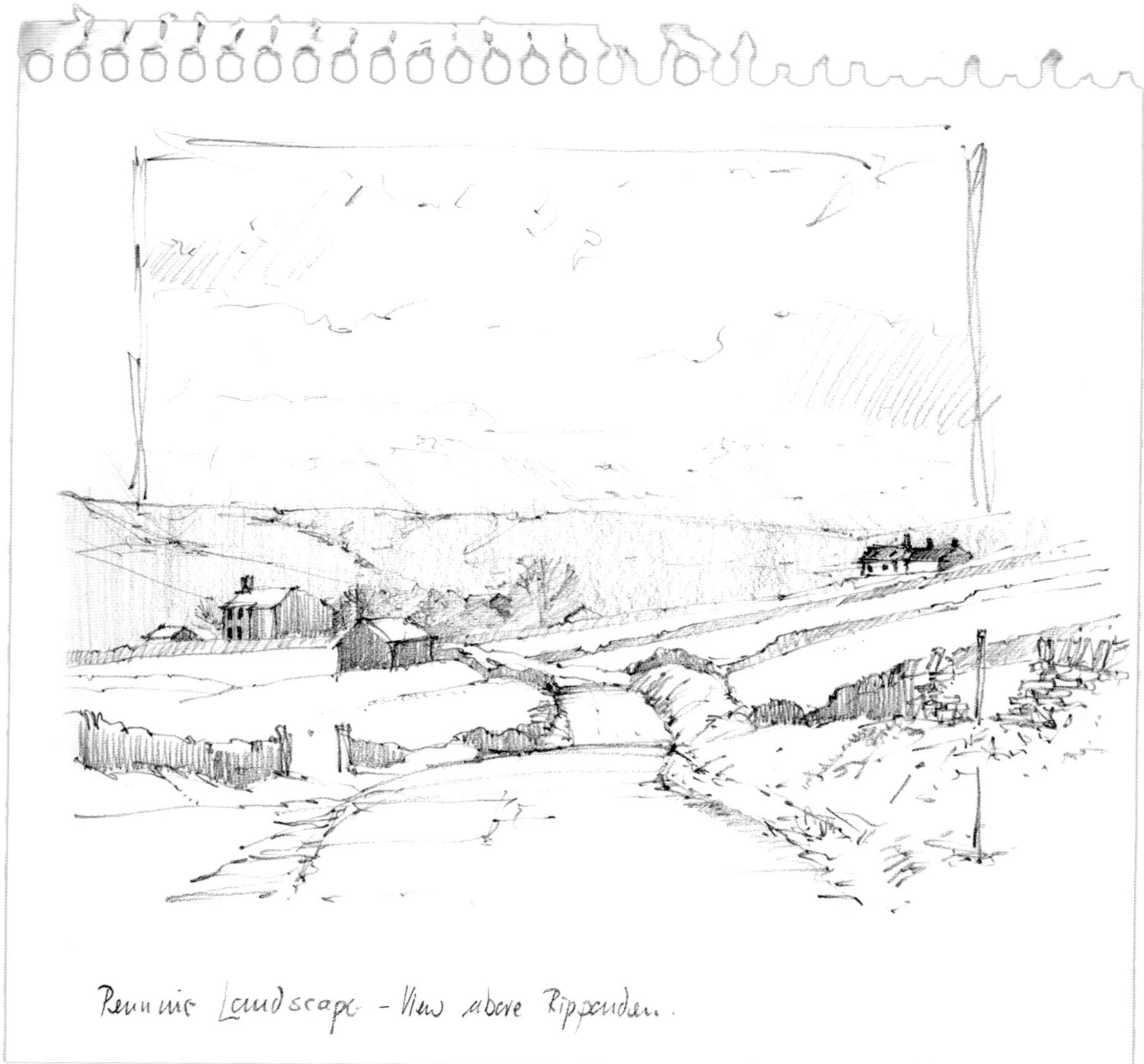
Pennine Landscape - View above Ripponden.

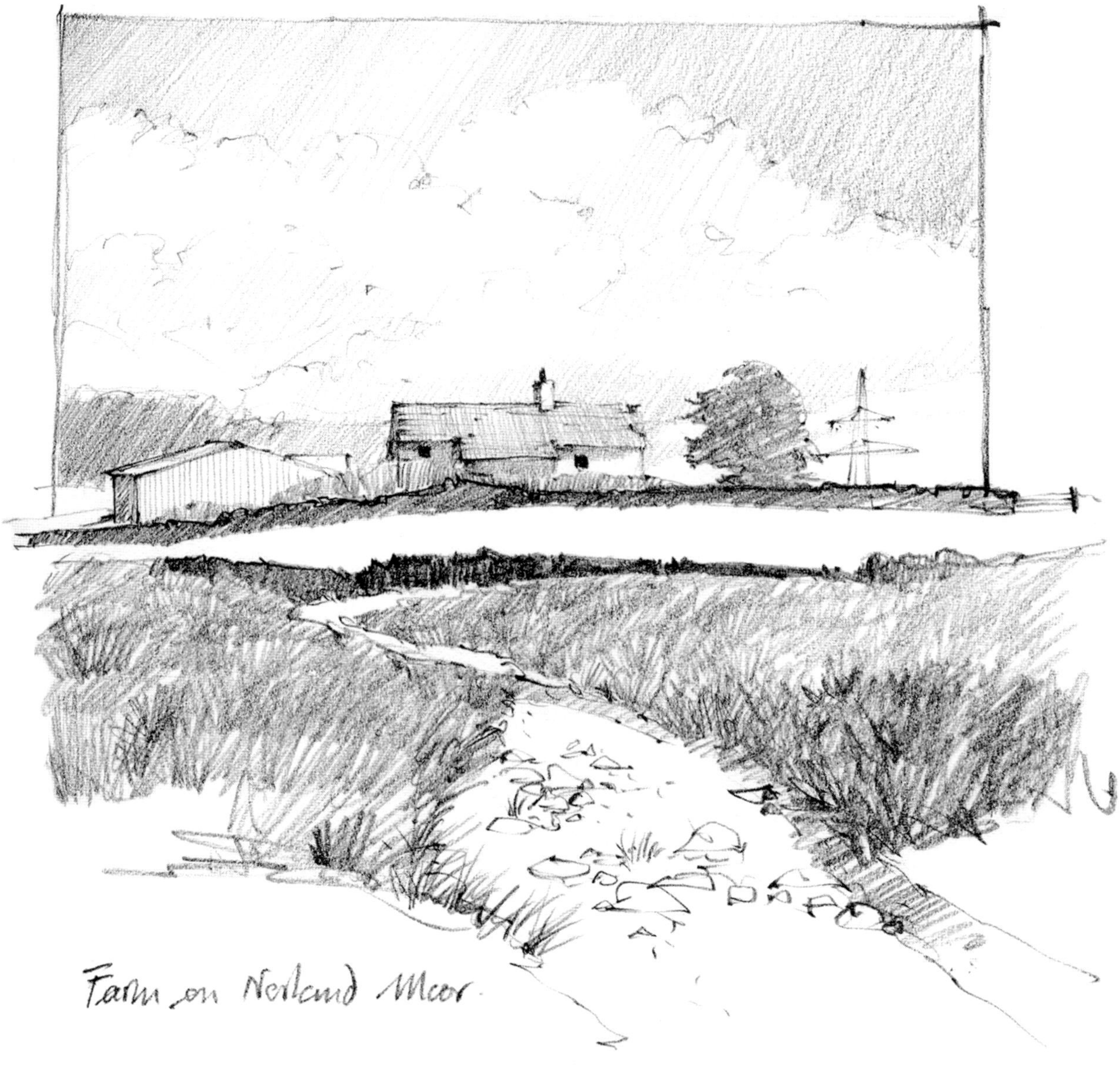
Farm on Norland Moor

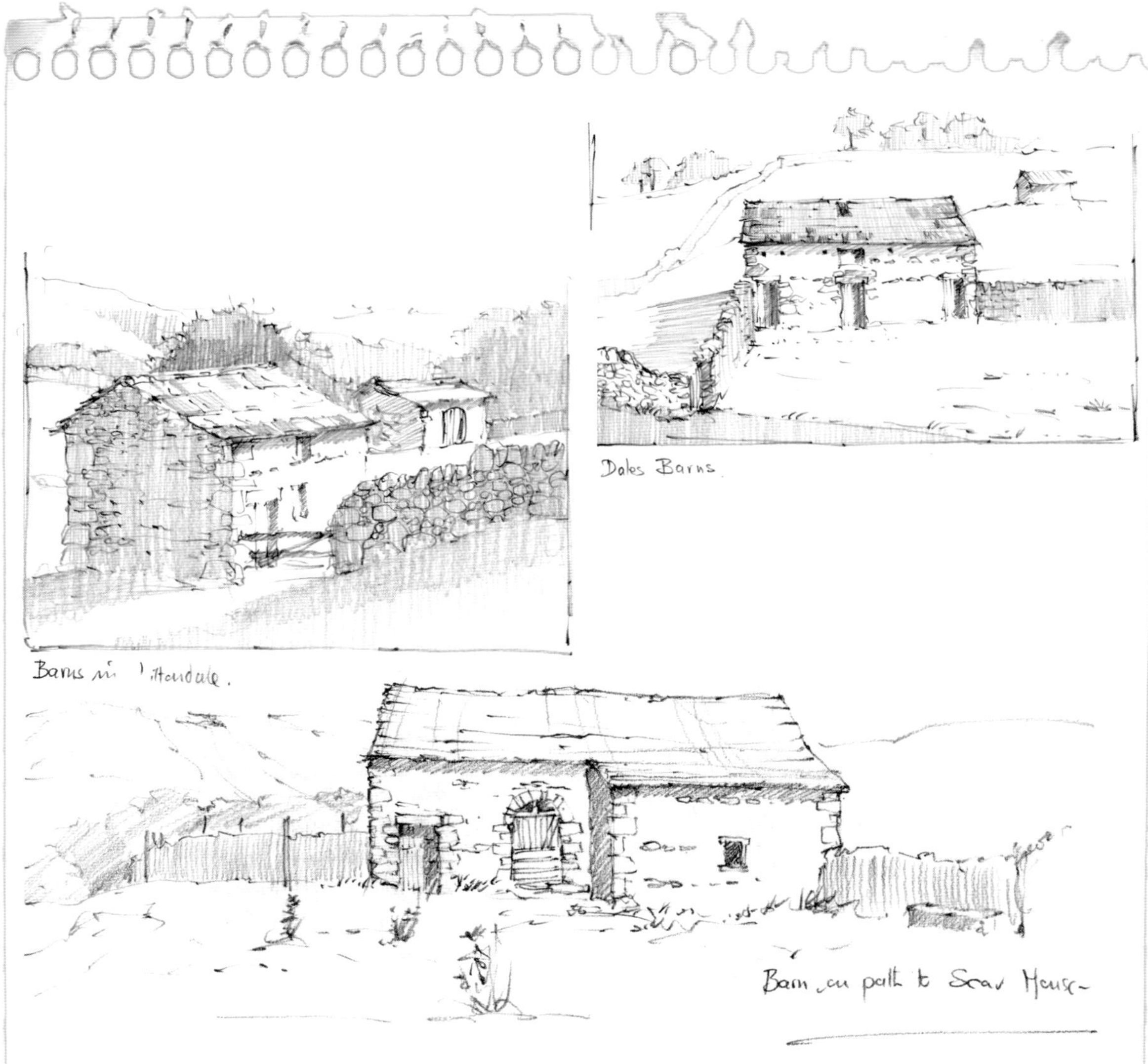
Dales Barns
Barns in Littondale.
Barn on path to Scar House

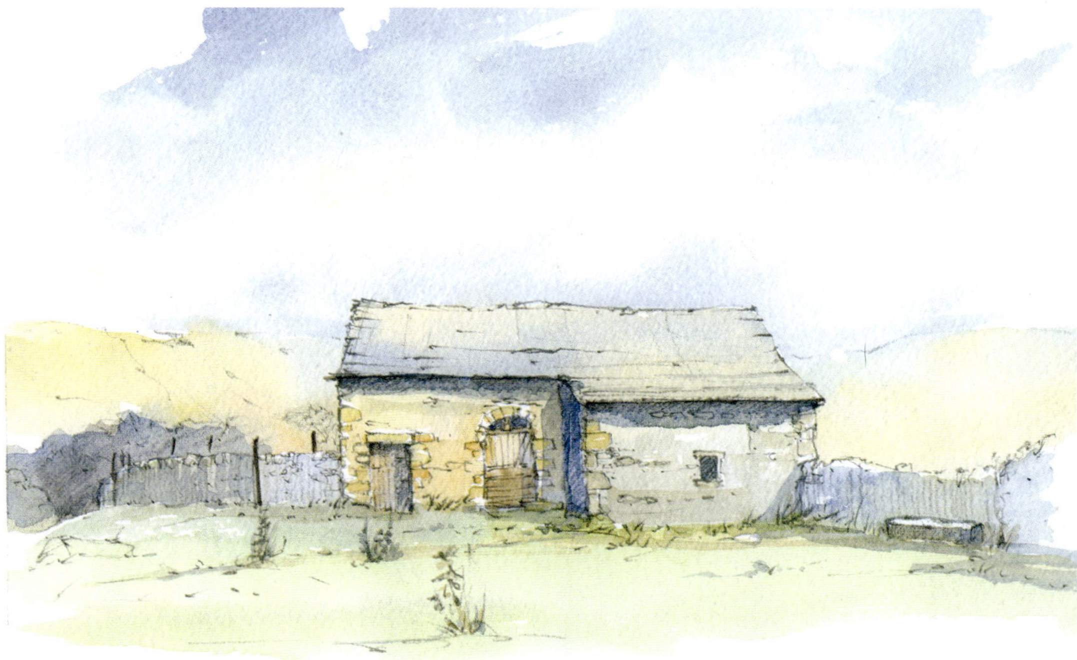

Barn Near Cray.

Dales barns. Simple, elegantly functional buildings. Not architect designed but built by generations of builders who knew just how it should be done. They look timeless, as if they had grown out of the very rock from which they had been built. Originally cattle were kept there and milking was often done there. Now all that has ended, it not being considered hygienic. Some are now simply used to store equipment, whilst many have been converted into accommodation. I cannot resist including the soft grey limestone walls and lichen covered roofs in my paintings. In short barns and landscape go together like fish and chips!

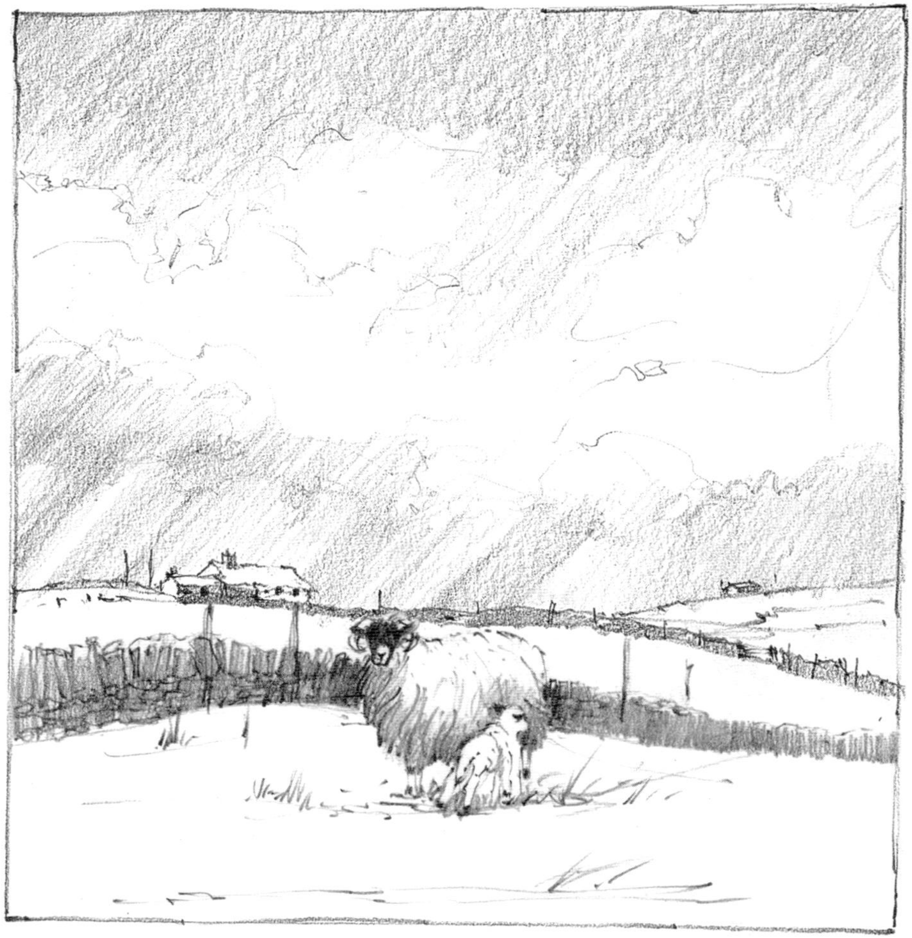

From winter's cold, dead hand
Springs life anew.
The annual miracle.

Summer

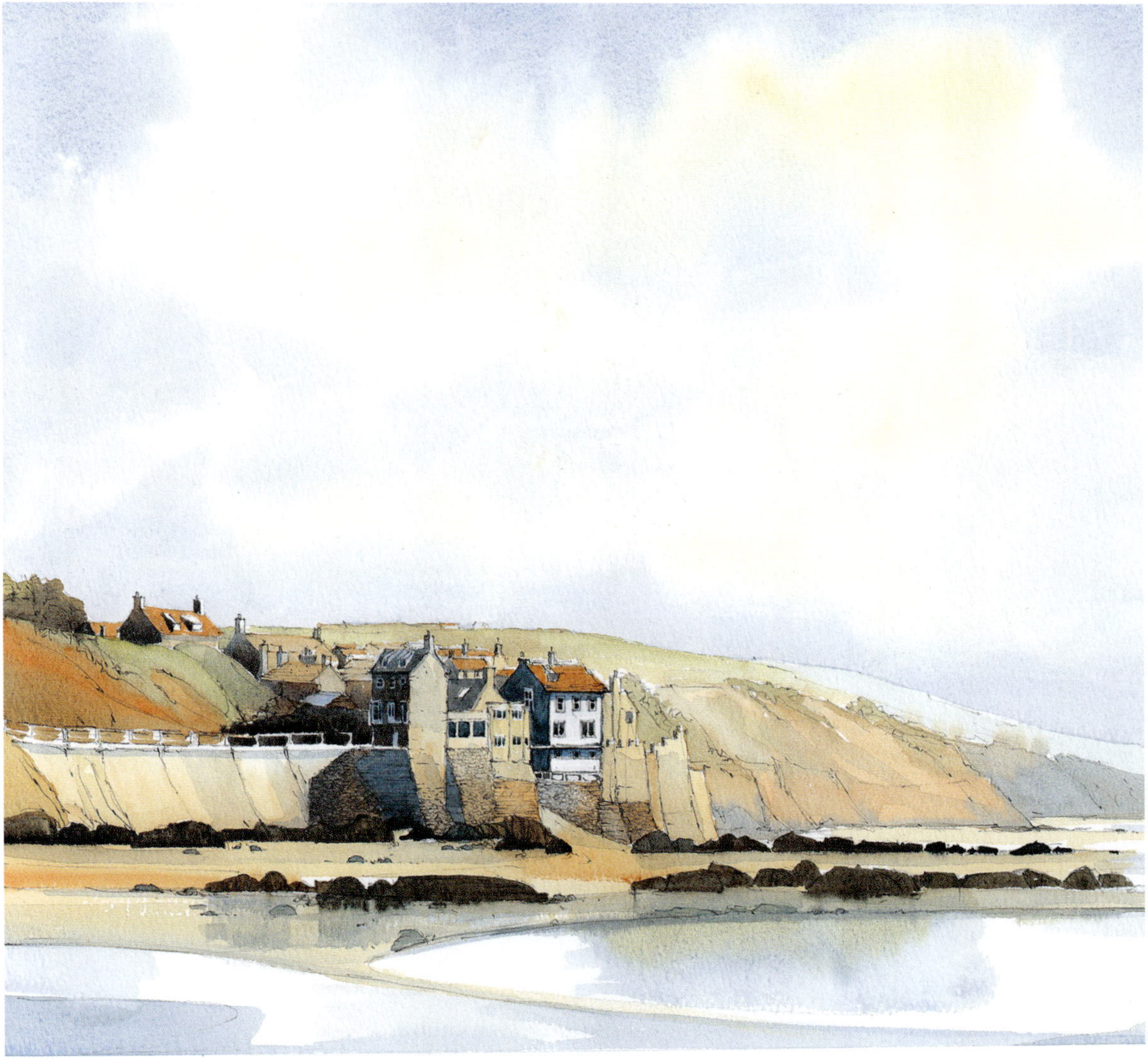

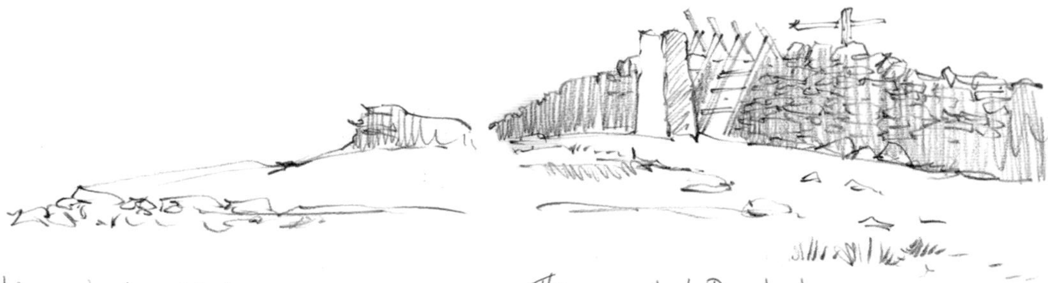

The summit of Penyghent.

Not much of a picture,
but I felt like doing it.
I always used to think that if
I didn't return with at least
three sketches, then I hadn't
been trying. (One more to do!)

A really good climb- windy
but with pleasant sun. Not a
lot there when you get to the top!

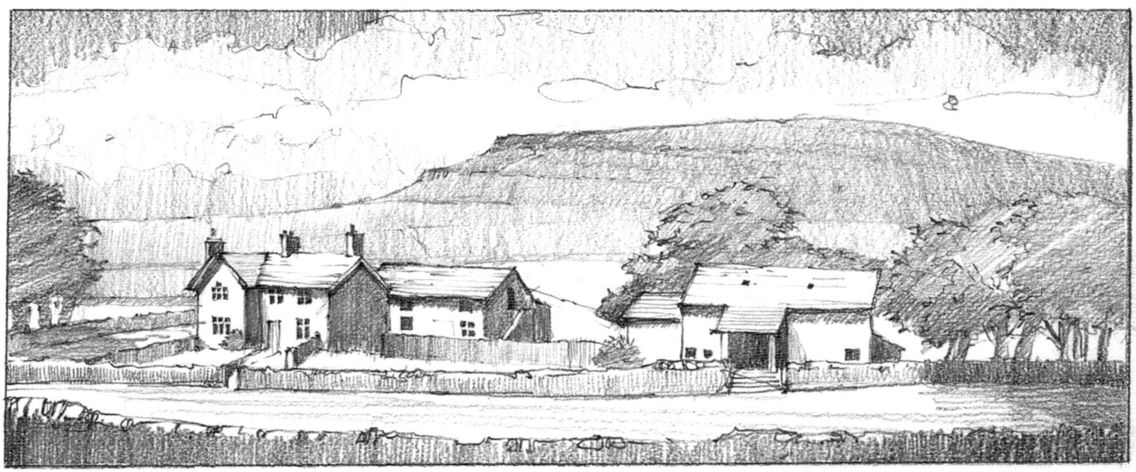

Penyghent on a sunny, summer's day.

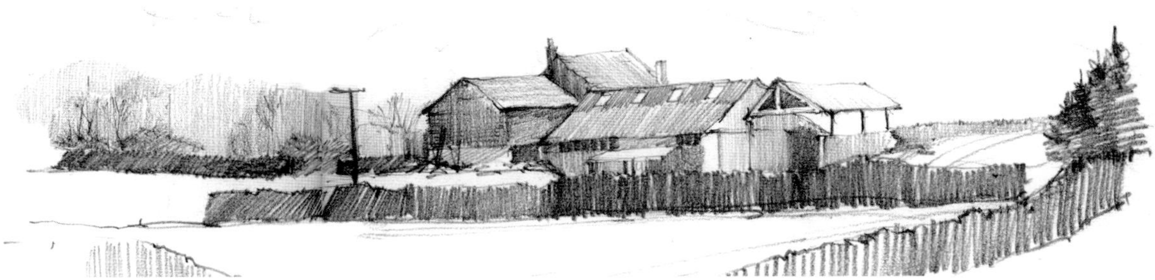

Farm Near Haworth.

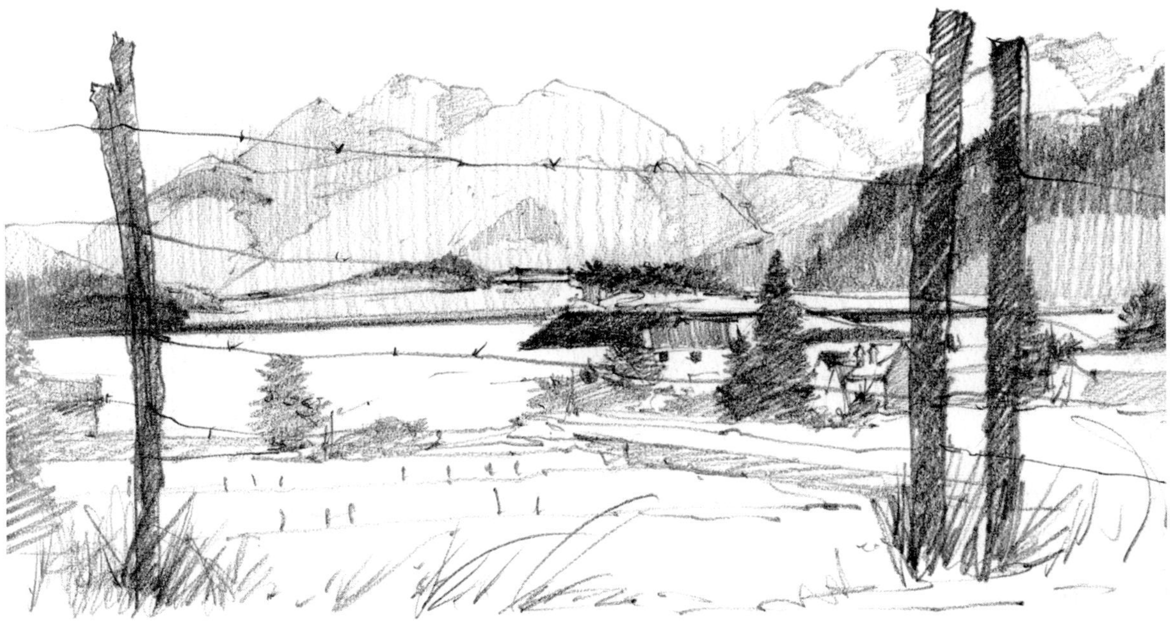

Bridge at Ballachulish.

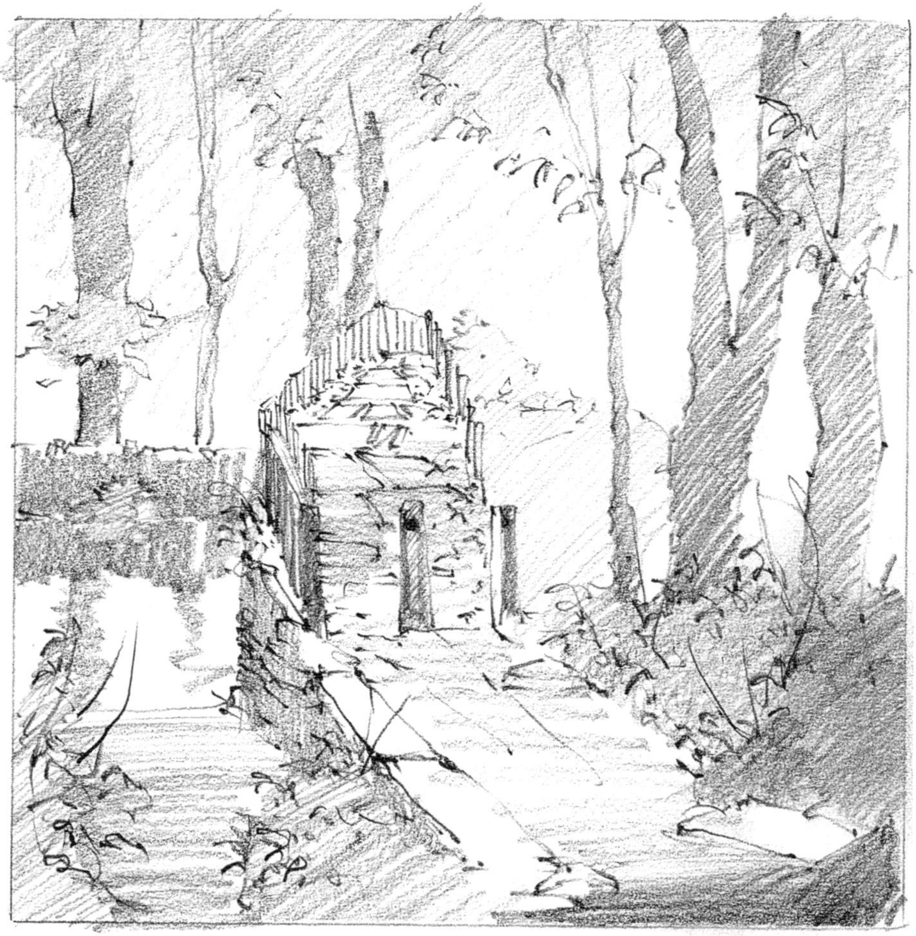

Beckfoot Bridge - Bingley
(A 10 minute quickie)

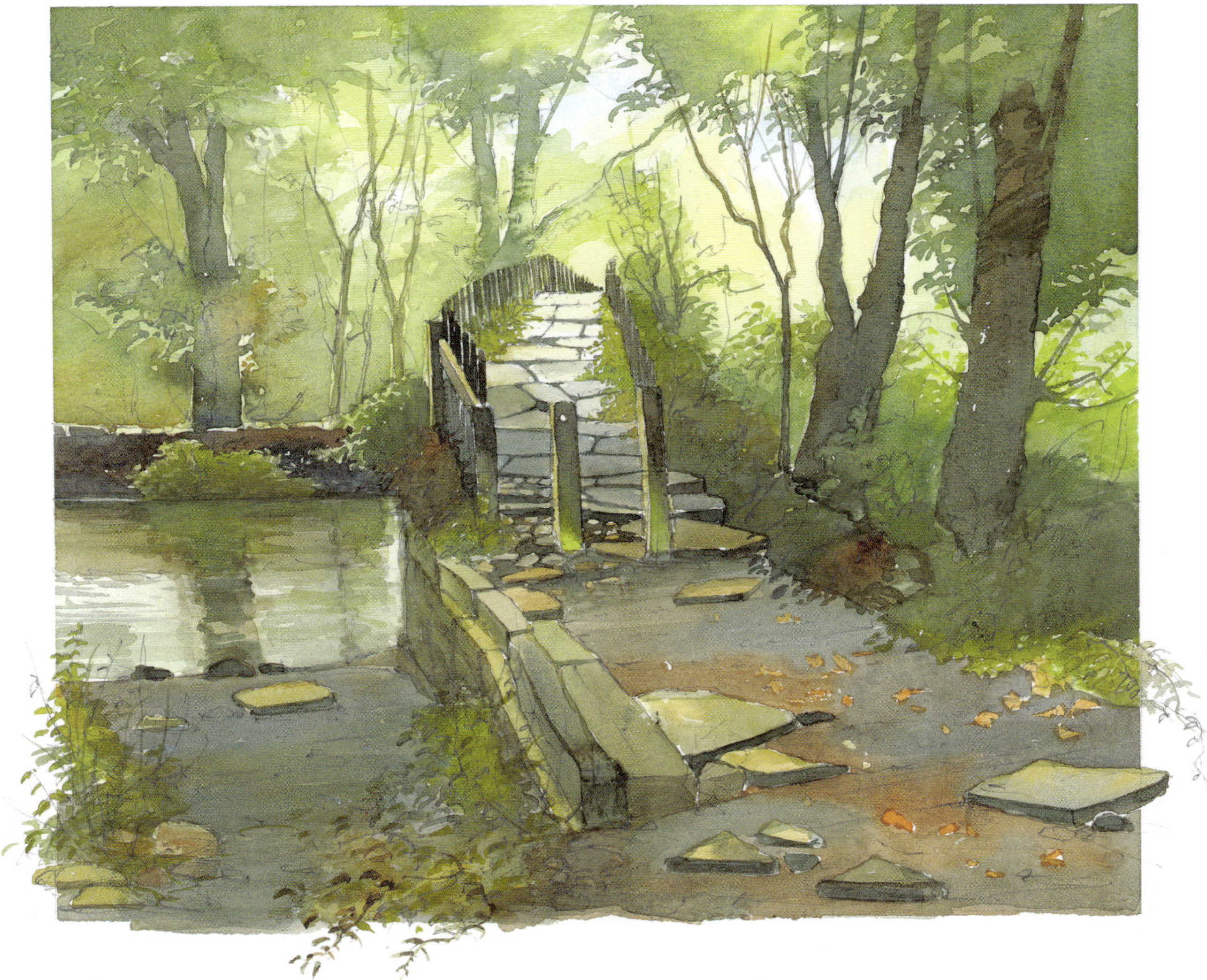

Beckfoot Bridge - Bingley

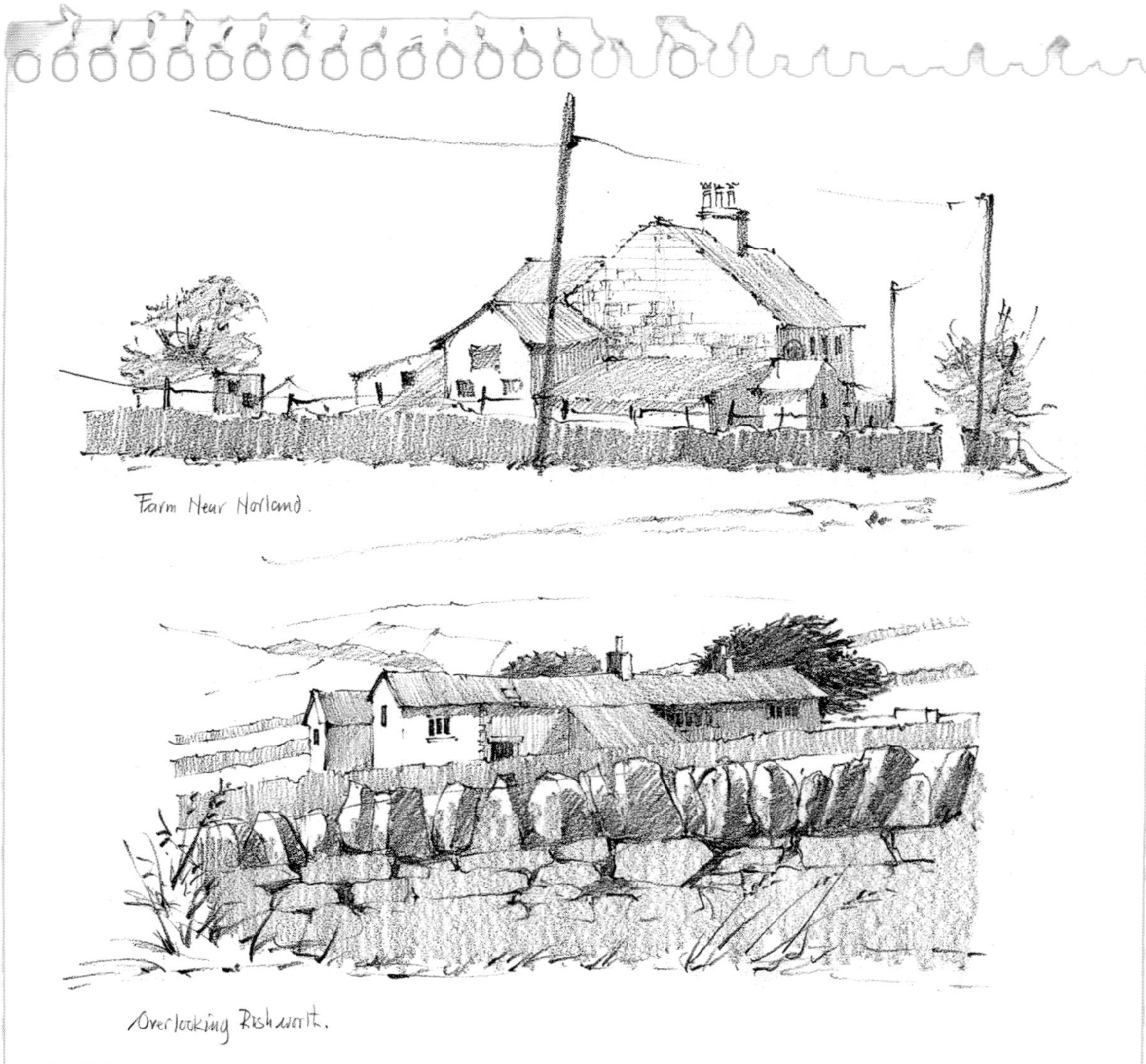
Farm Near Norland.
Overlooking Rishworth.

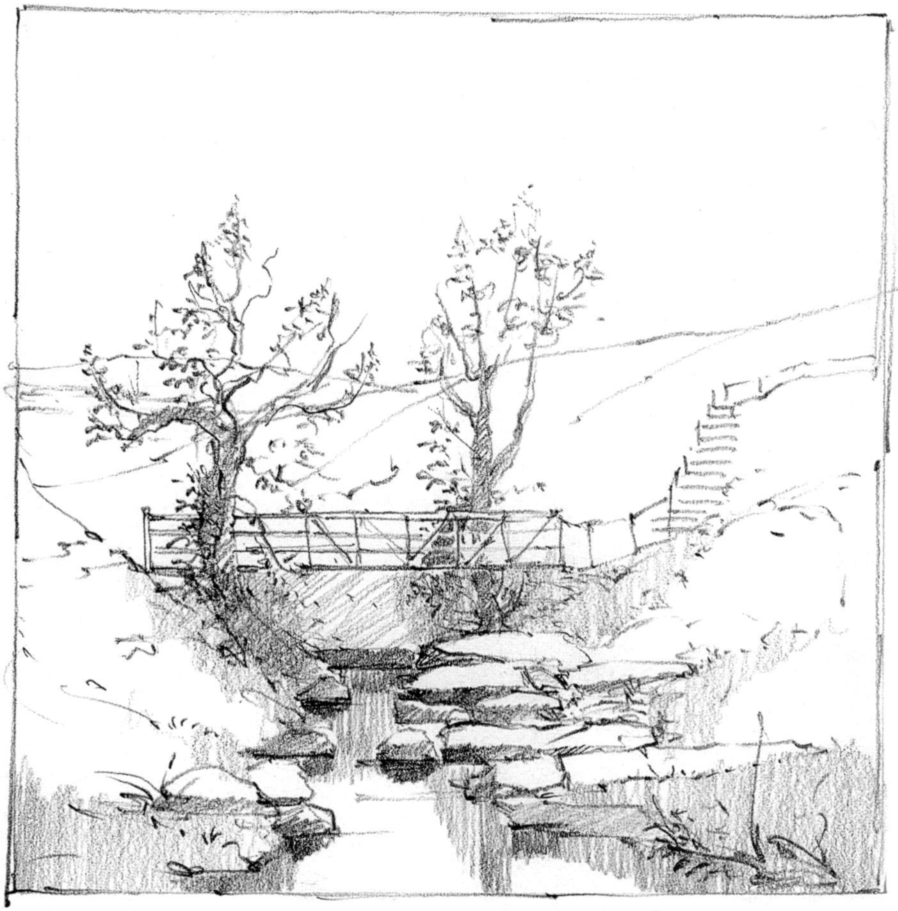

Very quick sketch.
Sun behind me
shining onto the
paper. Too bright
to draw

Bridge over the River Twiss
View up Kingsdale above
Thornton Glen - Ingleton.
5.6.07.

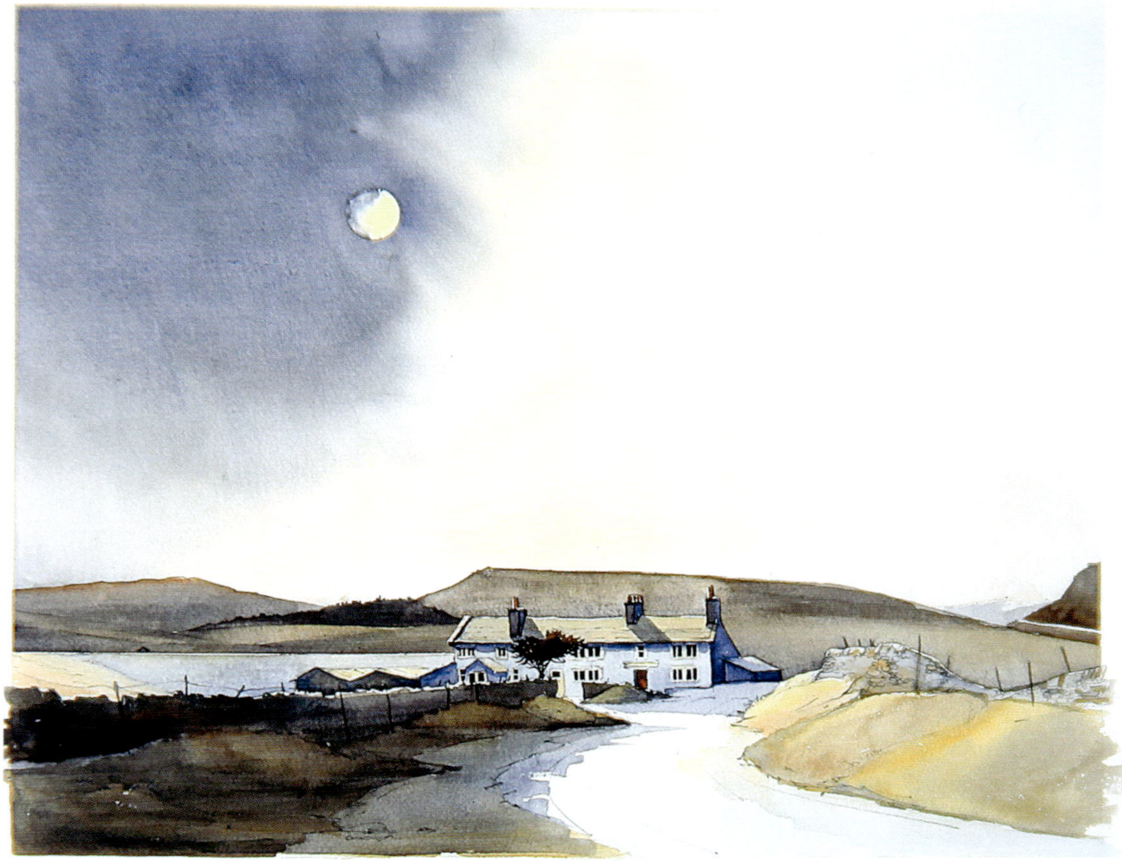

The Pack horse Inn – Widdop.

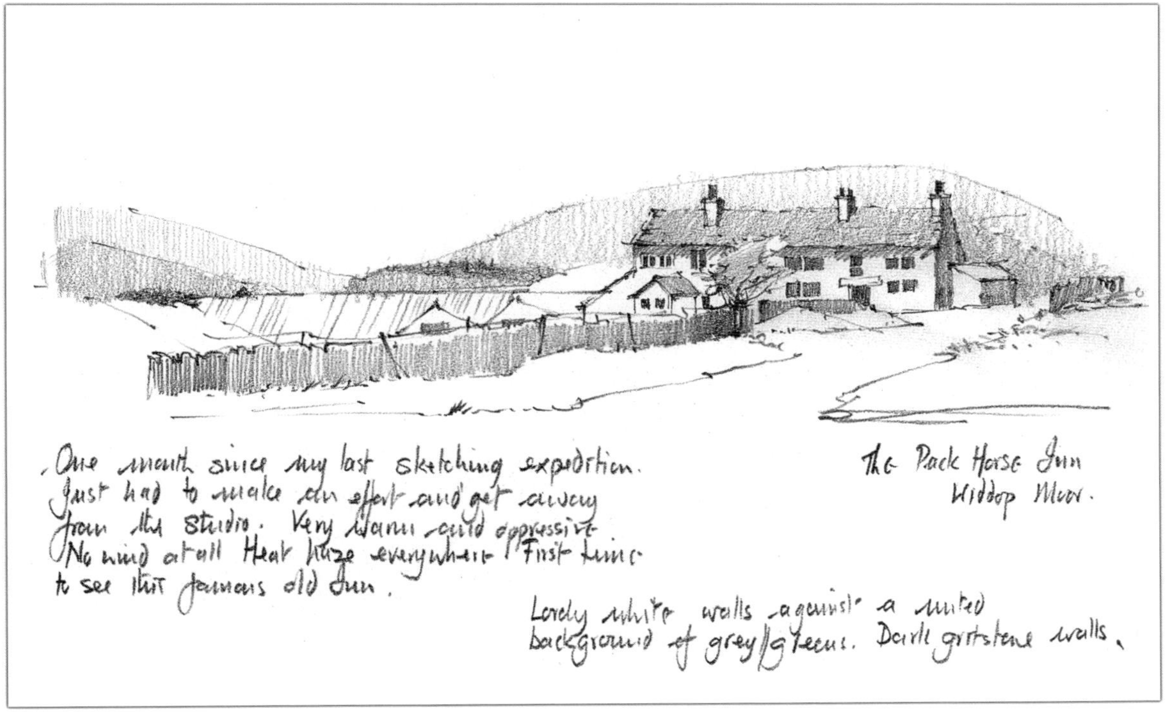
One month since my last sketching expedition.
Just had to make an effort and get away
from the studio. Very warm and oppressive.
No wind at all Heat haze everywhere First time
to see this famous old Inn.
The Pack Horse Inn
Widdop Moor.
Lovely white walls against a muted
background of grey/greens. Dark gritstone walls.

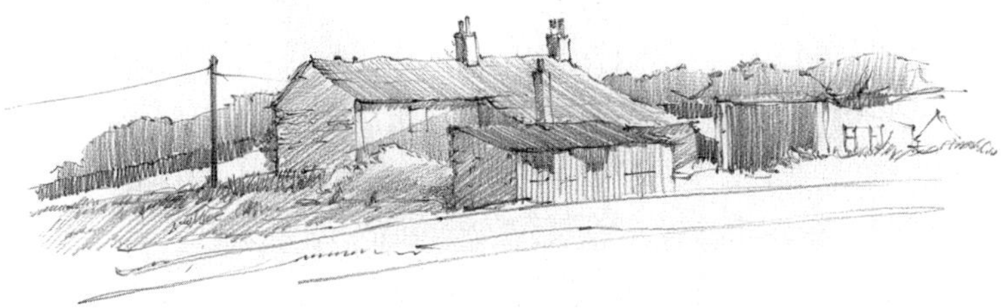

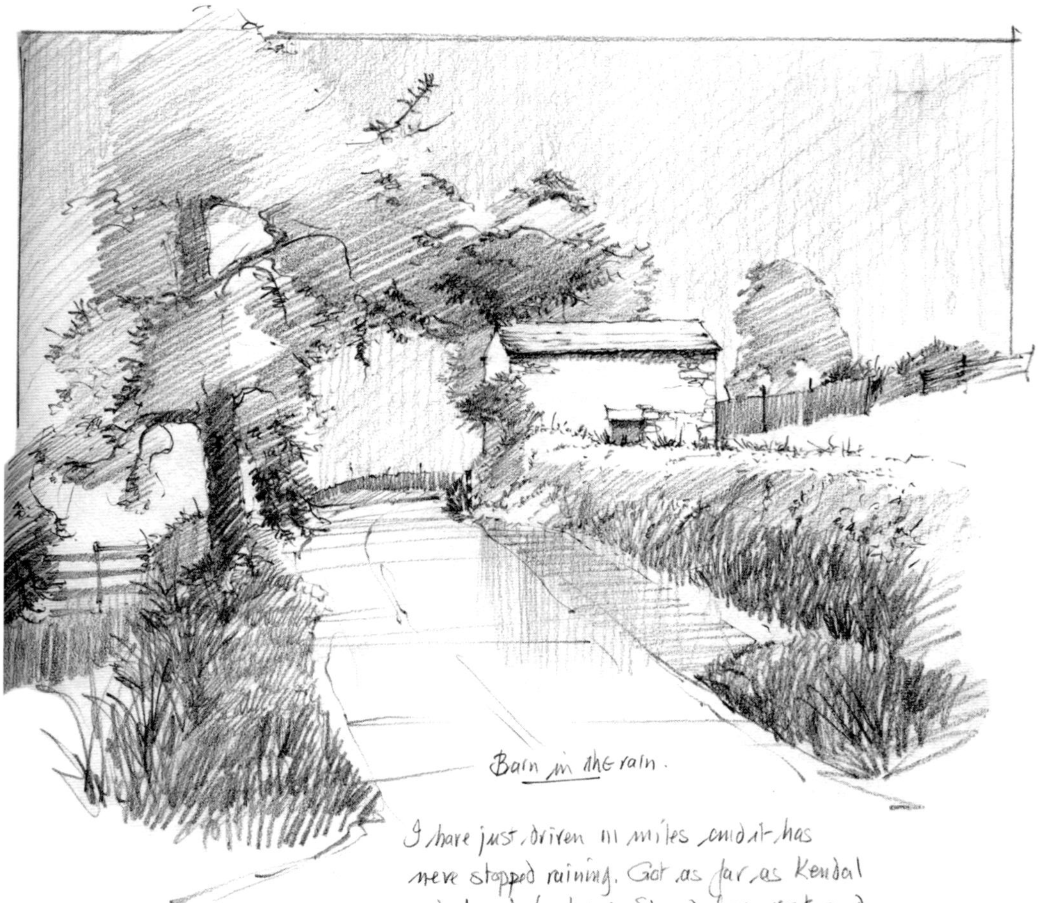

Barn in the rain.

I have just driven 111 miles and it has
neve stopped raining. Got as far as Kendal
and turned for home. Stopped for a rest and
made this drawing. If it hadn't been for
Classic F. M. (Sibelius and Brahms) it would
have been a wasted day.
The gloom has just been swept away by
Janet Baker singing Brahms Alto Rhapsody.

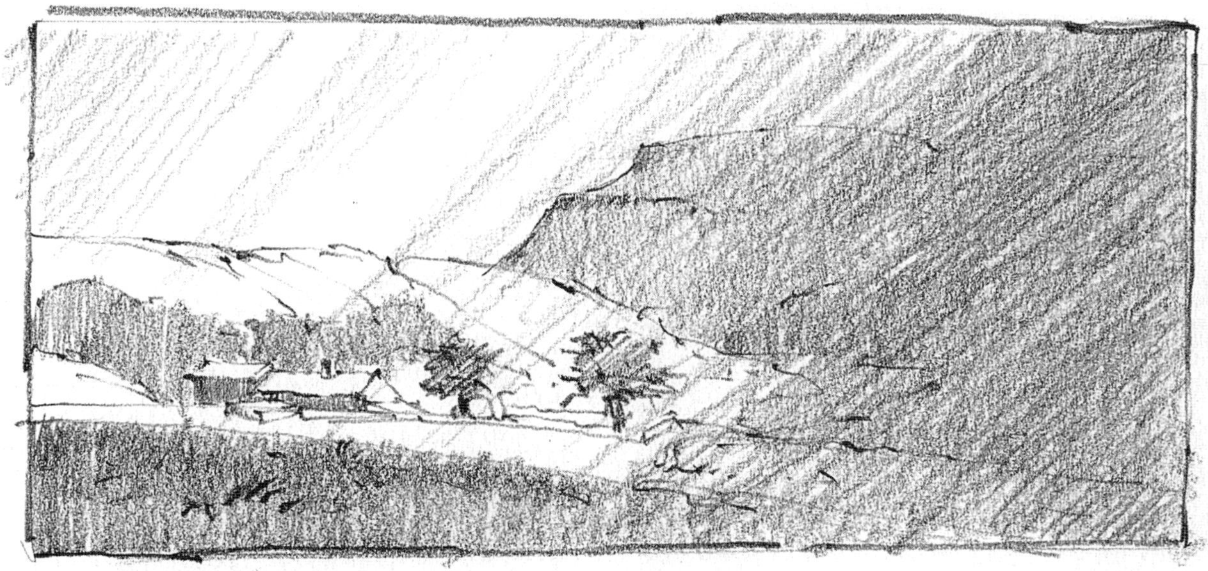

Rain Over Ingleborough.

It might be summer, but this is England (and in my case Yorkshire) where the weather can change many times a day. The hill walker should always have a waterproof in his rucksack. The very fact that you are walking in hill country, which has it's own climate, means that beautiful mornings can often turn into windy and rainy afternoons. The best advice is to keep your eyes open and be aware of what the wind is blowing in your direction.

My sketch shows Ingleborough with bad weather approaching. Time to get into waterproofs whilst your clothes are still dry.

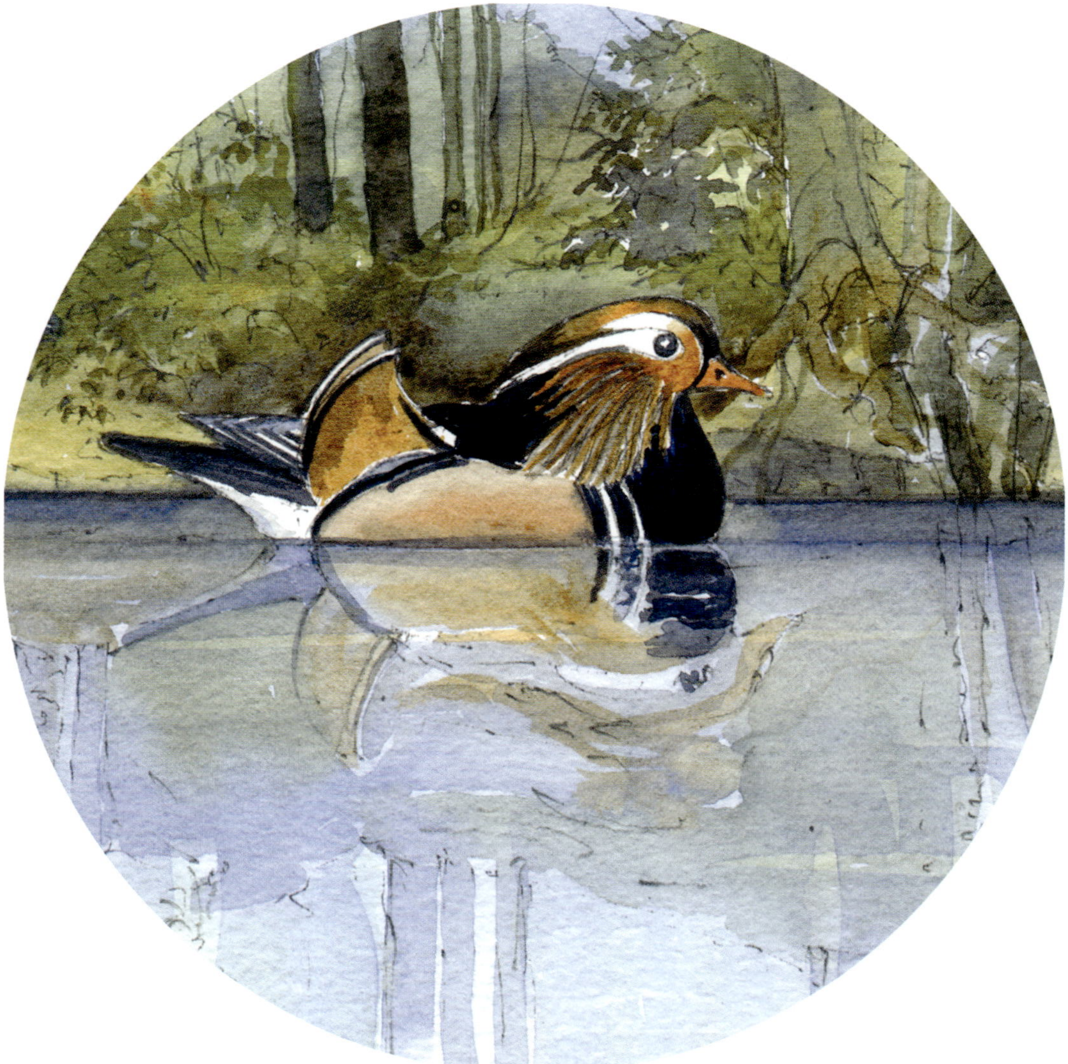

A World Within a Circle

I gaze entranced, at a world within a circle,
Bright as a jewel.
Unlike the astronomer, who, lying
Beneath his telescope in the dark of the night,
Looks at a world distant, cold and dead.
My world is bright with life abundant.

I watch this world within a circle,
Busy living it's own life.
Quite unaware of me, the watcher in the hide.
Lifting the spirit with it's dazzling beauty.
Reality enhanced by the effect of light and lens,
This world within a circle, bright as a jewel.

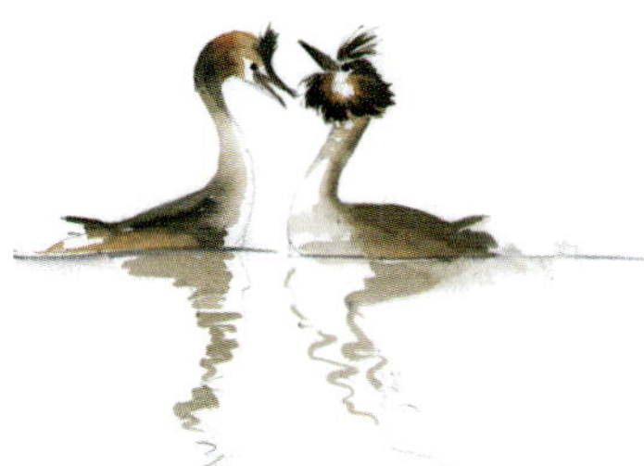

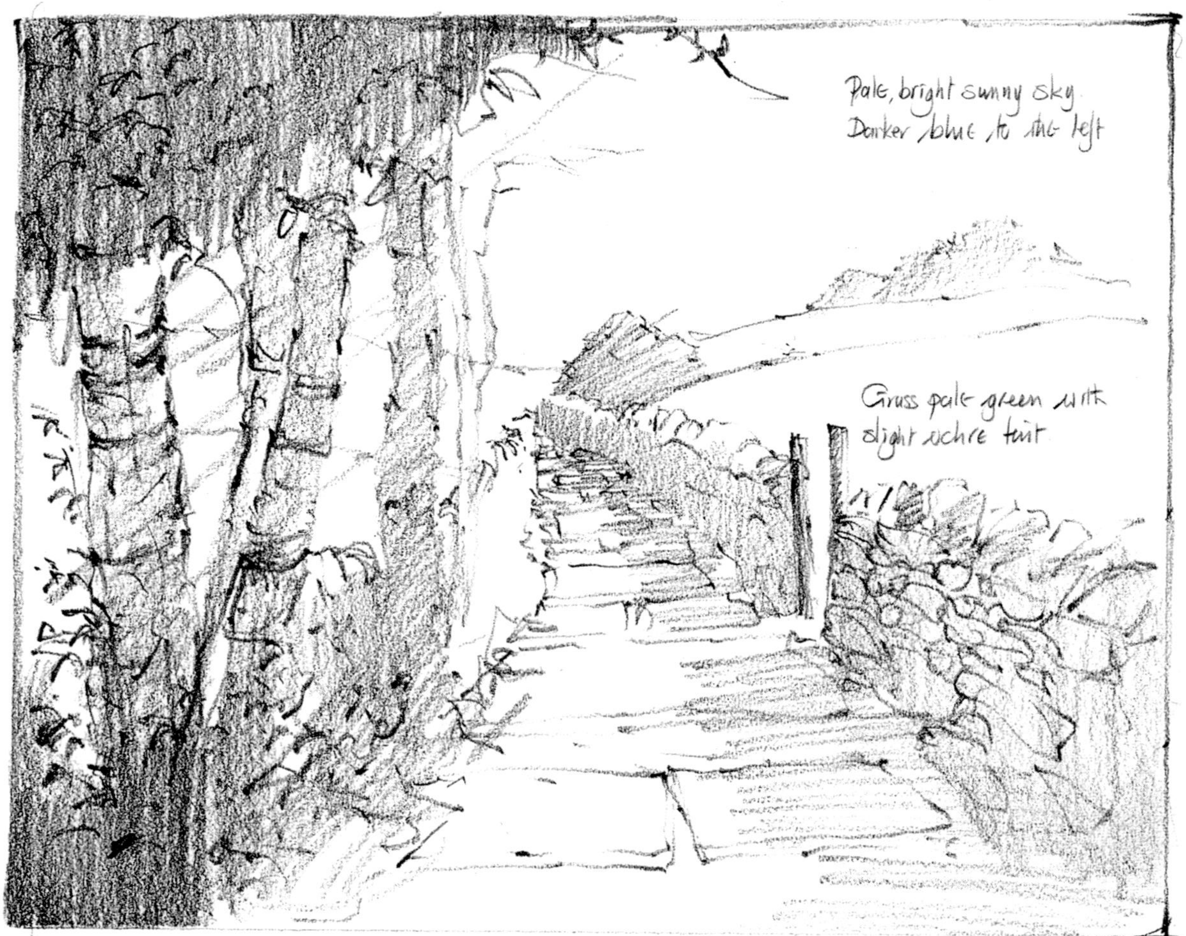

Sunlight flickering down through the trees. Drawing does'nt work - hope the painting will.

Path from Linton Falls to Grassing ton. Probably has a name. (Locals call it the "snake path".

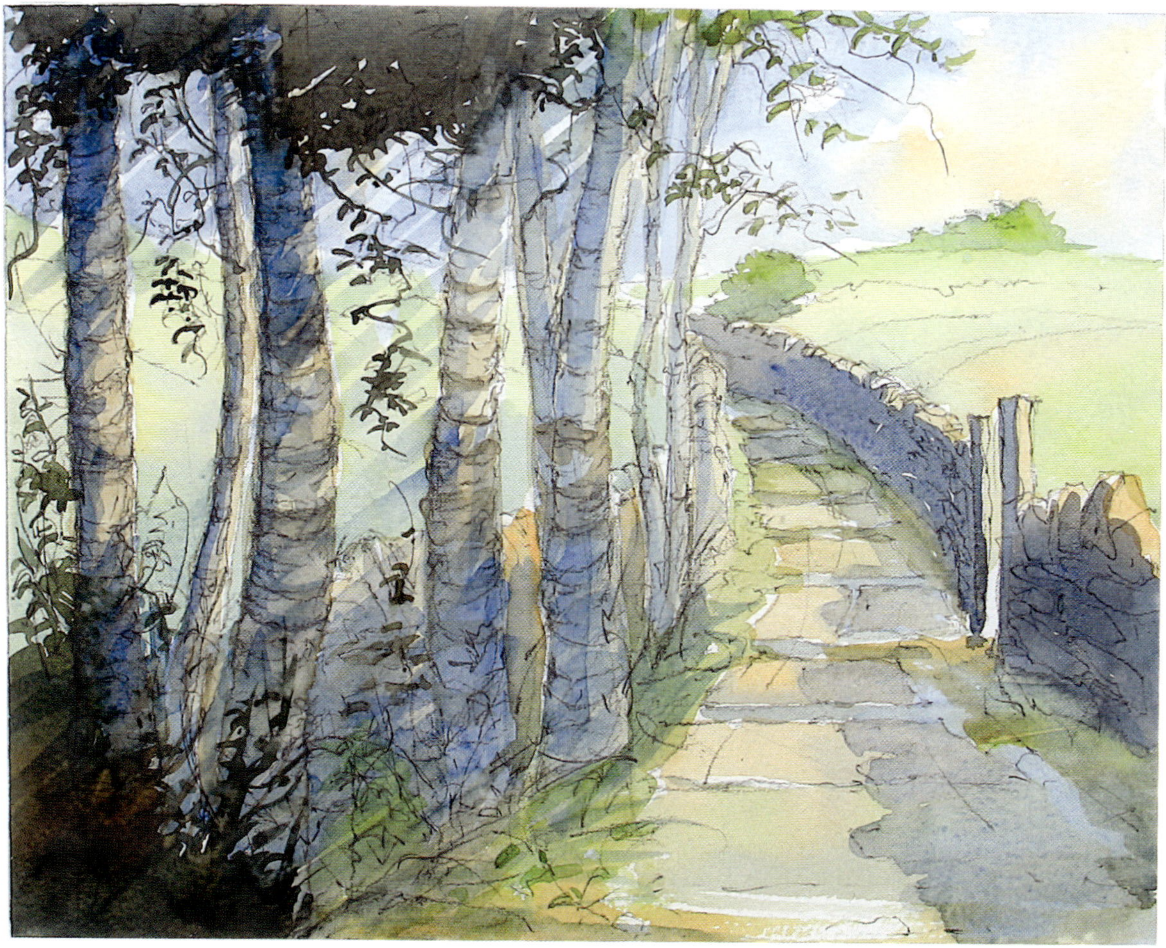

The "Snake Path" to Grassington.

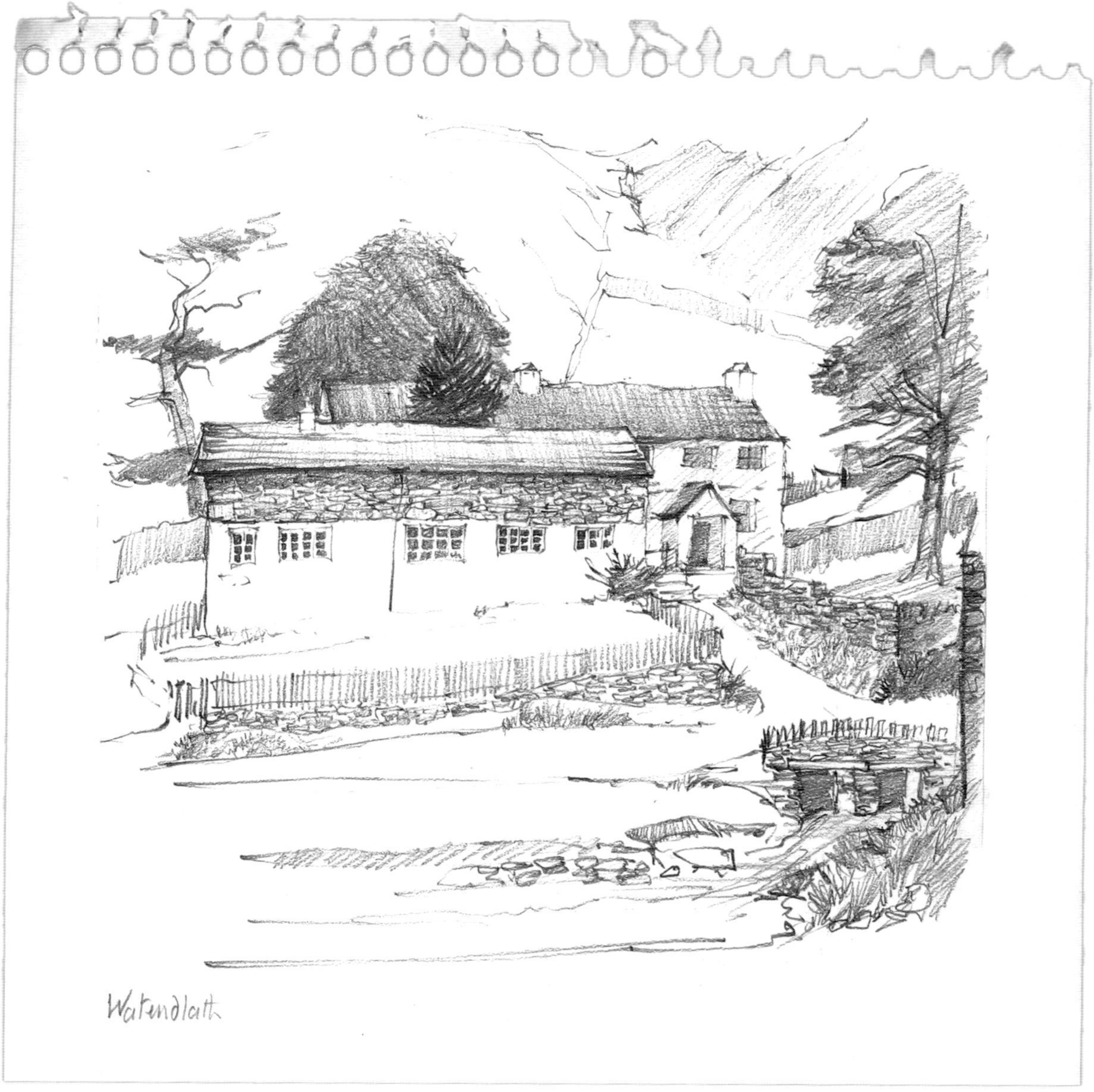
Watendlath

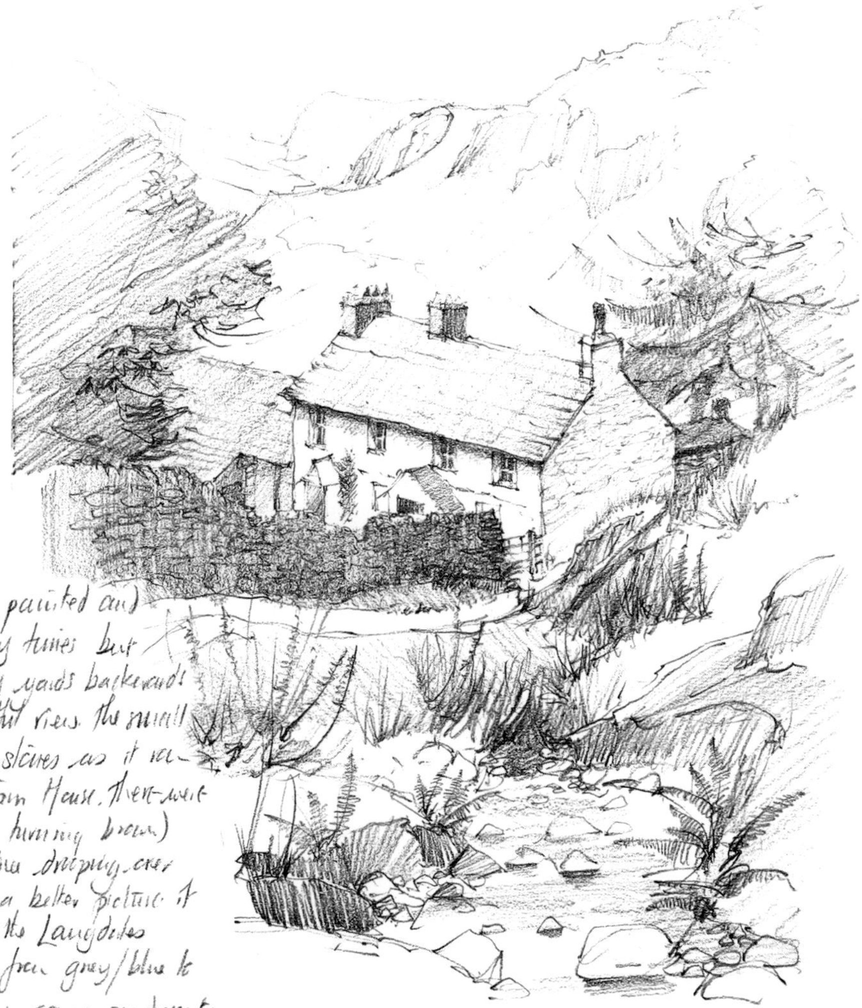

Blea Tarn House.

I have drawn and painted and photographed this many times but today I walked twenty yards backwards and found this delightful view. The small stream chattered over stones as it ran down towards Blea Tarn House. There were ferns and nettles (now turning brown) and the famous larch tree drooping over the building – what a better picture it makes. The high hills of the Langdales continually changing from grey/blue to apple green as the sun came and went.

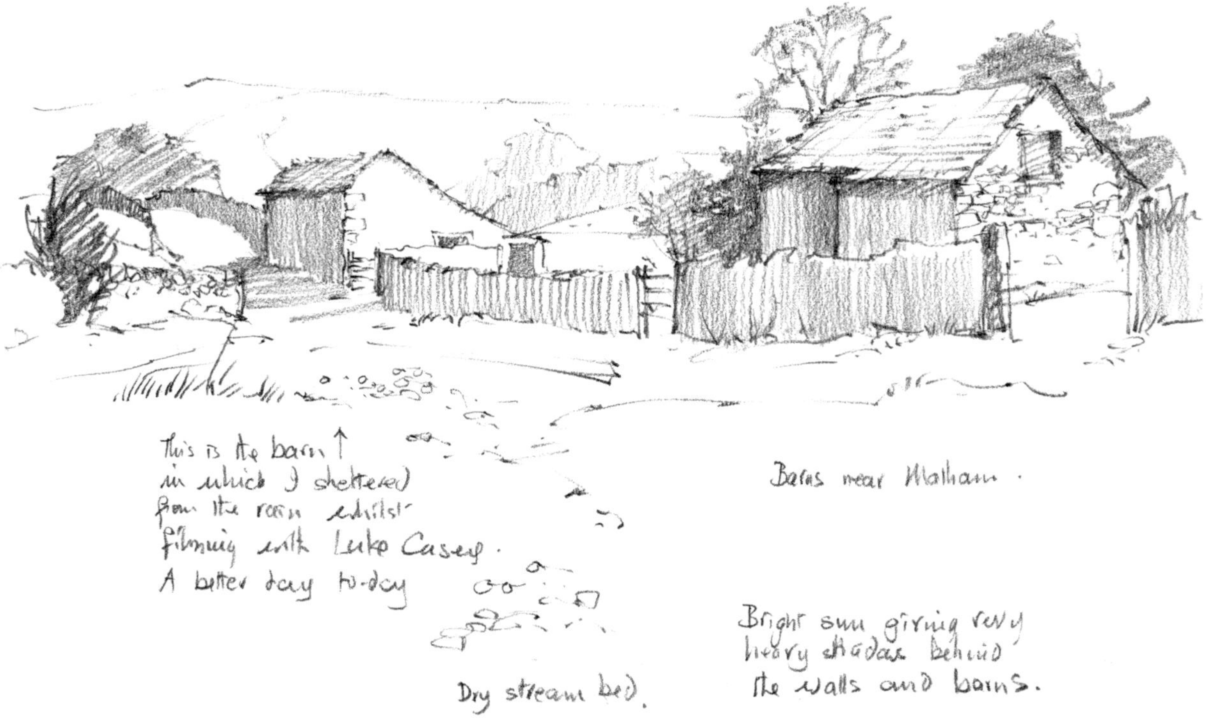
This is the barn ↑
in which I sheltered
from the rain whilst
filming with Luke Casey.
A better day to-day
Barns near Malham.
Bright sun giving very
heavy shadows behind
the walls and barns.
Dry stream bed.

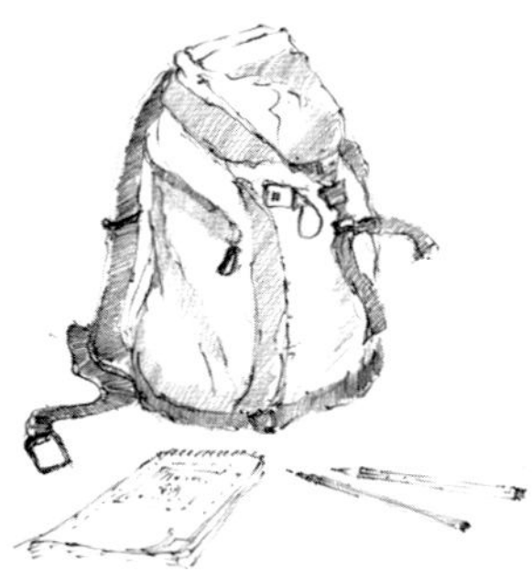

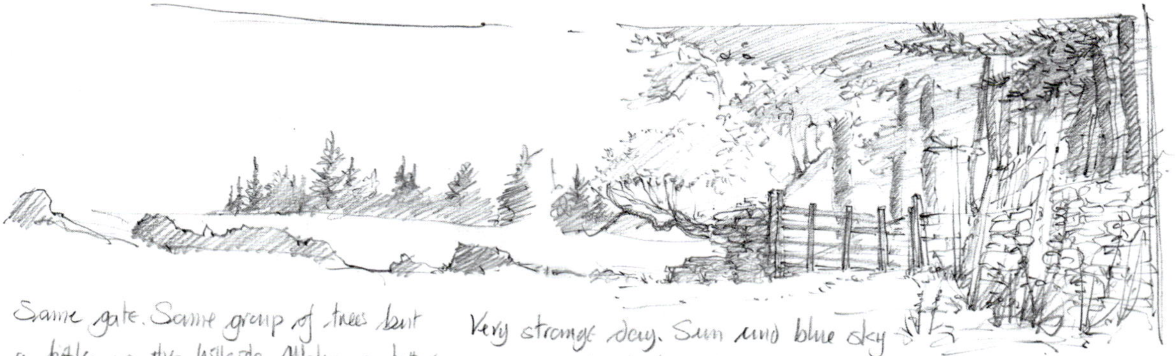

Same gate. Same group of trees but a little up the hillside. Makes a better picture.

Very strange day. Sun and blue sky on my side of the valley. Great banks of grey mist on the other side. Strange - drizzle out of a blue sky.

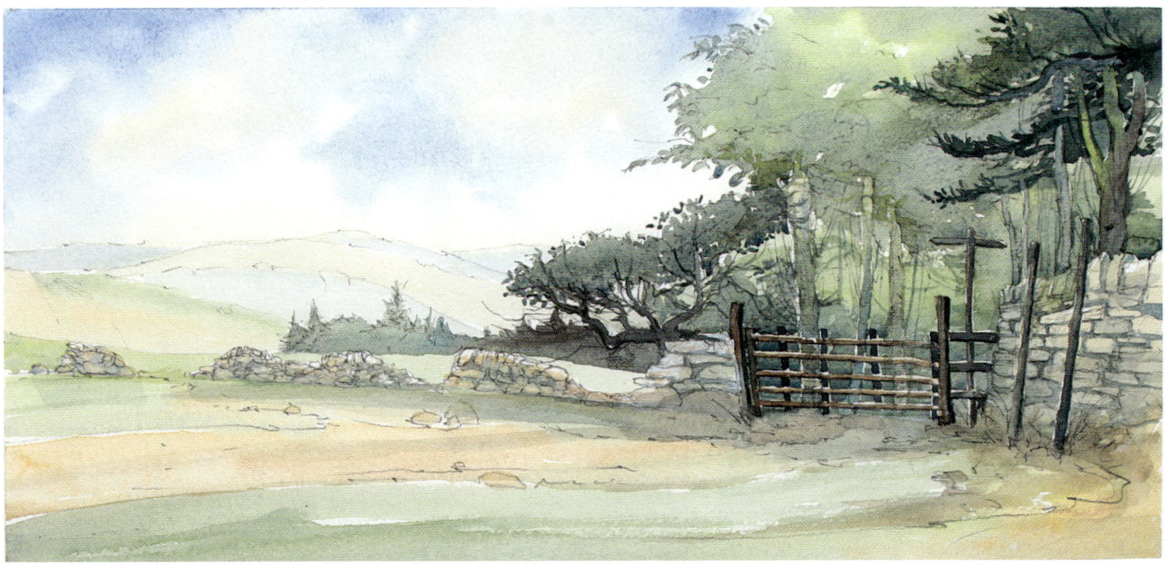

The "Dalesway" to Kettlewell

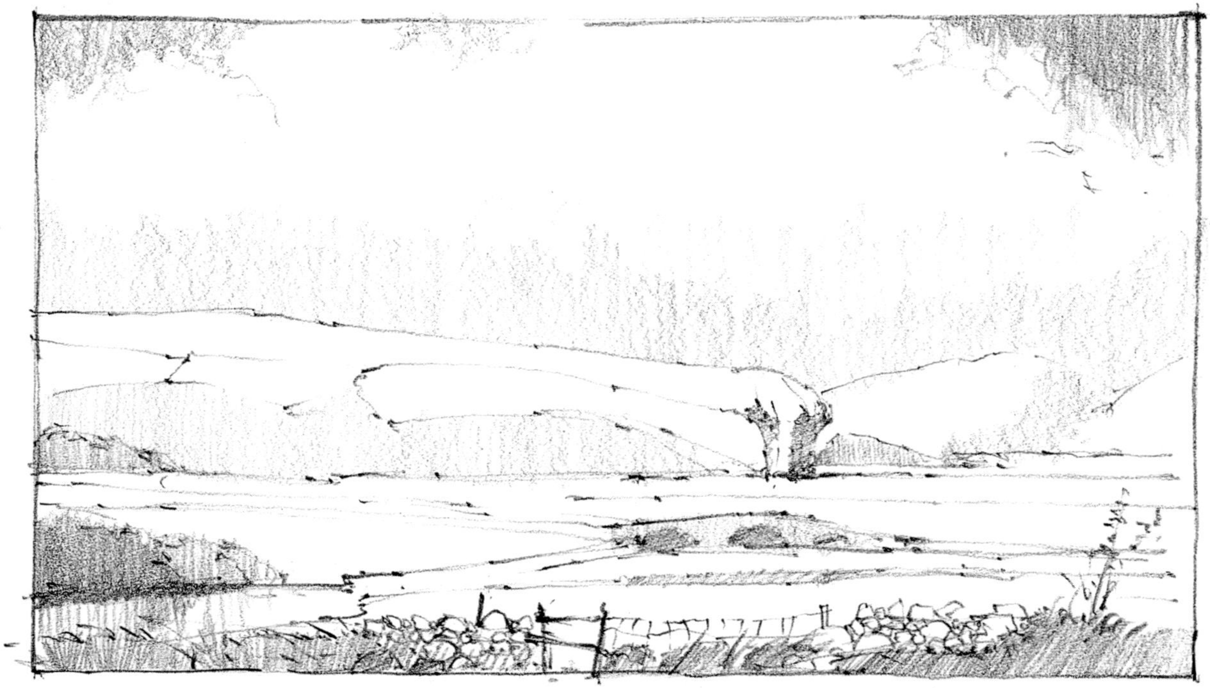

Kilnsey Crag.

It took a long time to find this place
I think it was this very spot where
J.M.W.T painted Kilnsey Crag on his
tour of Yorkshire. I am going to try it for myself.

In Memory Of J.M.W.T.

To tread in the footsteps of someone so famous
Was a humbling experience.
Could I possibly make something of the scene
Which he had viewed and painted, so many years before?

In all those years, so little has changed.
Now I am standing where he once stood.
And it worked - perhaps he was there lending a hand.
The pencil took control and I held on - going for the ride!

Now I sit in my cottage looking at the painting,
remembering another day spent in this beautiful dale,
Whilst over it hovers the ghost of J.M.W.T.
A gentle reminder of a greater talent.

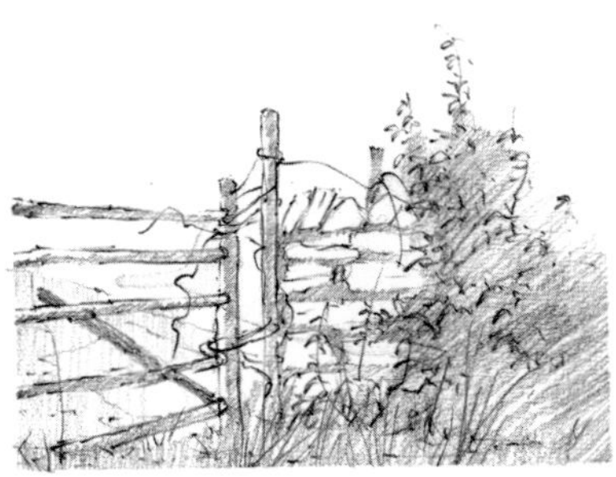

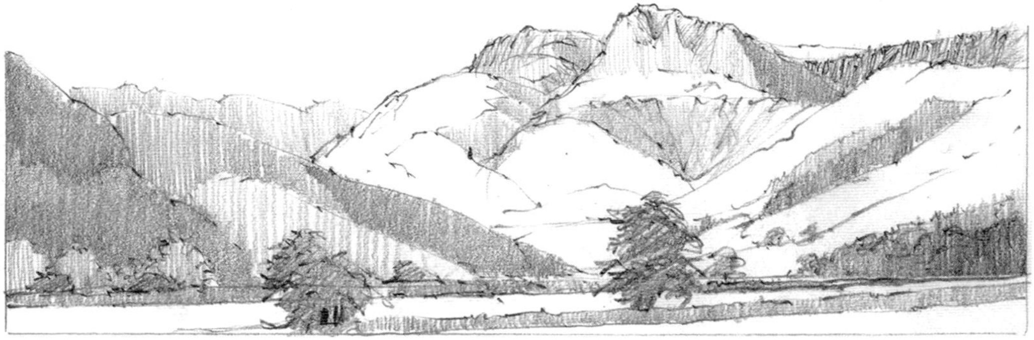

Langdale Pikes from Mickleden

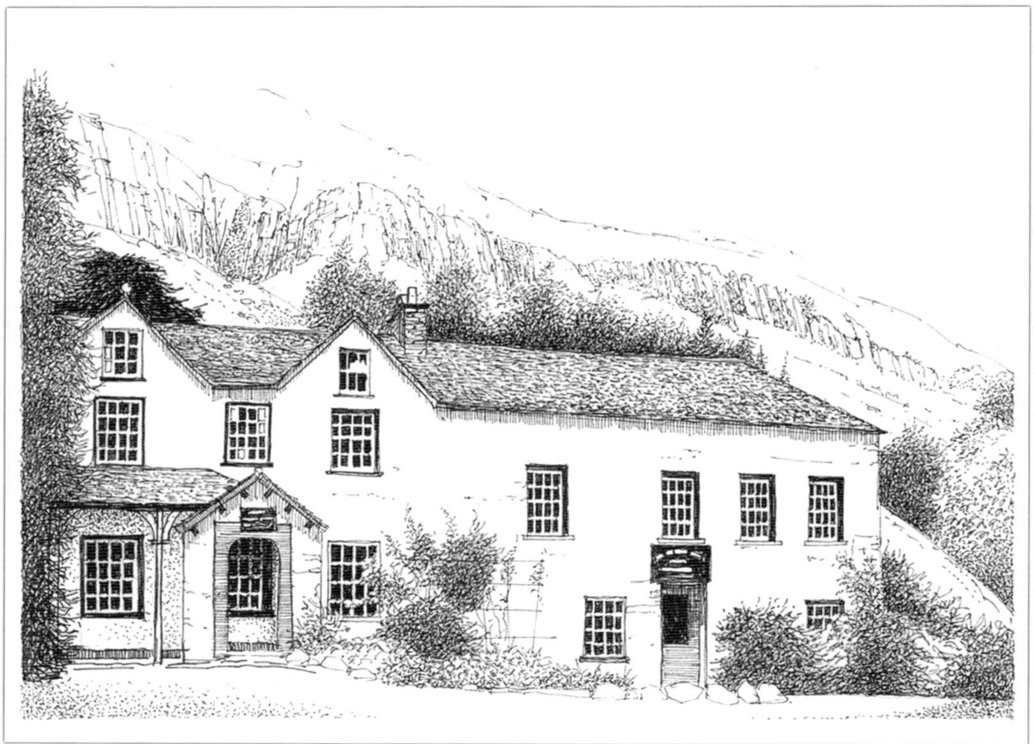

Dungeon Ghyll Hotel

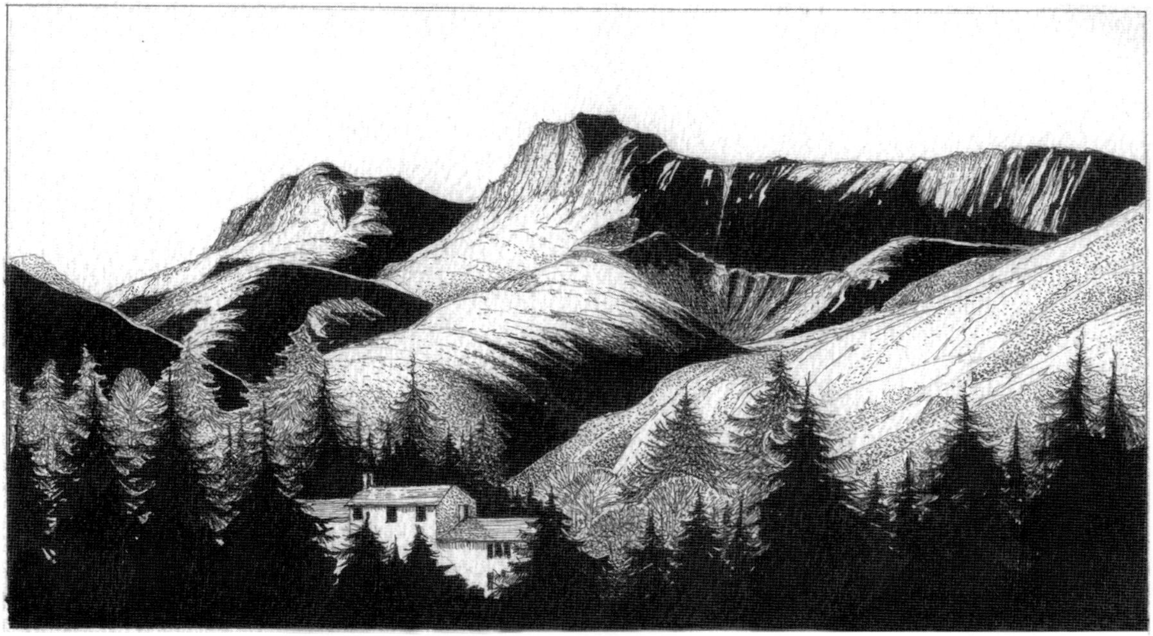

There are often occasions when the brain becomes lazy and bored. At times like this, a change of medium is often all that is required to start it thinking again. Pencil drawing is the most wonderful activity. It is simple, spontaneous and can be executed very quickly. Even so, when your brain becomes bored the quality of the drawing decreases.

A challenge is needed.

After producing a number of pencil sketches, I decided to get out the Staedtler technical drawing pen. Drawing with this pen is completely different to using a pencil. You can not get the tonal range simply by using a lighter touch. The two drawings show what the drawing pen can do. Neither will become paintings.

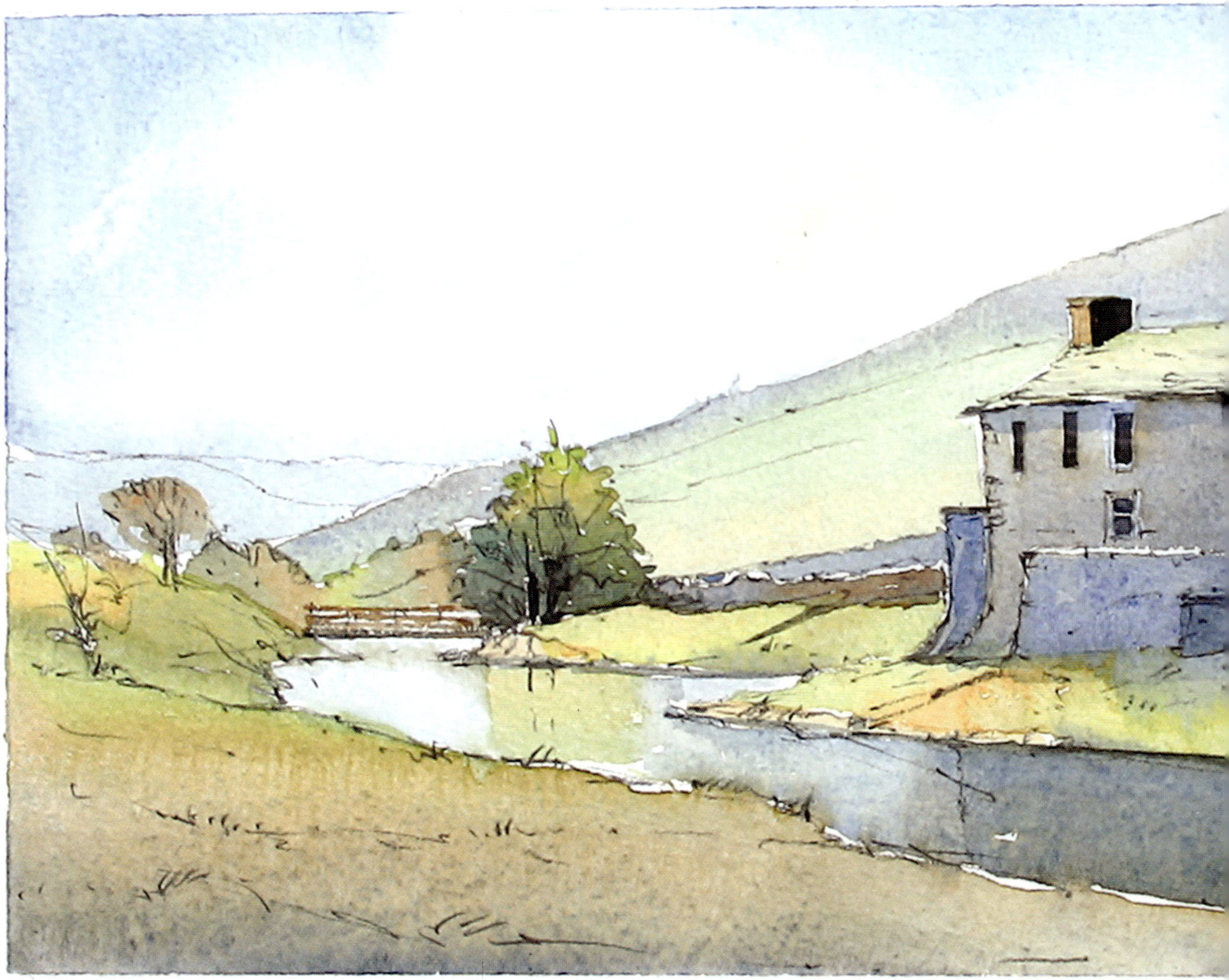

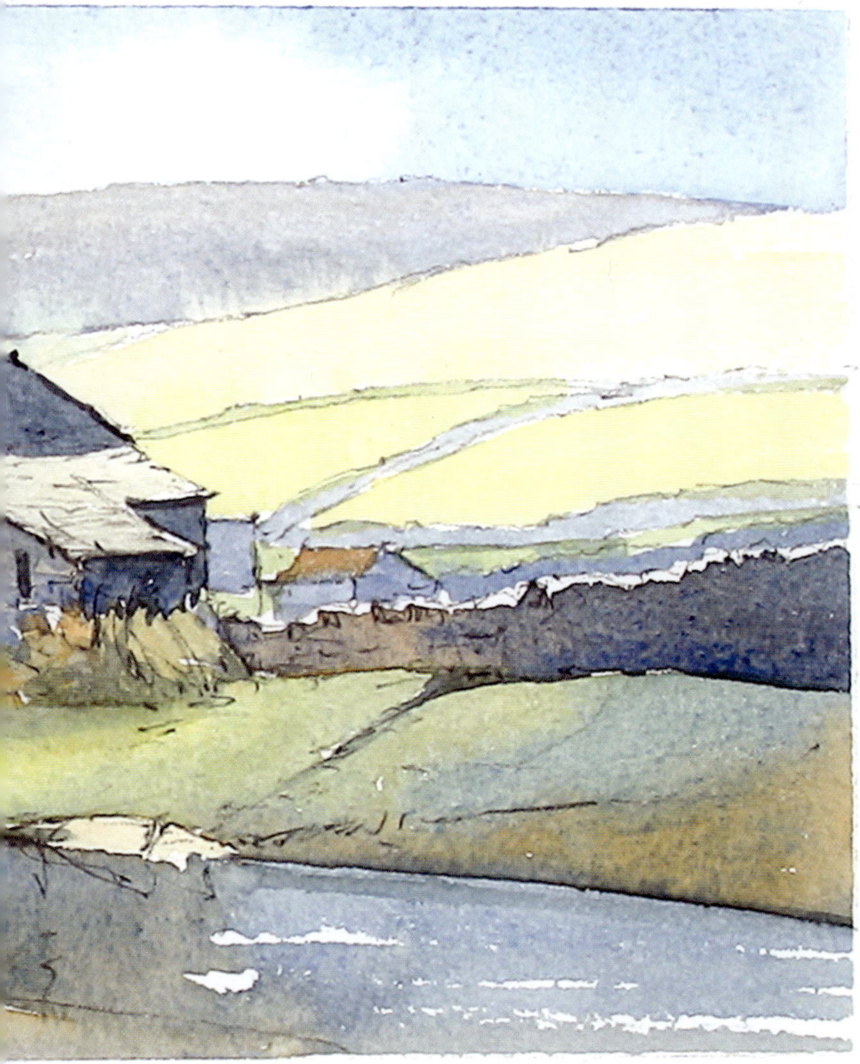

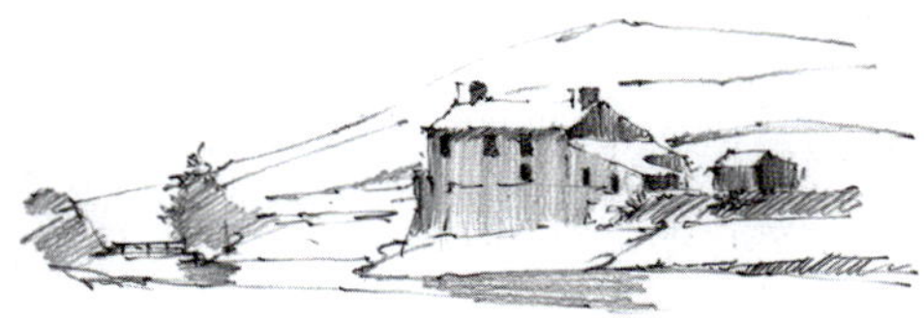

I have visited New House Farm, Langstrathdale, on several occasions and made at least four drawings. Not one of which produced a worthwhile painting.
All it needed was to change my view point, and look at the farm from the opposite side.

And it worked!

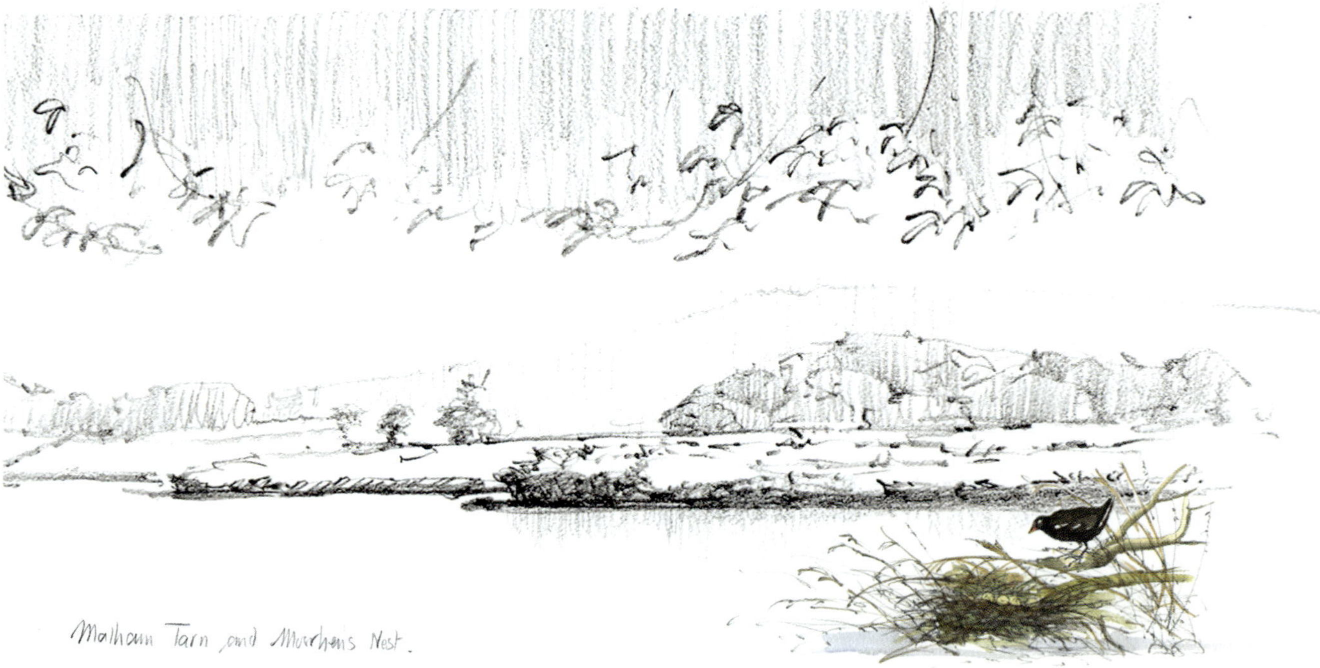

Malham Tarn and Moorhen's Nest.

From an early age I have been interested in bird watching. I love sitting in the hide with binoculars and telescope, whilst the birds go about their busy lives.

One day, on entering the hide at Malham Tarn, I found a lady with two young daughters looking very excited. "Look down out of the window", they whispered. There, almost at the foot of the hide, was a Moorhen with it's nest containing five eggs. It took absolutely no interest in the occupants of the hide, but settled down to brood it's eggs. Wonderful !

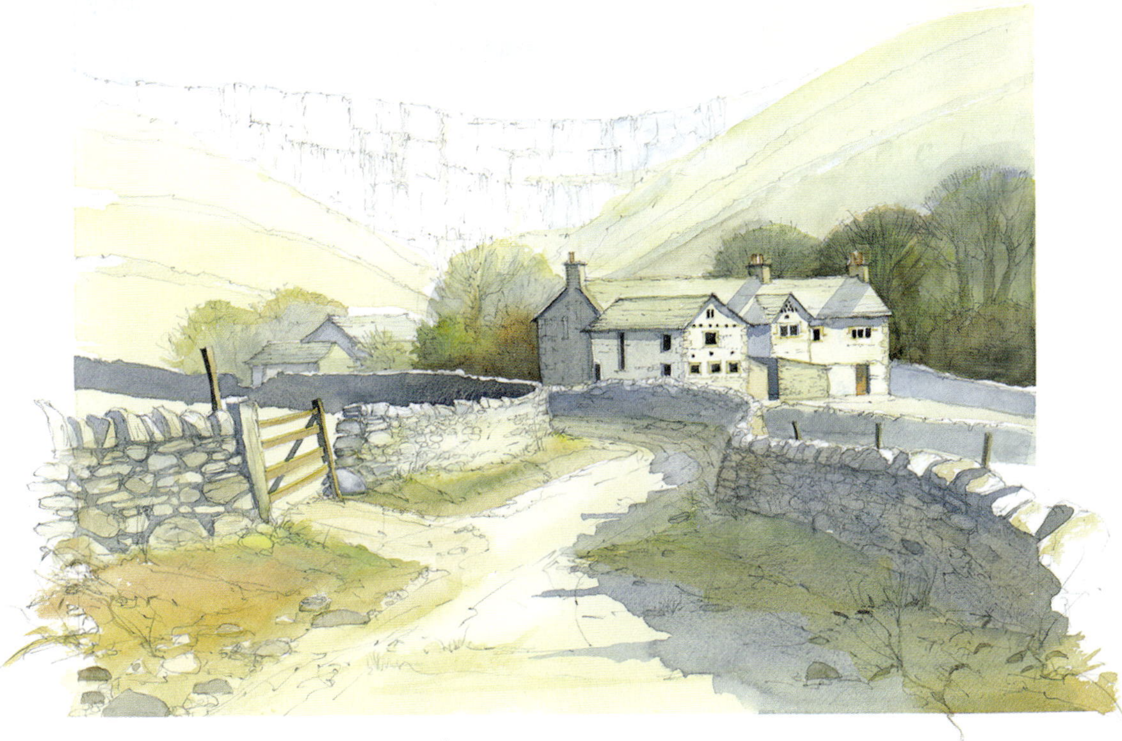

Malham in Summer.

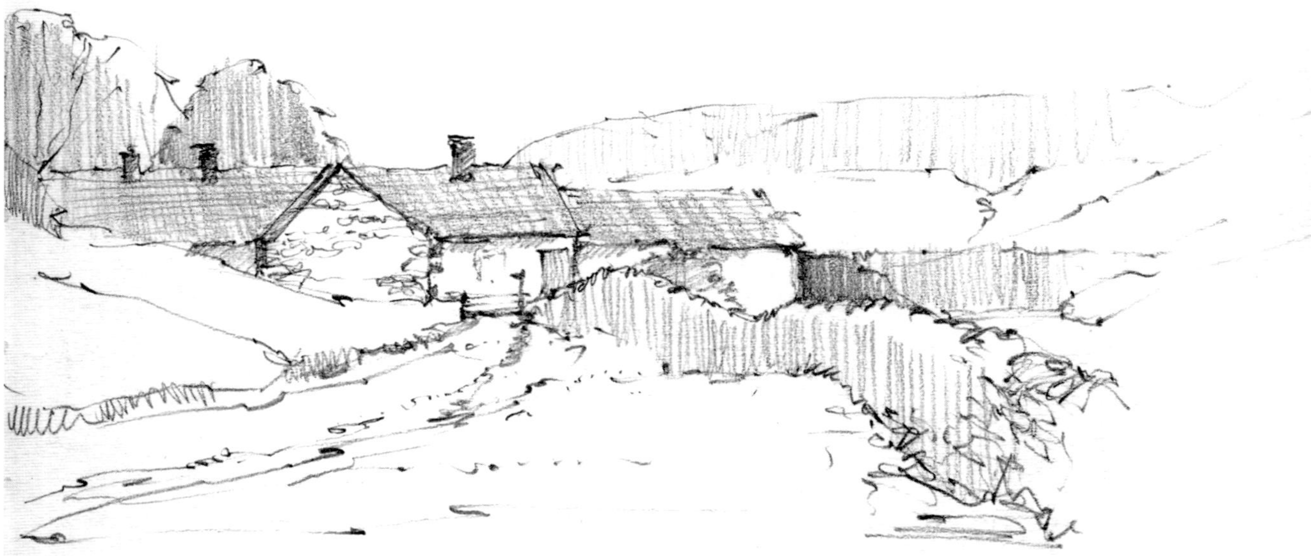

Moor End Farm

Old Cote Moor (I think - check the map).

One of the most remote farms I know. Came last week without camera or sketch book!. Not much of an artist am I. Then it was sun and blue sky all day. Now - cold wind grey day and heavy showers all the way here.

Blue sky, hazy sun and
clouds low down near
the horizon.

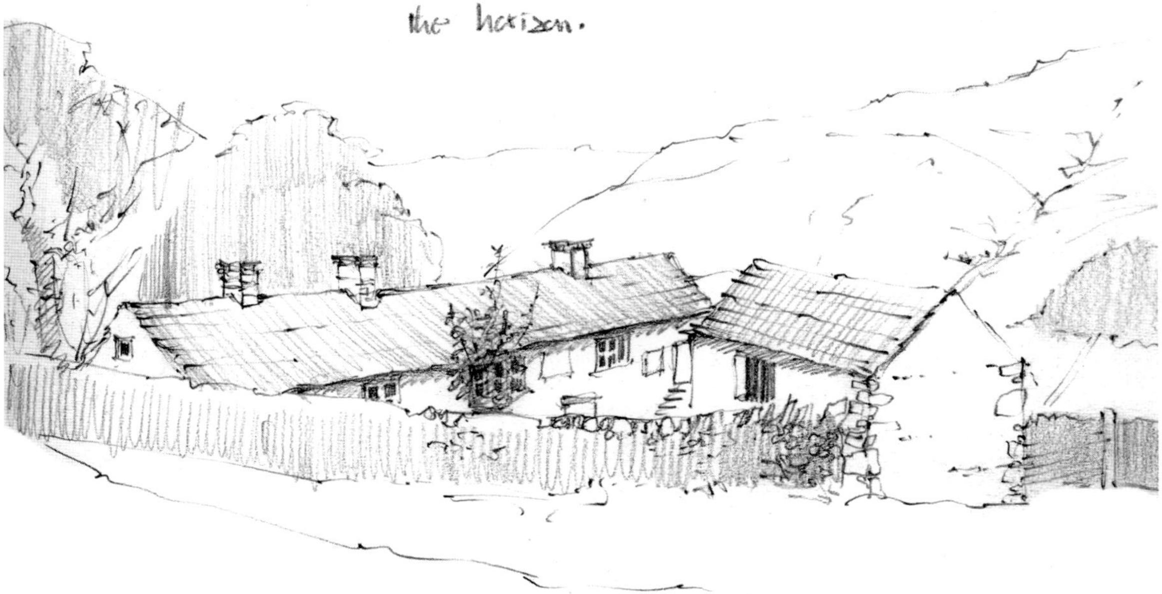

Moorend Farm – Again!

The third time in as many weeks.
Intrigued by this place. Each time the
weather has been good but today it
has been the best of all. Blue hazy sky
with white clouds. Cool wind but just
right for walking.

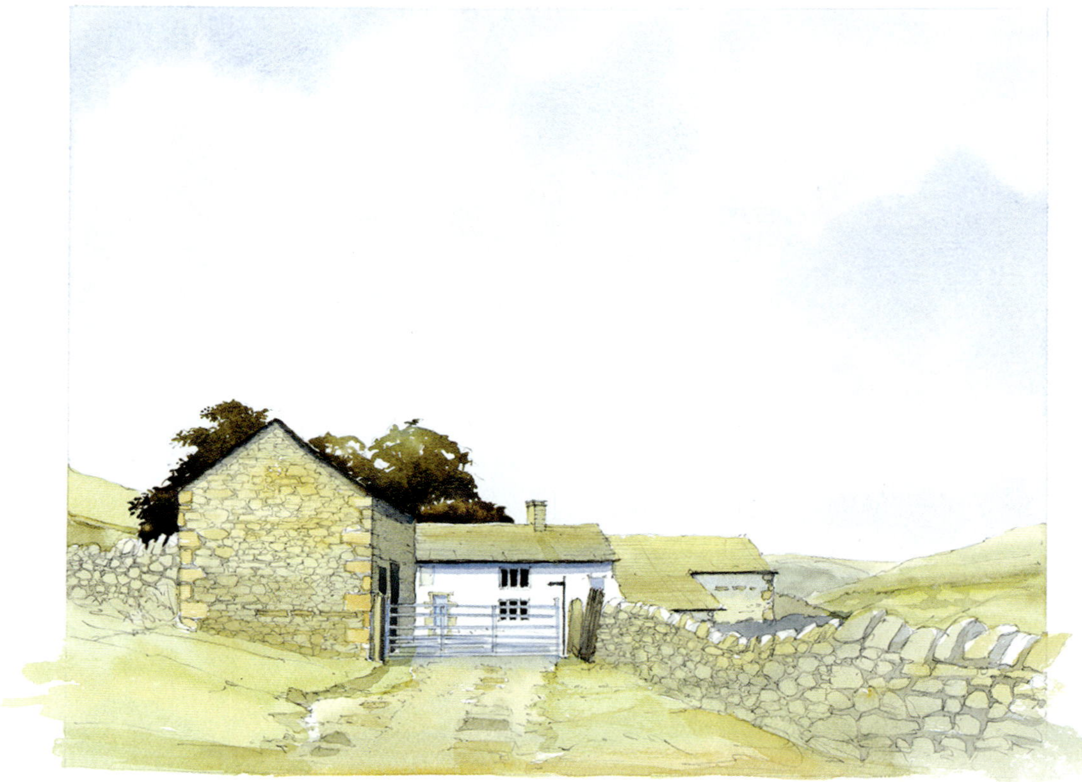

Moor End Farm

Moorend Farm

The climb up was hard.
Not difficult, just hard.
The path impossible to all but quads or tractors.

Underfoot, the path was steep and had been
Repaired many times,
With cobbles from the river.

Yorkshire farmers never waste money
And the cobbles were free
For the taking.

At last, the gradient eased
And once through the gate the path followed
A much easier route along the hillside.

In front of me stood the farm
Looking as if it had been built by nature
Not by the hand of man.

It crouched infront of a small copse of trees,
Seeking shelter from the north winds.
Its windows like eyes watching my approach.

All now was silent.
No bark of sheepdog. No excited call of children
Welcoming home their father from the high fells.

Only the silent, deserted farm.
Man had tried to tame nature but had failed.
Nature had won. Man had retreated - beaten.

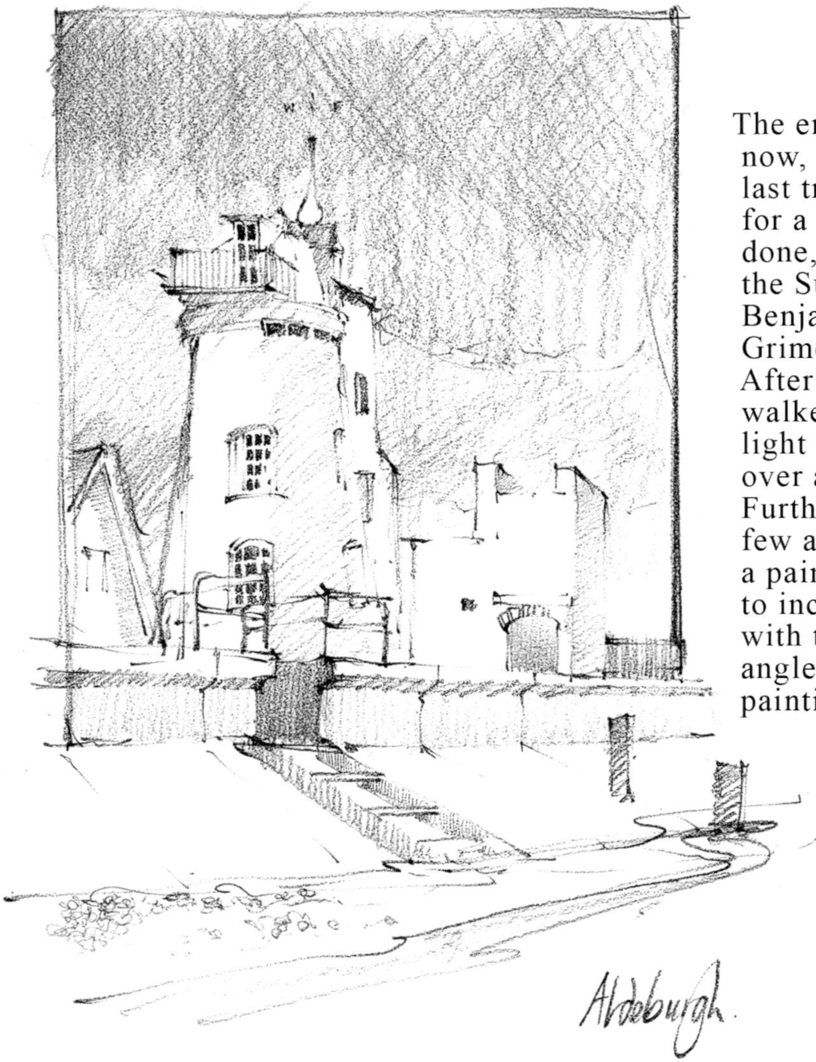

Aldeburgh

The end of a lovely summer and now, on the verge of autumn, one last trip to complete a painting for a calendar. Once that was done, my wife and I motored to the Suffolk coast to the land of Benjamin Britten and "Peter Grimes".

After an evening meal, we walked along the beach. The light was wonderful. A clear sky over a very calm sea.

Further down the beach were a few anglers. Later, when making a painting of the scene, I decided to include the anglers. Combined with the coloured wind break, the anglers provided the interest the painting needed.

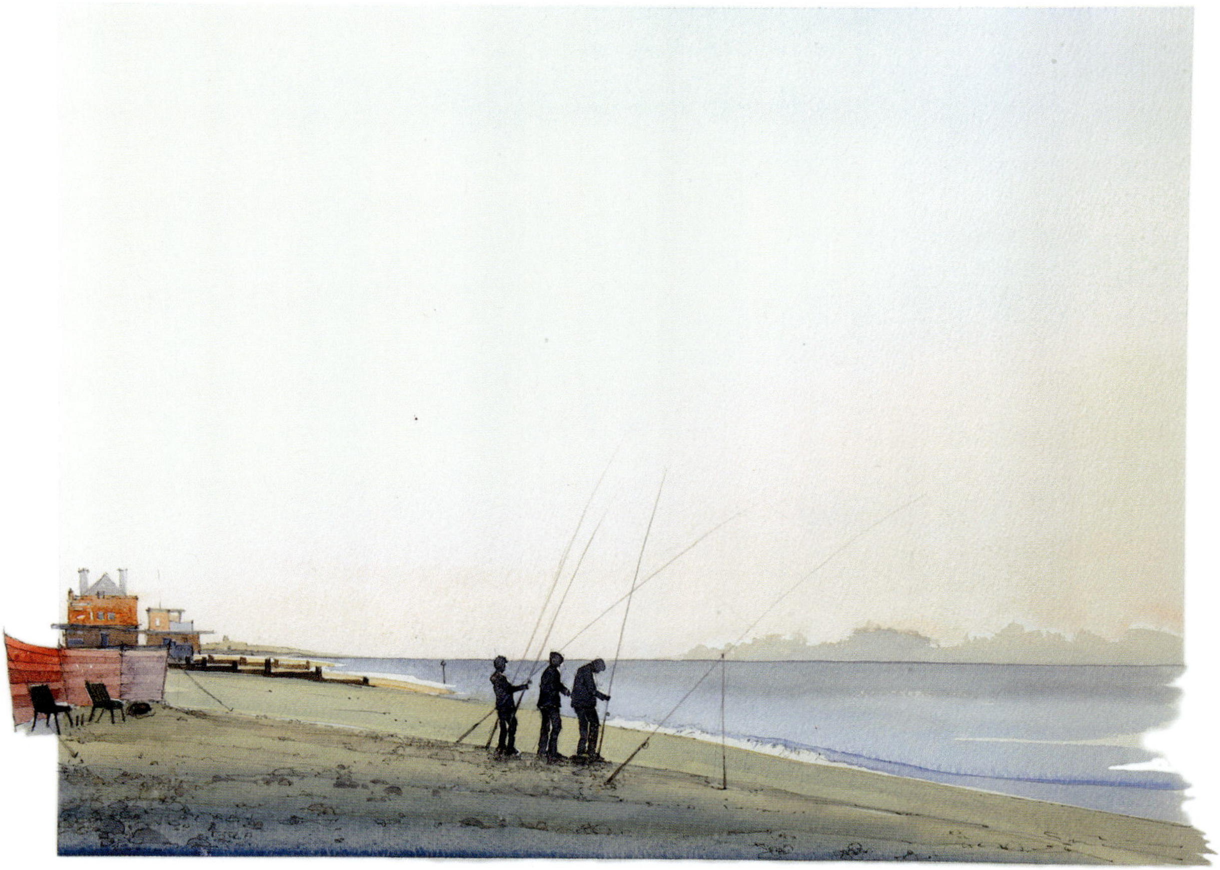

Evening on the Beach - Aldeburgh.

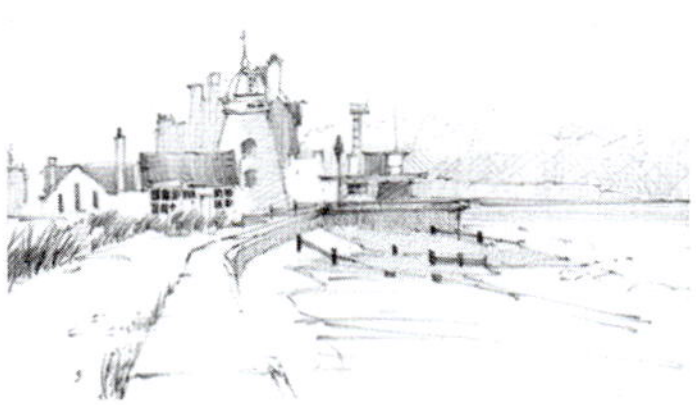

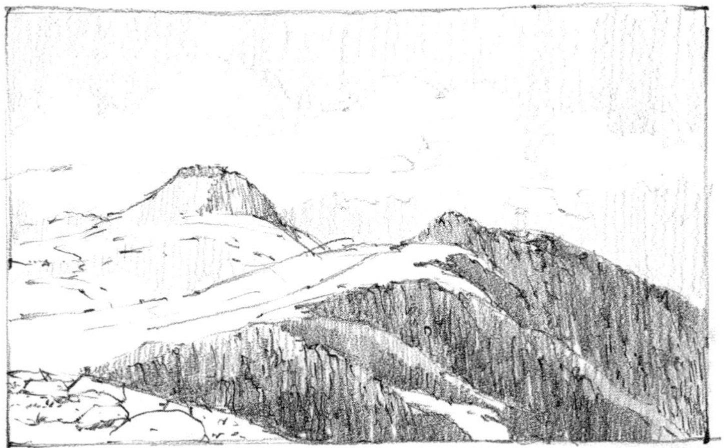

Harrison Stickle from Pike o' Stickle

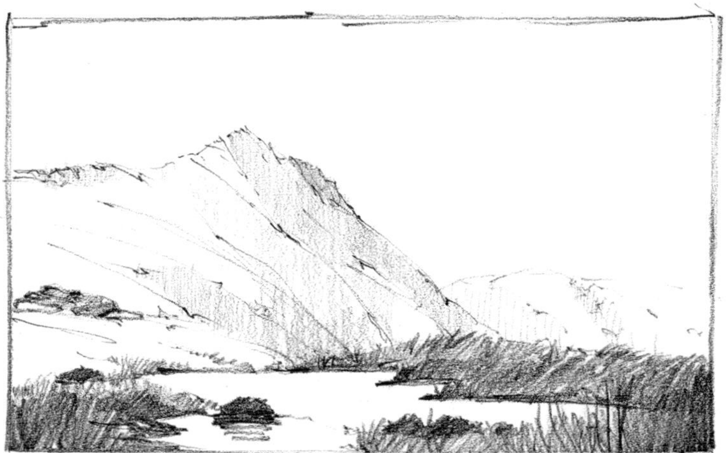

View from the top of Rossett Ghyll
towards Pike o' Stickle A long slog to get here but worth it for this view

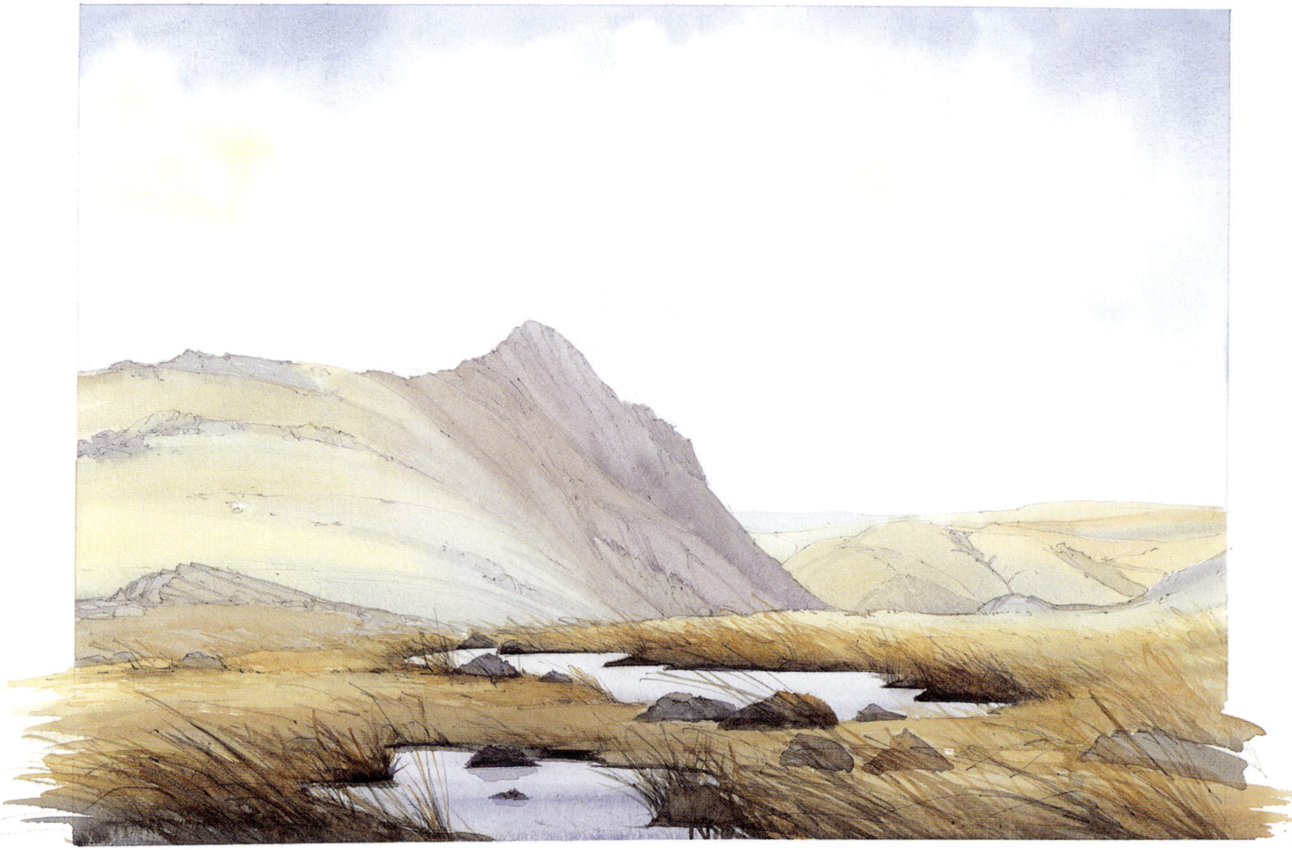

View From the Top of Rosset Ghyll towards Pike o' Stickle

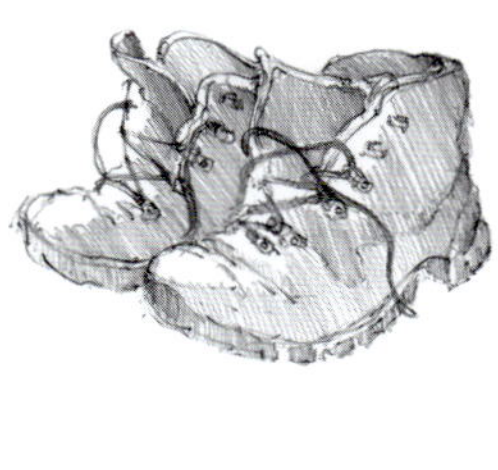

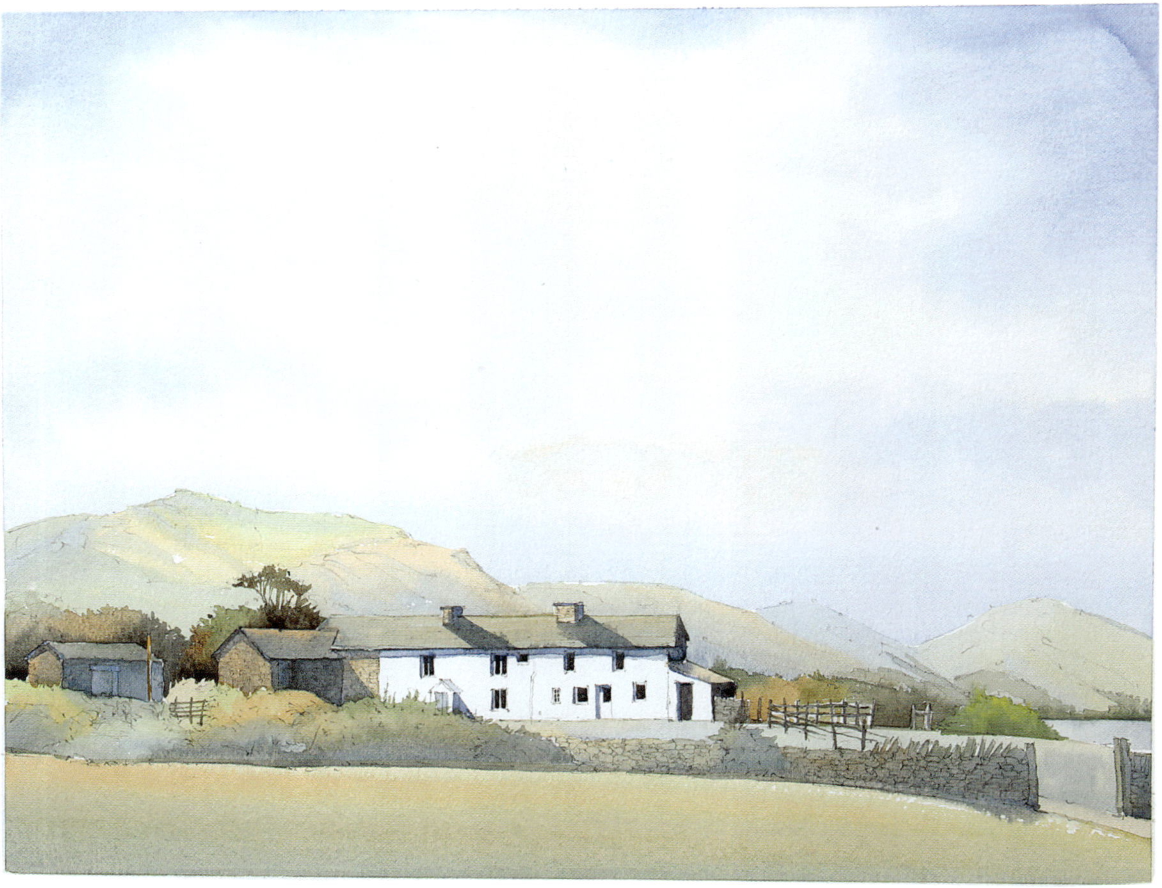

Summer Afternoon near Ullswater.

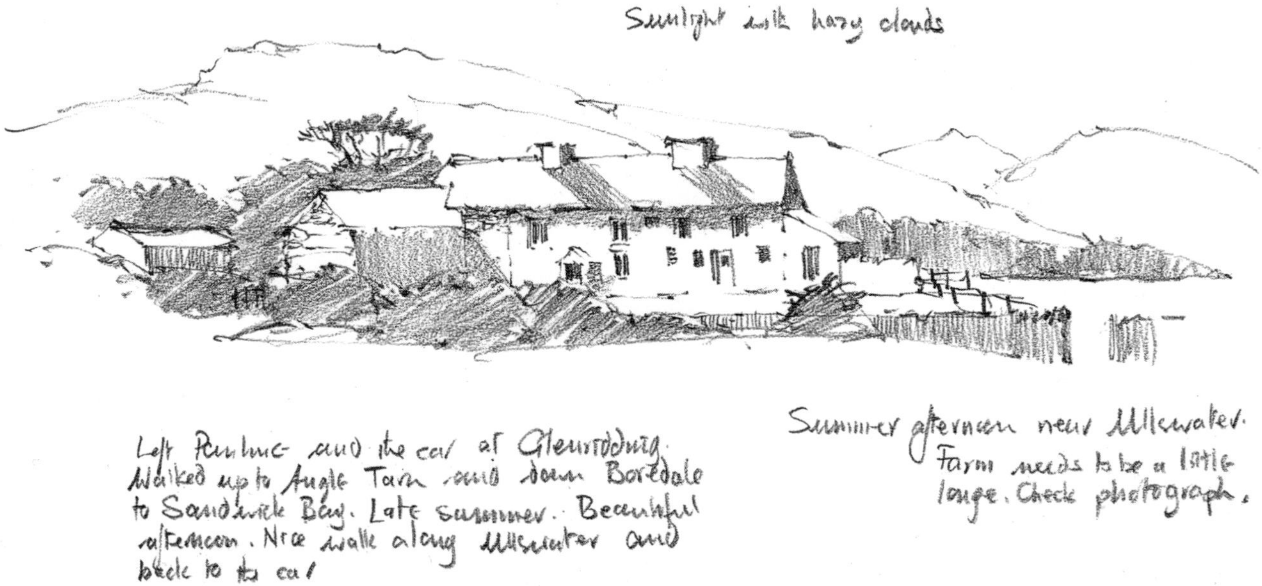

Leaving my wife in the car at Glenridding, I crossed the valley and began the ascent to Angle Tarn. It was a slow steady climb and the tarn was just the place to have lunch. Feeling refreshed, it was now downhill to the old church in Martindale and then on to Sandwick Bay. The sun was lighting up the old cottages and I knew that eventually they would make a painting.
After the sketch and photograph it was on with the rucksack to continue the walk along the shores of Ullswater, over Silver Point and back to Glenridding.

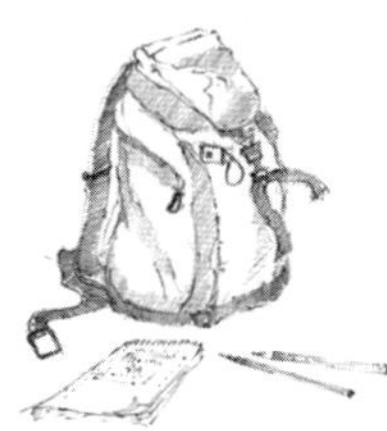

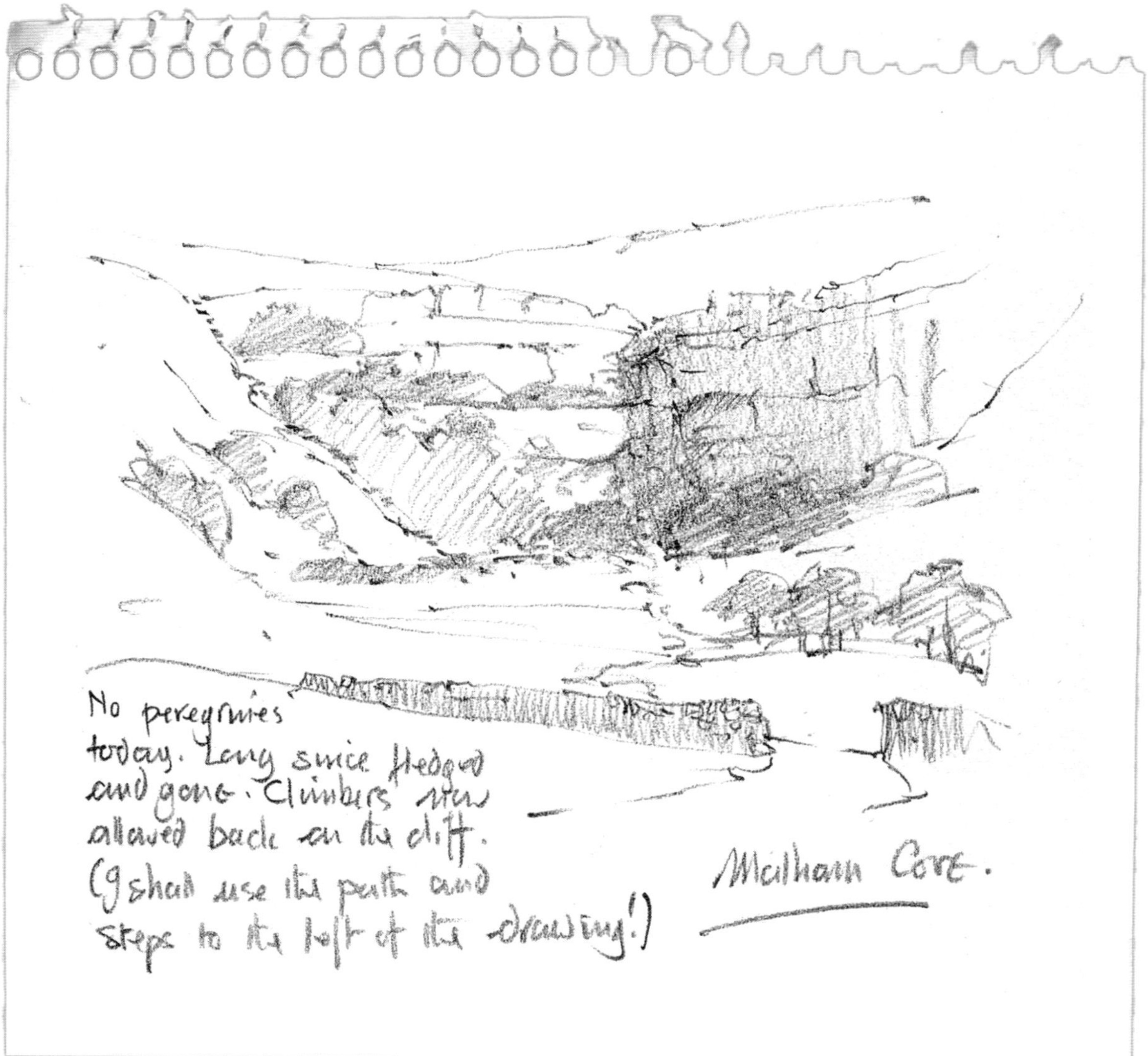
No peregrines
today. Long since fledged
and gone. Climbers now
allowed back on the cliff.
(I shall use the path and
steps to the left of the drawing!)
Malham Cove.

The Ascent of Malham Cove
(By the steps!)

"Twentyone - twenty two - twenty three."
    The pace is easy at first.
    Remember - start slowly.

"Forty three - forty four - forty five."
    The legs are beginning to feel the pain
    And still a long way to go.

"One hundred and one - one hundred and two."
    How much longer before I stop to admire the view?
    Keep pushing on!

"Two hundred and fifteen - two hundred and sixteen."
    People coming down.
    Pretend there is no pain.

"Four hundred and twenty one - four hundred and twenty two."
    Almost there.
    Have I miscounted? - It feels like more.

"At last" The limestone pavement.
    Sit and admire the whole of Airedale
    Whilst the pulse returns to normal.

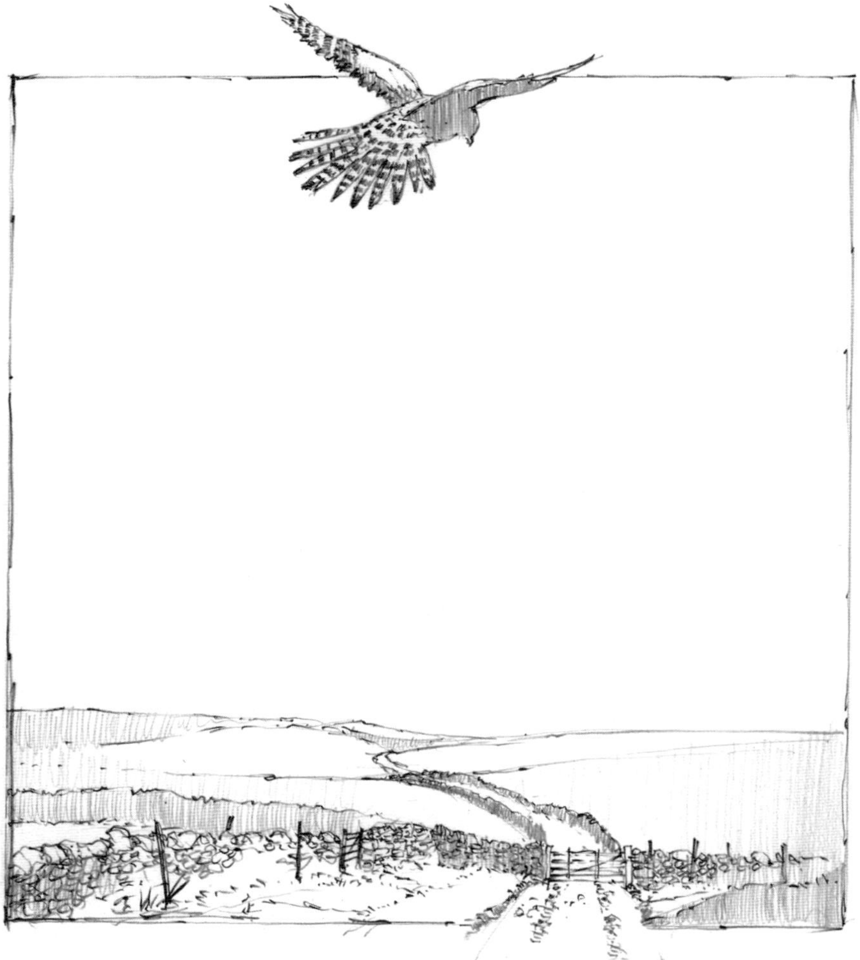

I know a place where the winds run free
And the bright-eyed Kestrel
Rides the morning light.

Autumn

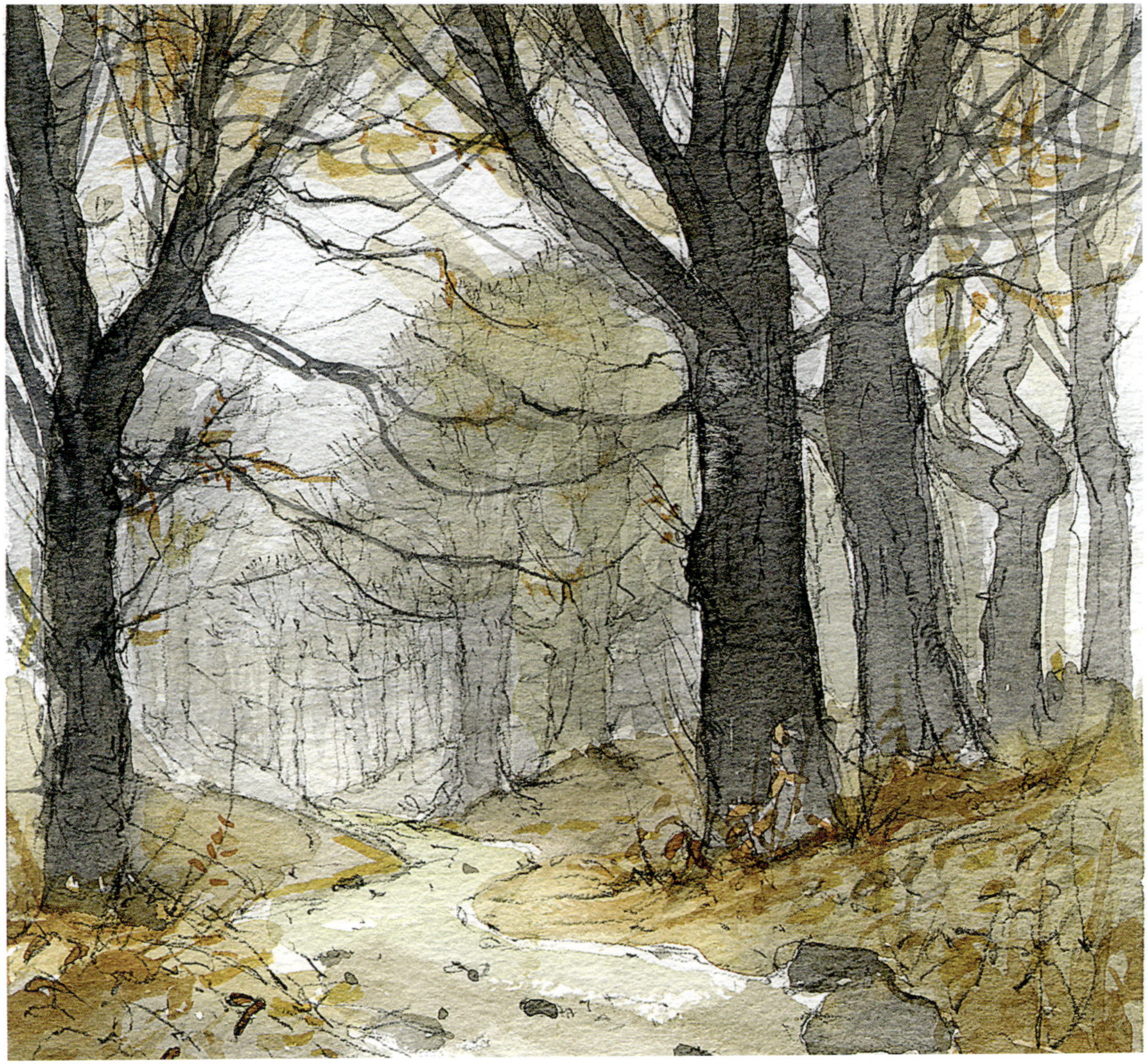

Autumn

I have always found Autumn to be a pleasant season. The trees and fields are beginning to change colour. The vibrant greens of summer are giving way to the soft autumn shades of ochre and sienna. In the woods, all is silent except for the slight rustle of leaves floating gently down to join those already carpeting the ground.
Although there can be cold mornings, the "nip in the air" seems to encourage walking. The afternoons are often suffused with that beautiful golden light which I love to try and capture in paint. Even when autumn mists hang over the hills it does not make me feel sad. It lends an air of mystery to the landscape which I find exciting. Nothing is what it seems. Things appear out of the mist and just as quickly disappear.

Keats described it perfectly as:

"The seaon of mists and
mellow fruitfulness"

One morning, leaving the car at Burnsall, I followed the river Wharfe downstream towards Howgill and Bardon Tower. A pleasant October day with alternating sunshine and showers. After sheltering for a few minutes under the old outbuilding I was pleased, when the rain stopped and lovely autumn sunlight flooded the scene. As my rucksack incorporated a folding stool, I did not have to sit on the wet grass when making my sketch. The leaves were just begnning to turn into their autumn colours and the grass was no longer a bright green. I found this collection of buildings very interesting with the white walls of the farmhouse reflecting the bright sunlight and highlighting the scene.

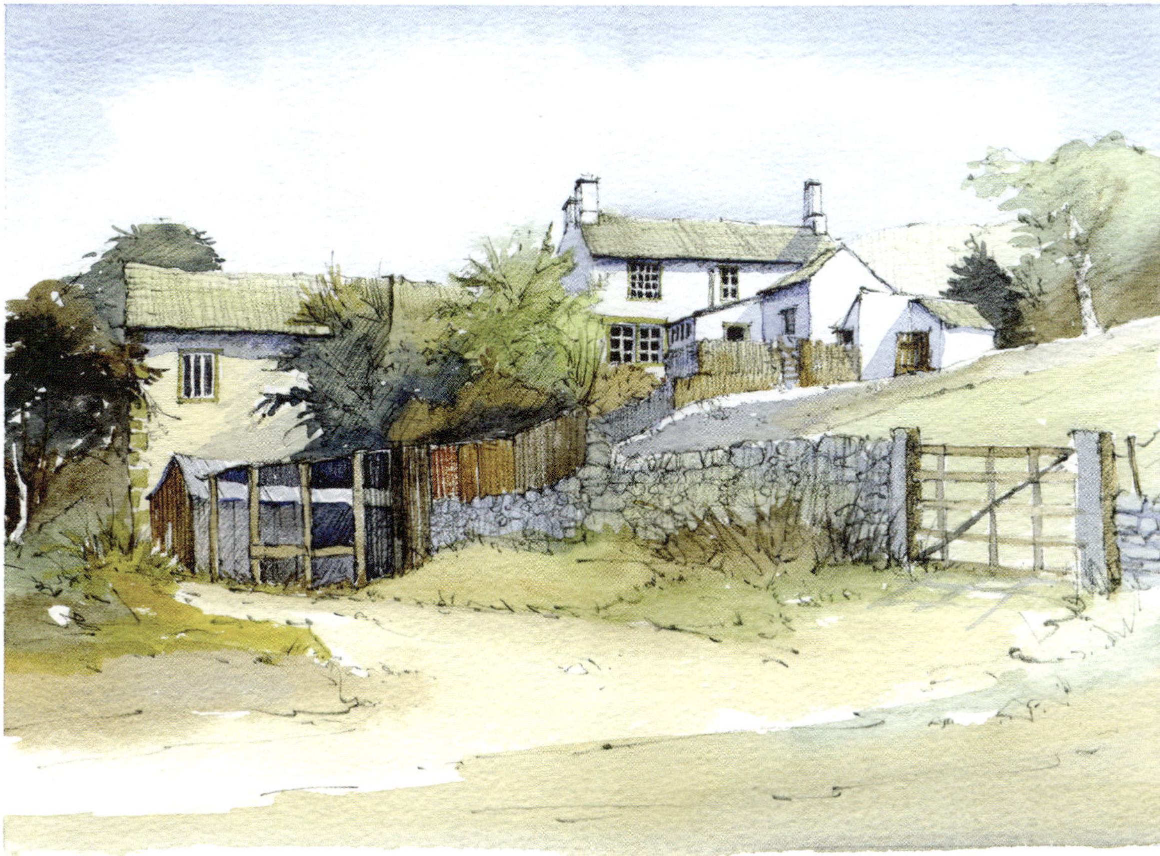

Sunshine After the Showers - Howgill.

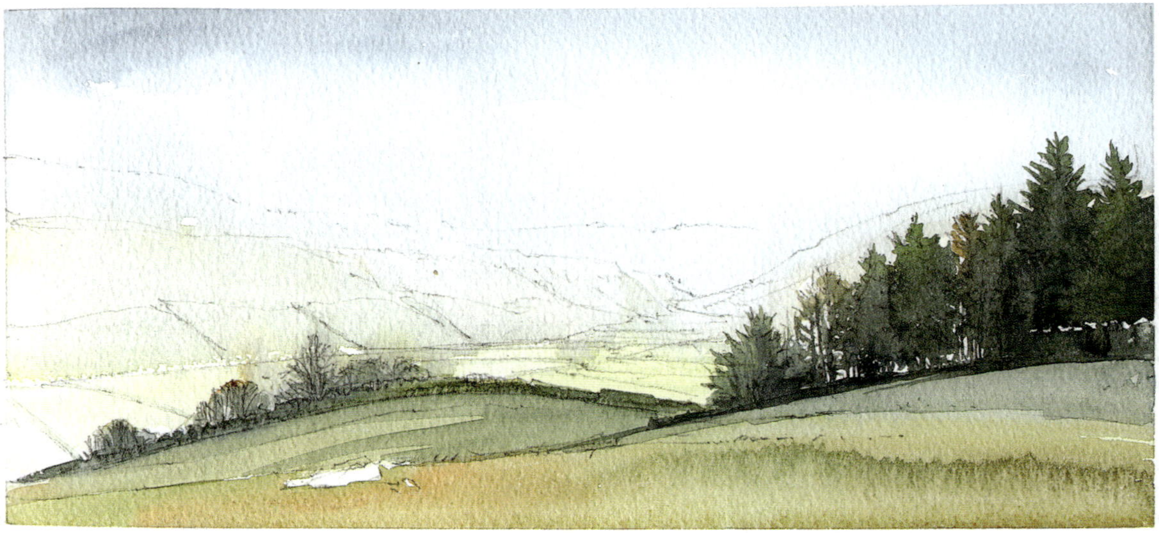

Grey Autumn Day. Upper Wharfedale

Autumn

Autumn and the mist sits
Gentle on the high tops.
Trees stand without movement in the still air.
Wall to wall silence fills the valley.

The journey uphill is slow,
Only the sound of my boots breaks the silence
Until a whirling cloud of Jackdaws
Drifts from the huge limestone cliff,
Shouting “Jack.” “Jack.” “Jack.”

These are magical days.
A quietness, which allows my mind to wander,
Settles on me, whilst the miles drift past.
A Heron, disturbed by my passing,
Floats away on broad wings.

Through my mind flashes a kaleidoscope of images
From times long gone.
Memories of days on the hills, in good weather and bad.
Of friends and conversations and unforgettable moments,
"The stuff as dreams are made on."

And so the day passes
Until, all too soon, it is down hill
Toward the church, the village, the car park,
With another wealth of memories for those days
When the legs will no longer be able to cover the miles.

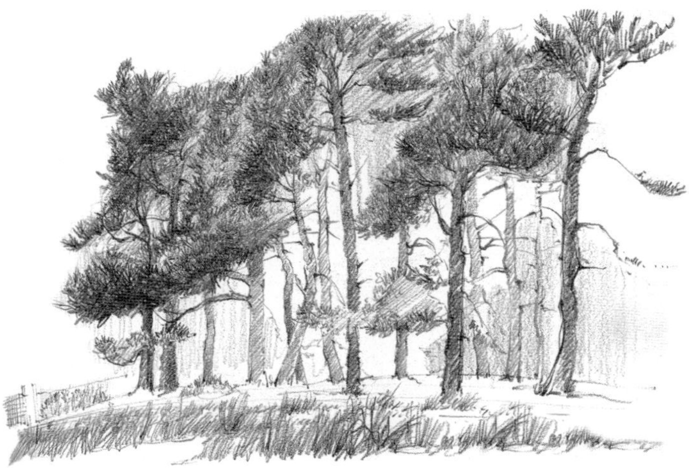

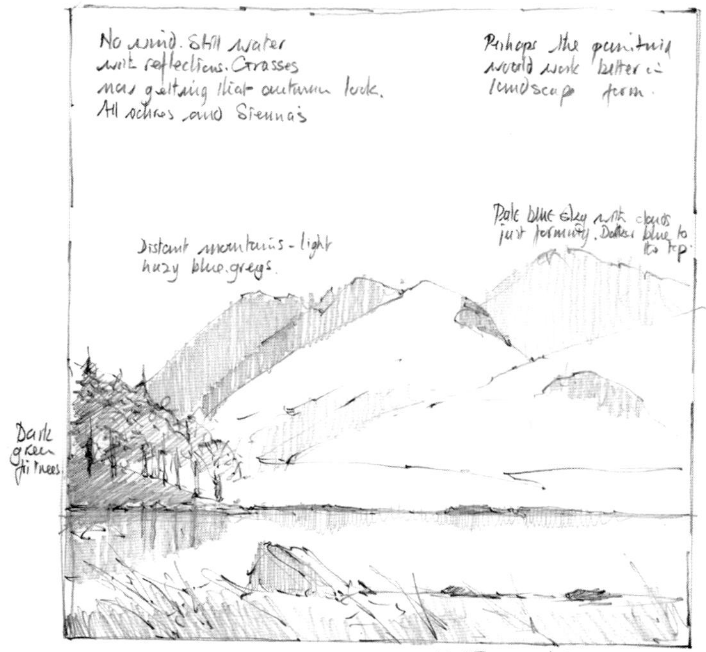

Blea Tarn - Autumn Day.

So many times, the idea you have in your head, gets lost on its way to your fingers. You start with the best will in the world but seldom do the results on paper live up to the idea.
American painter Andrew Wyeth, also had this problem.

He said - *"The way I feel about things, is so much better than the way I have been able to paint them. The image I had in my head before I started, is not quite - never quite - completely conveyed in paint."*

It is good to know that this problem is not mine alone.

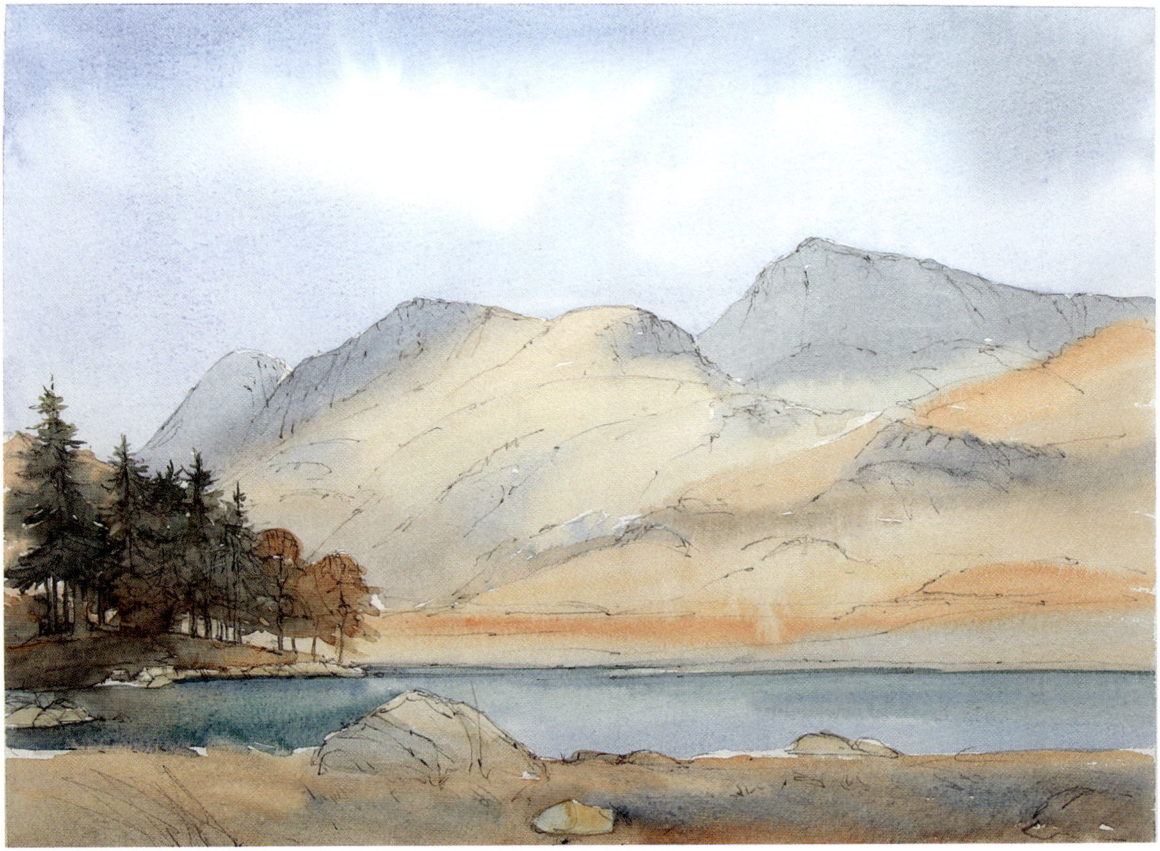

Blea Tarn - Little Langdale

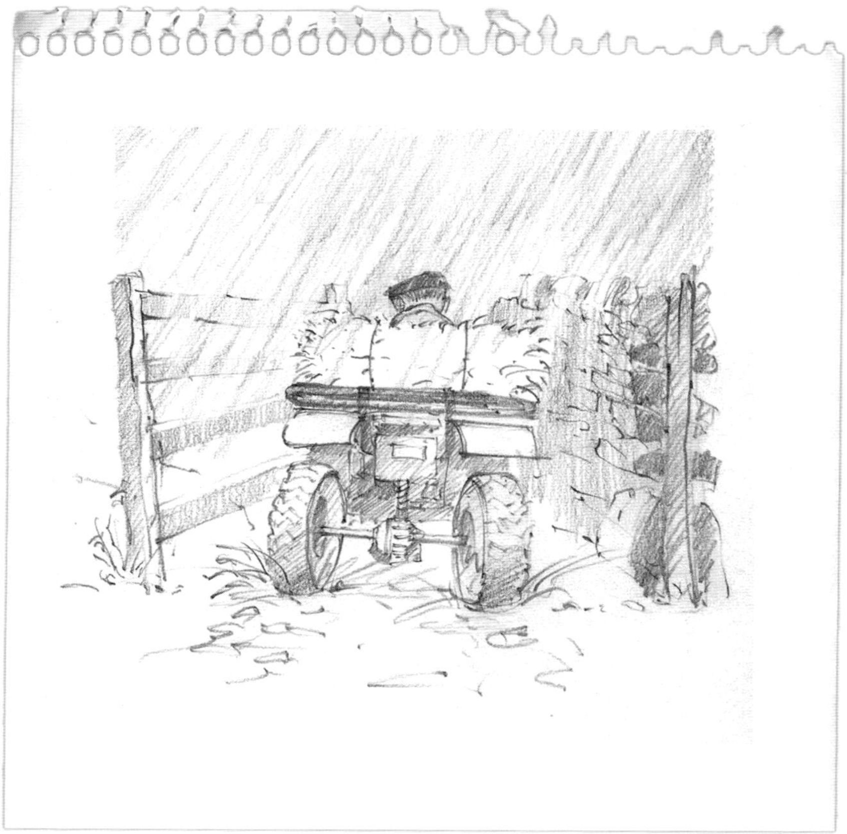

The weather plays an important part on any day spent in the hills. Knowing that it always helps to get local knowledge, I once asked a farmer friend of mine in the Lake District, what the weather was going to do. He looked across to the Langdale Pikes and said,

" If you can see the Pikes it's going to rain.
If you can't see them it's raining already."

"A've Nawn Better"

The forecast was not good.
The isobars explained it all but as hope springs eternal,
I set off.

Beyond Skipton and still no rain.
Perhaps they had got it wrong, forecasting not being an exact science.
Now I was hopeful.

As I entered the car park at Buckden,
The first small drops hit the windscreen.
It must have been waiting for me.

Perhaps it would pass over.
I was putting off the struggle into waterproofs.
Reaching the tops I knew I had made a mistake.

And so it continued.
Rain, steady, continuous, persistant, without a break.
Lunch under a tree - wet sandwiches!

The noise of the quad made itself heard
Above the gentle hiss of the rain.
I opened the gate for the farmer.

"It's a foul day" I said,
"It's never stopped raining since I left the car".
"Aye - A've nawn better" said the farmer as he drove away.

And that said it all.

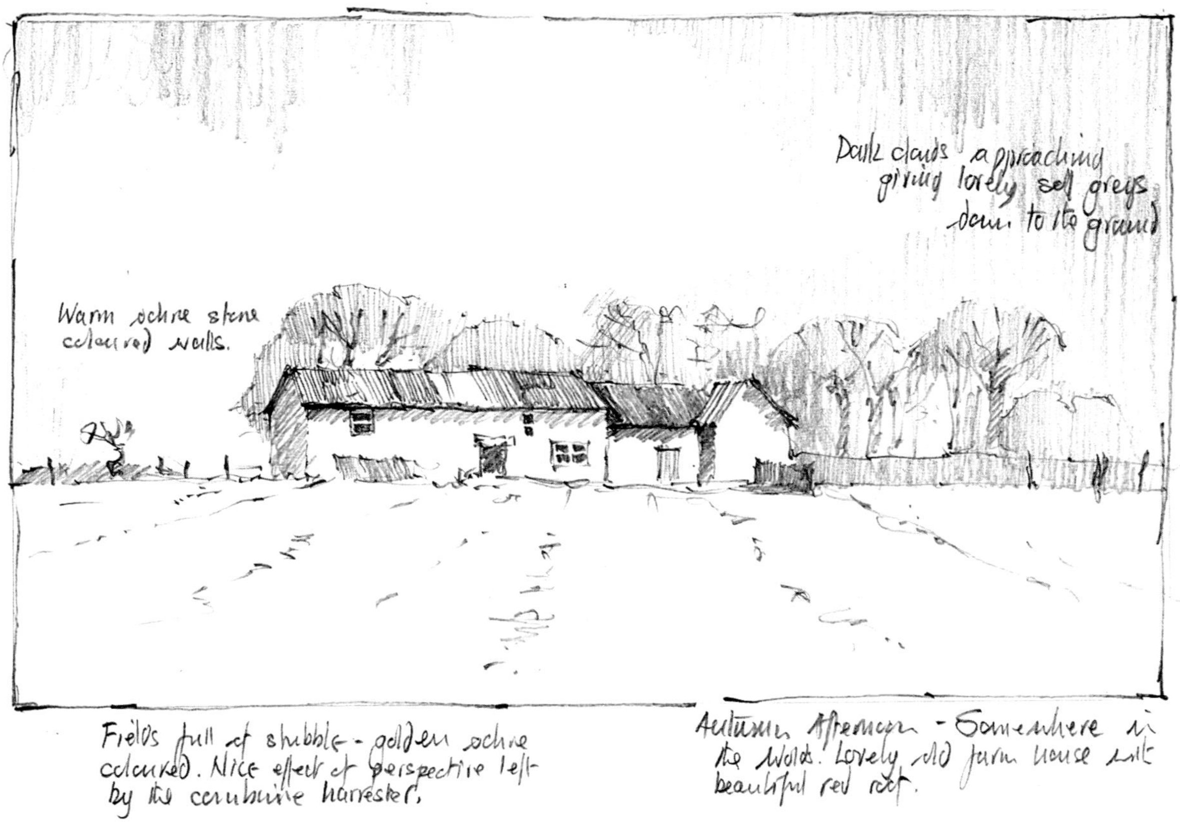

Driving back from the coast across the Yorkshire Wolds, I glanced to the right and there was this scene. Beautiful in it's simplicity! Stopping the car, I reached for the sketch book, but one glance in the rear view mirror showed me that, with all the traffic, this was no place to stop and make a sketch. Changing the sketch book for the camera, I quickly took a photograph which I worked up into a drawing in the studio at a later date. It was to be much later (about ten years later) before once again I saw the drawing and made the painting.

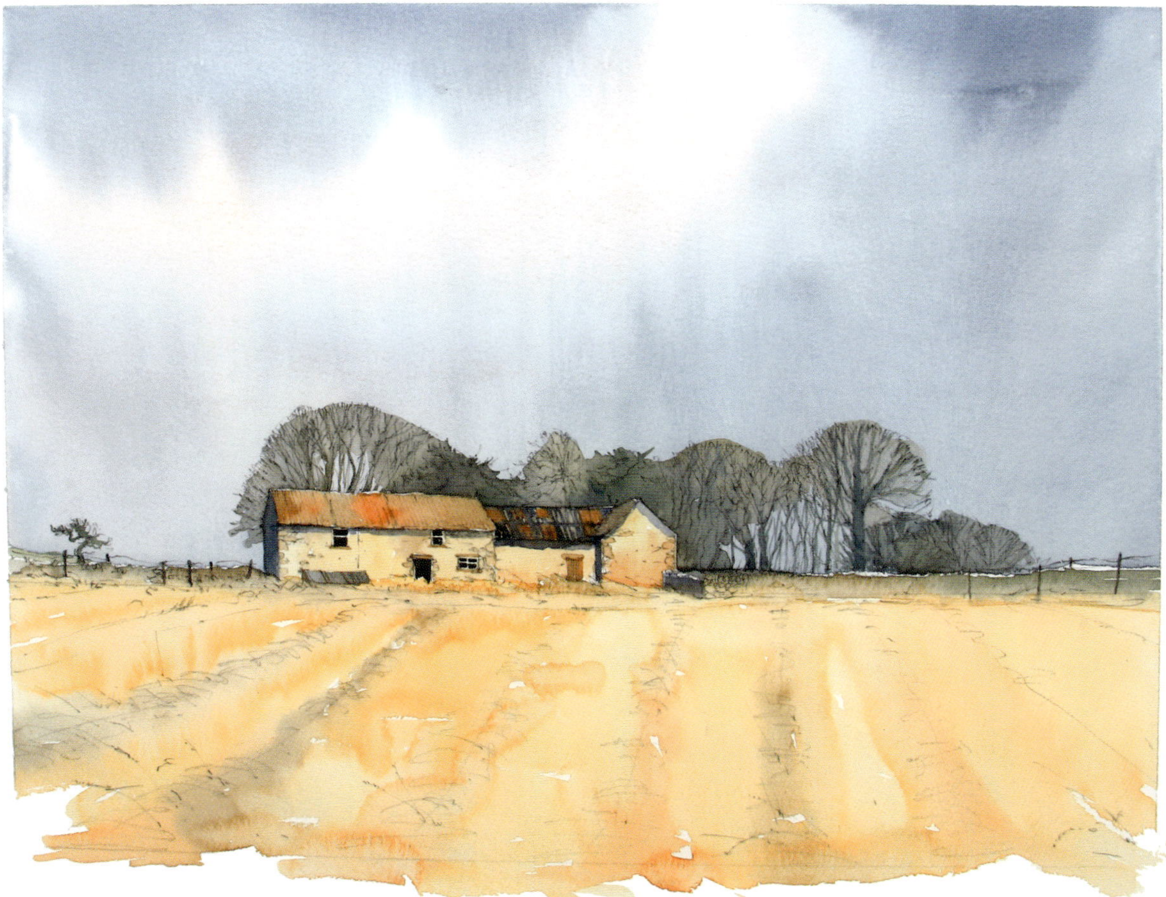

"All is safely gathered in" – just in time!

Somewhere here lies Ingleborough!

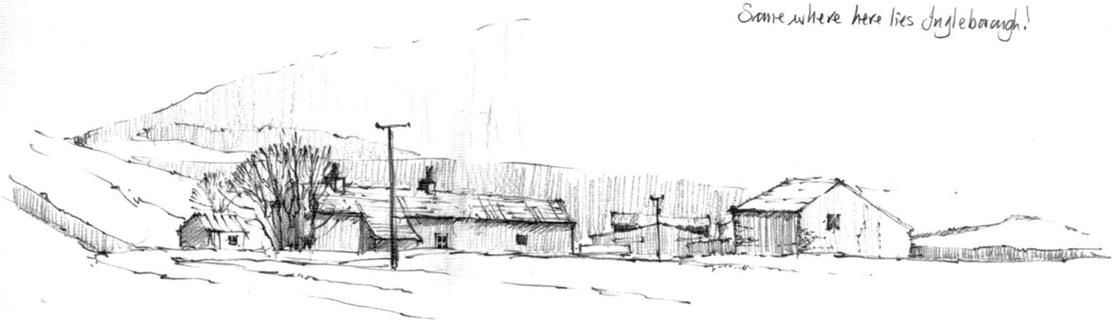

Farm at Gunnerfleet
on the route to Whernside.

There must be some reason why these two mountains have suddenly become shy. Walked down the valley to the "Old Hill Inn", and took some photographs - no sign of Ingleborough. I shall have to come back and have another go if the next 3 peaks prints are ever going to press.

(Very cold indeed and I just didn't have enough clothing, Silly mistake!)

Worse than last week! Good weather forecast but so far they got it wrong. Early morning mist which never cleared. Somewhere behind this farm lurks Simon's Fell, and Ingleborough. Cold and windy but the mist is not moving. Time to walk and get warm again.

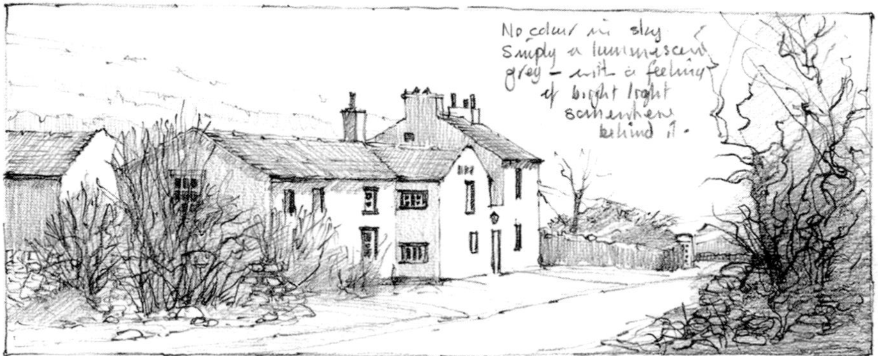

The Hill Inn – Chapel-le-dale
the end of autumn. Leaves all
fallen from the trees.

Winter on its way. No sign of Ingleborough.
Lost in the mist.

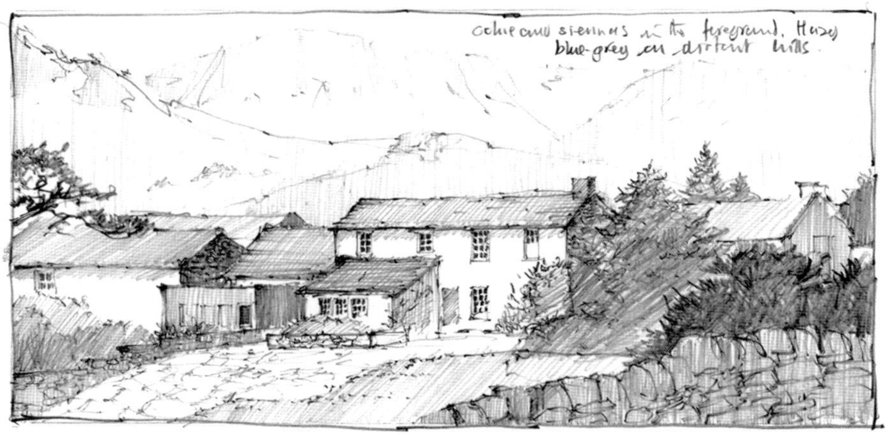

View from the bridge Grange-in-Borrowdale
Nice white painted buildings typical of
Lakeland. W.W. didnt like them. Cant
think why!

Hills beginning to show autumn colours
this contrasts nicely with the fir
trees which still retain their dark
greens

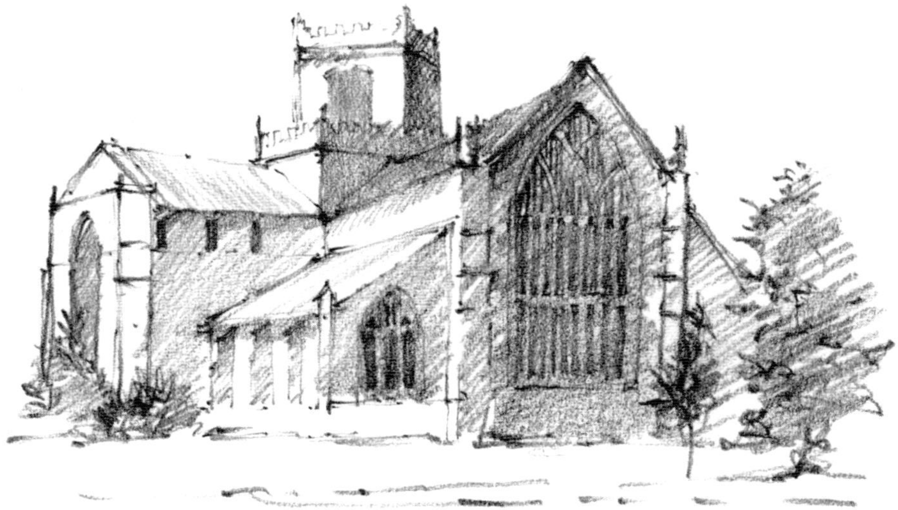

Cartmel Priory

A little to the south west of the main area of Lakeland, lies the small village of Cartmel. As well as being famous for it's "Sticky Toffee Pudding" and it's small racecourse, it also has an extremely attractive Priory. The Priory is unusual in that the upper part of the tower sits at an angle to the lower part. Some years ago, when repairs were being done to the wood-work in the bell tower, a large pile of old timber was placed outside ready to make a bonfire. I managed to buy a long length of this old oak which is now fixed over the Aga cooker in my kitchen. When my grandchildren were young, I used to tell them that, if you listened carefully on a windy night you could hear the bells ringing.

I don't think they believed me!

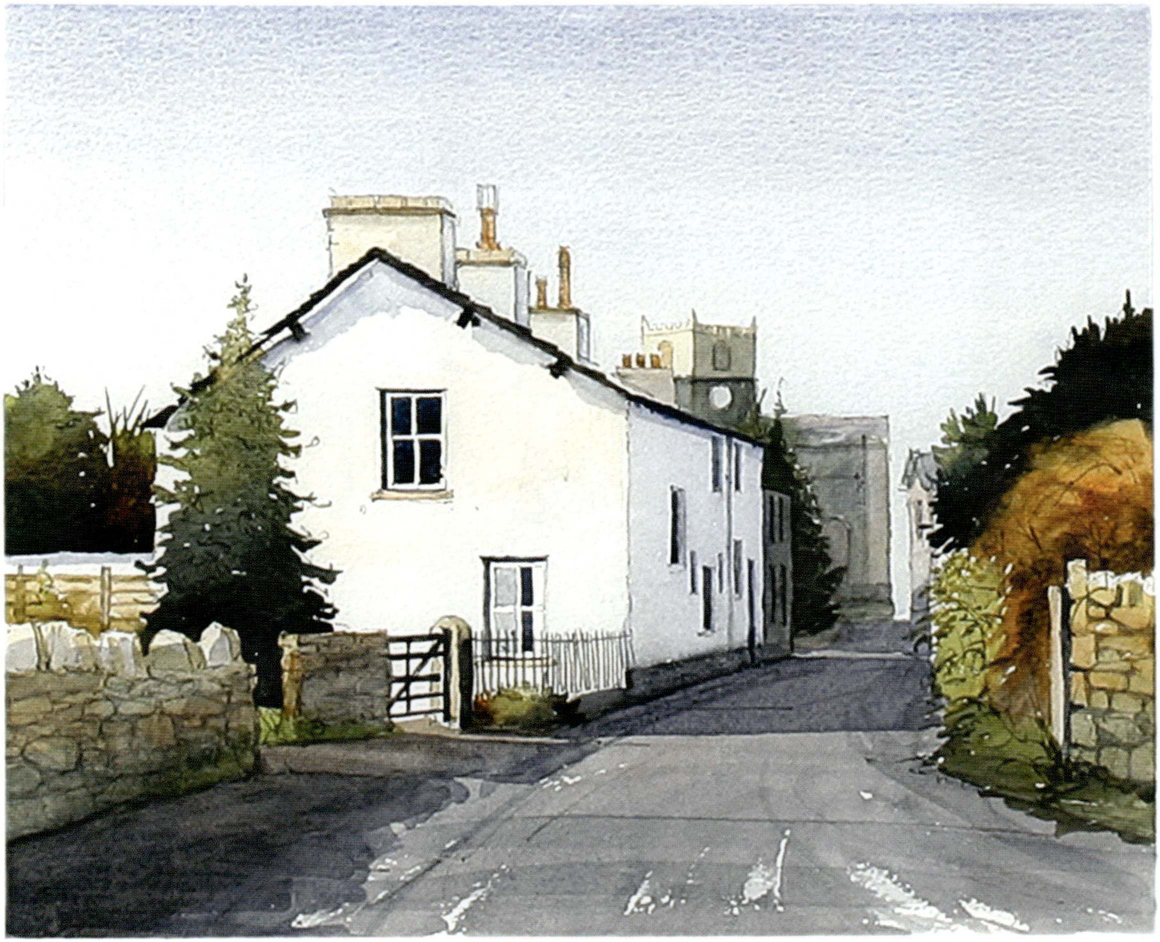

Early Morning - Cartmel

In Praise Of Binder Twine

You find it everywhere.
Lying behind walls.
Caught in hedges.
Blown high into trees.
Stuck on barbed wire -
Binder Twine.

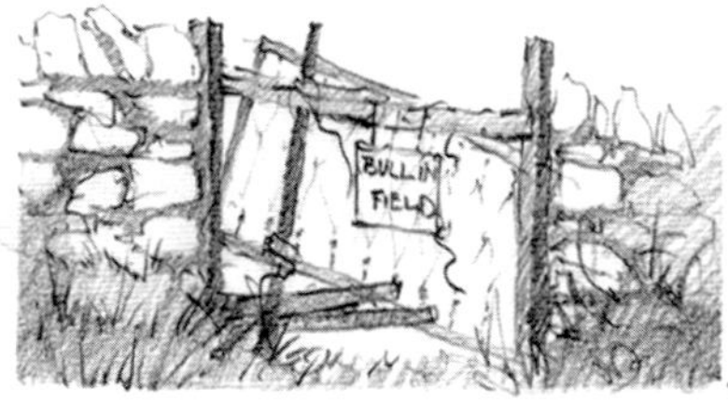

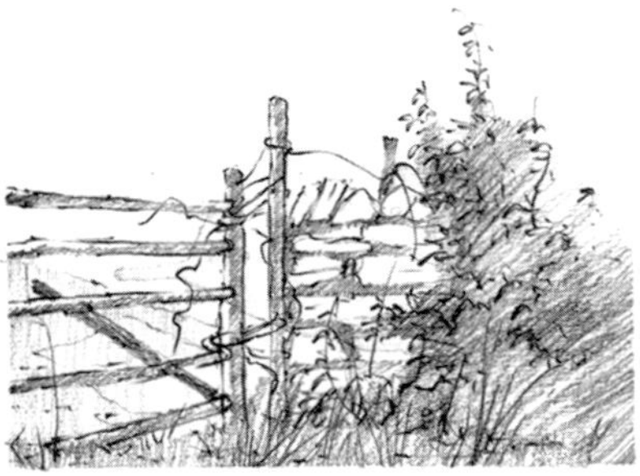

It comes in several colours.
Some in orange,
Some in blue.
Beloved by farmers
and even nest building birds -
Binder Twine.

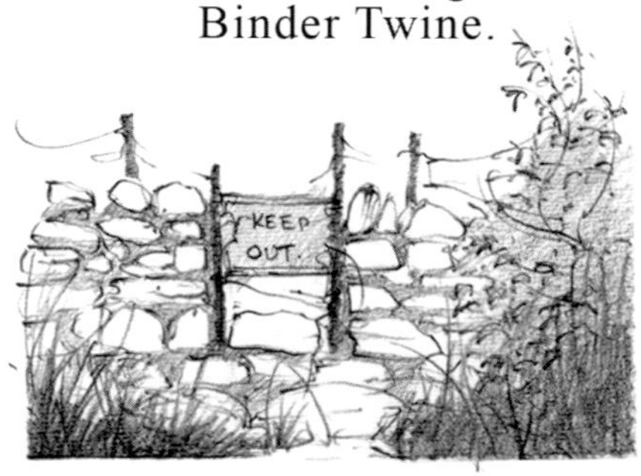

It has many uses.
Who needs locks?
Who needs hinges?
Who needs belt or braces?
Even bales on quads held safely -
Binder Twine.

There is no end to it's versatility.
Hysterical farm dogs secured to barn doors
To the relief of lone walkers.
"KEEP OUT" signs on gates
And warnings of "BULL IN FIELD" -
All owe a debt of gratitude to

UBIQUITOUS BINDER TWINE.

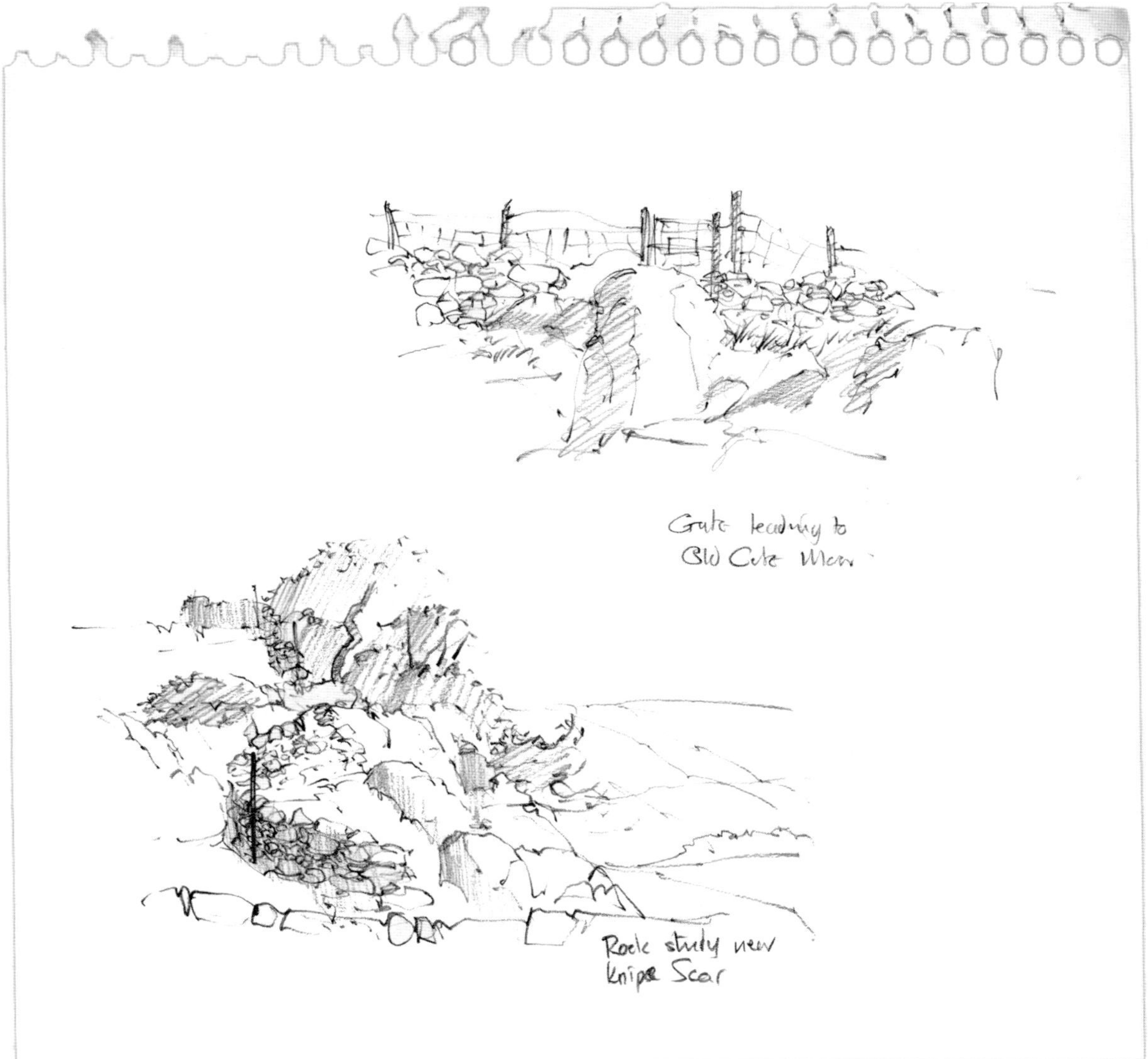
Gate leading to
Old Cote Moor
Rock study near
Knipe Scar

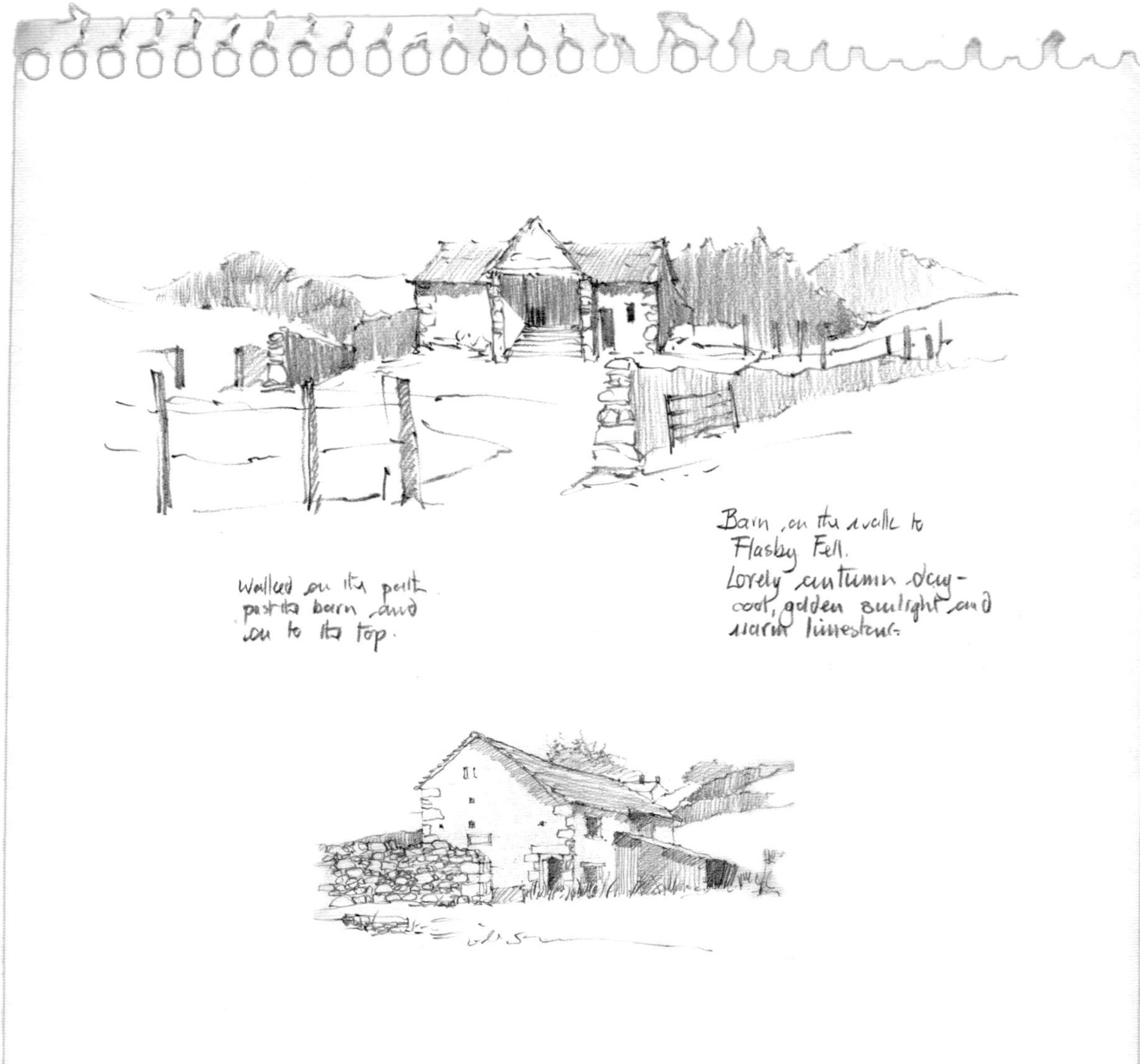
Barn, on the walk to
Flasby Fell.
Lovely autumn day -
cool, golden sunlight and
warm limestone.
Walked on the path
past the barn and
on to the top.

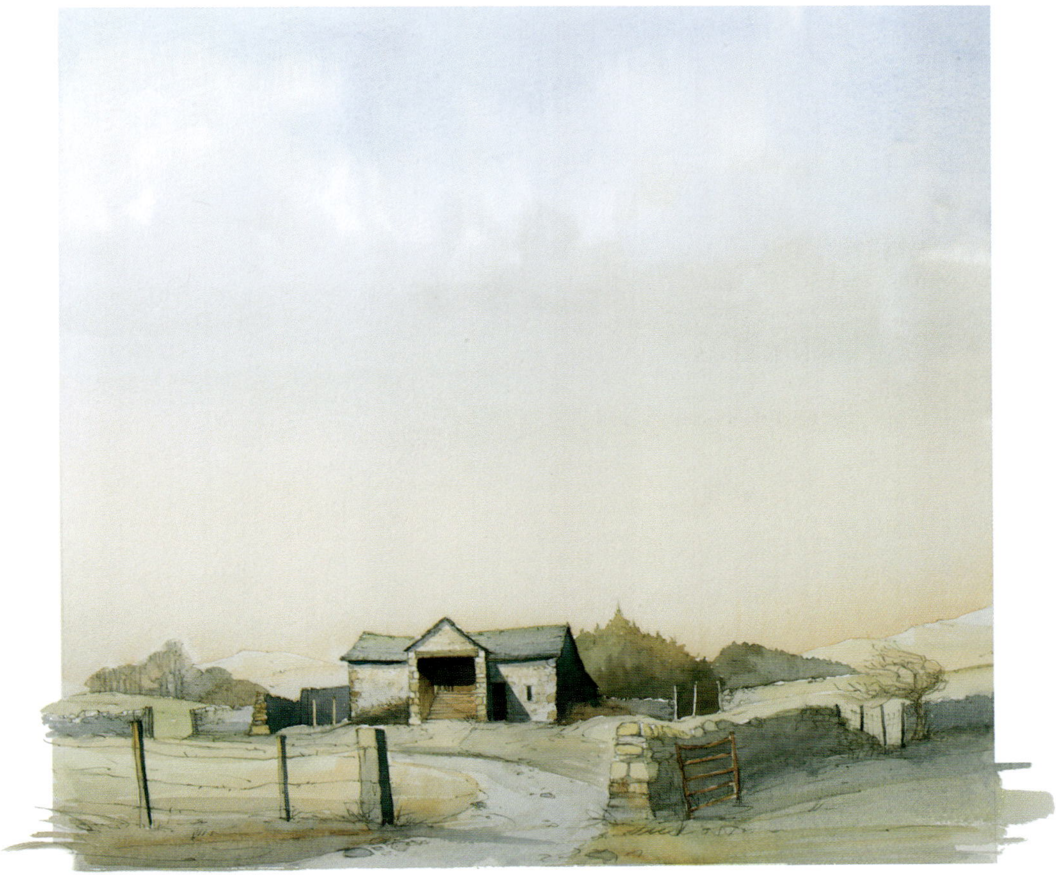

Autumn in Airedale.

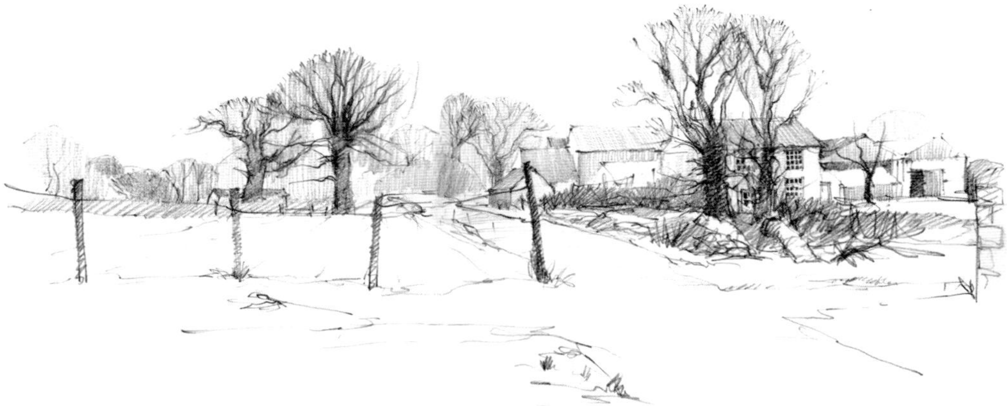

Farm Near Ripley
Warm autumn sun with some wind
The trees have lost their leaves, and
make interesting patterns against
the sky. Enjoyed making this sketch
(the best in the book so far) Too
many commissions have taken up
my time recently. If only I didn't
have to do them.

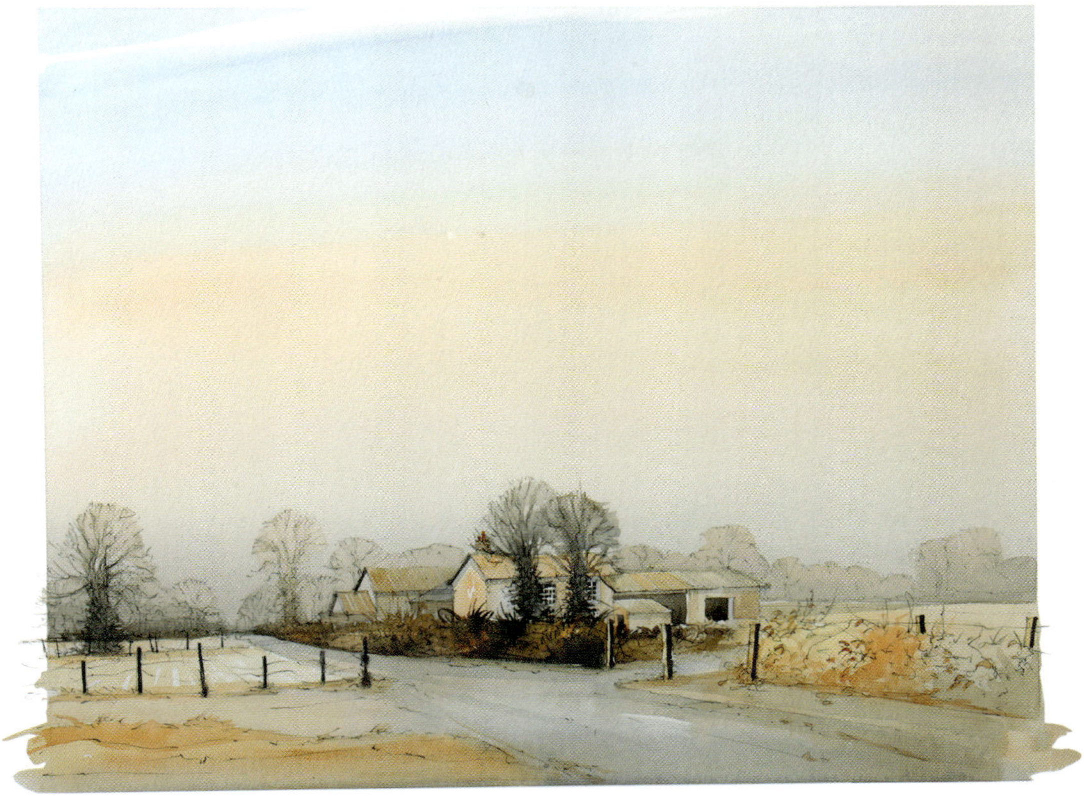

Autumn Near Ripley

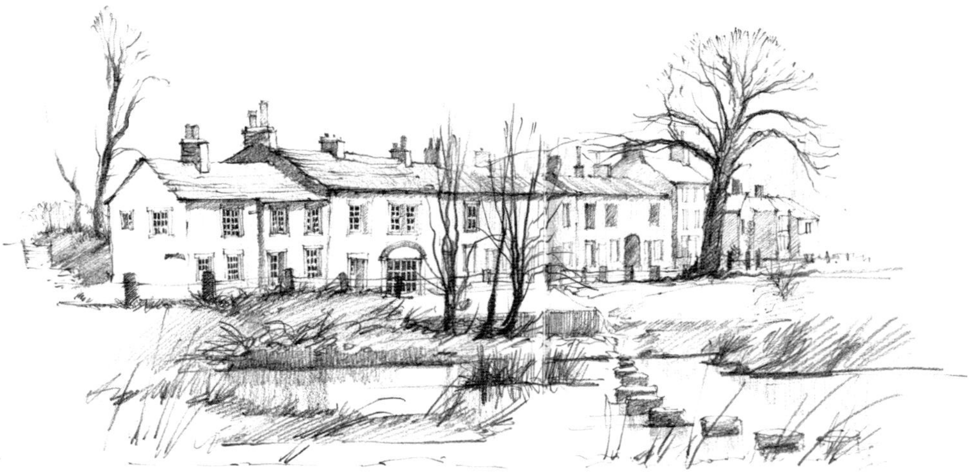

The Stepping Stones at Gargrave

Much colder than yesterday. Grey, overcast with sun trying to break through. Very complex subject. Had a go! Bad to begin with but began to improve as the drawing progressed. Perhaps it will make a small painting! Going for a walk now to get warm again

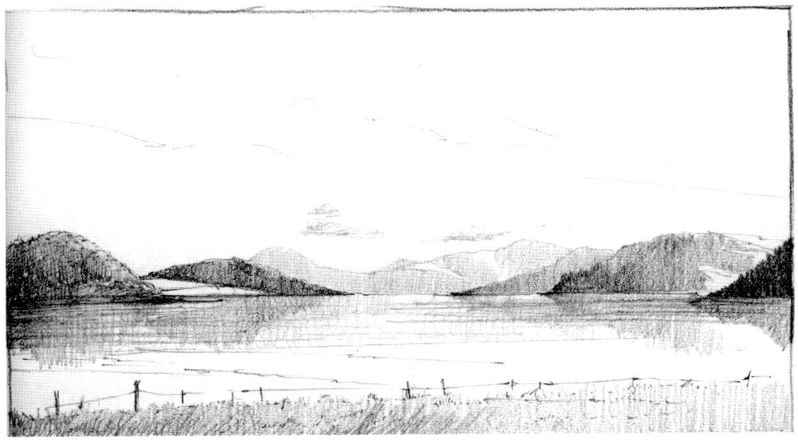

Evening Light Over Loch Linnie

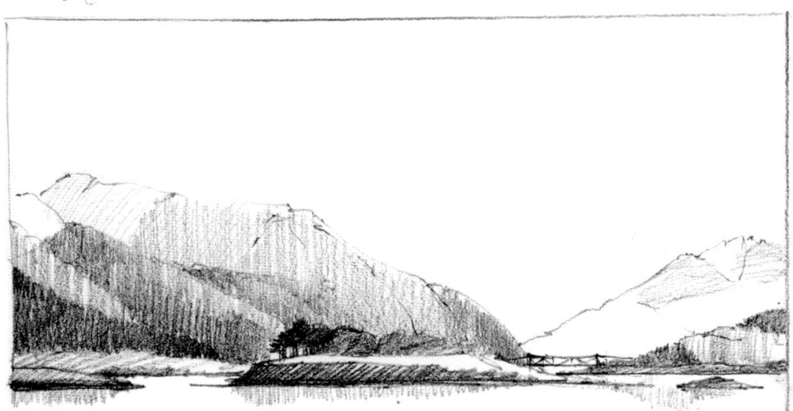

Bridge at Ballachulish

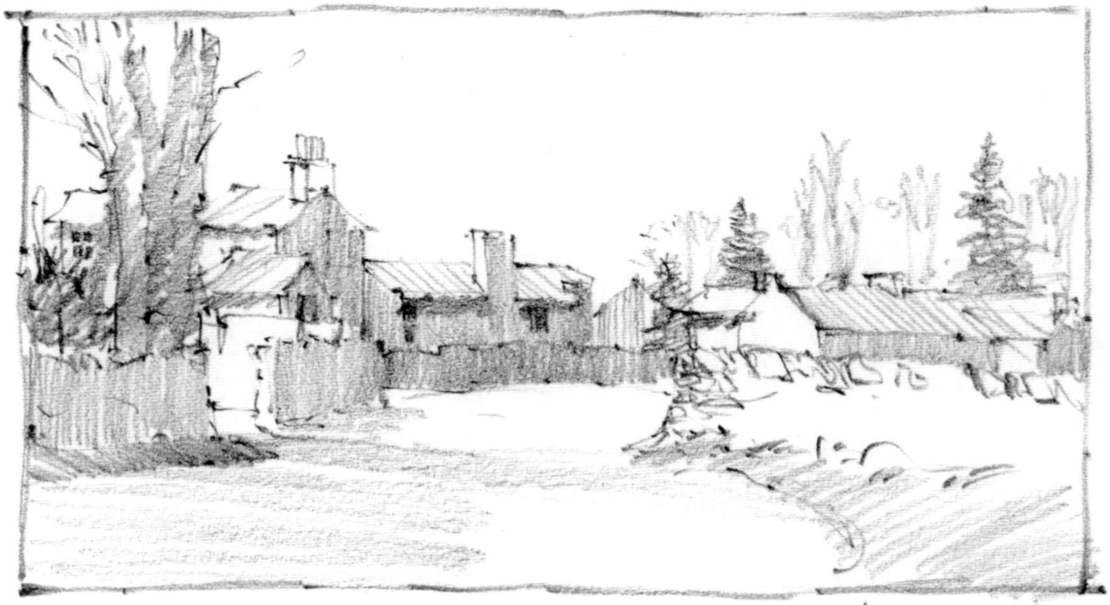

Autumn Afternoon - Near Sawrey

Beatrix Potter country. Late afternoon sunlight over Near Sawrey and just visible is the Tower Bank Arms. It was the quality of sunlight that made this view so appealing and raised the question - could I possibly capture this in paint?

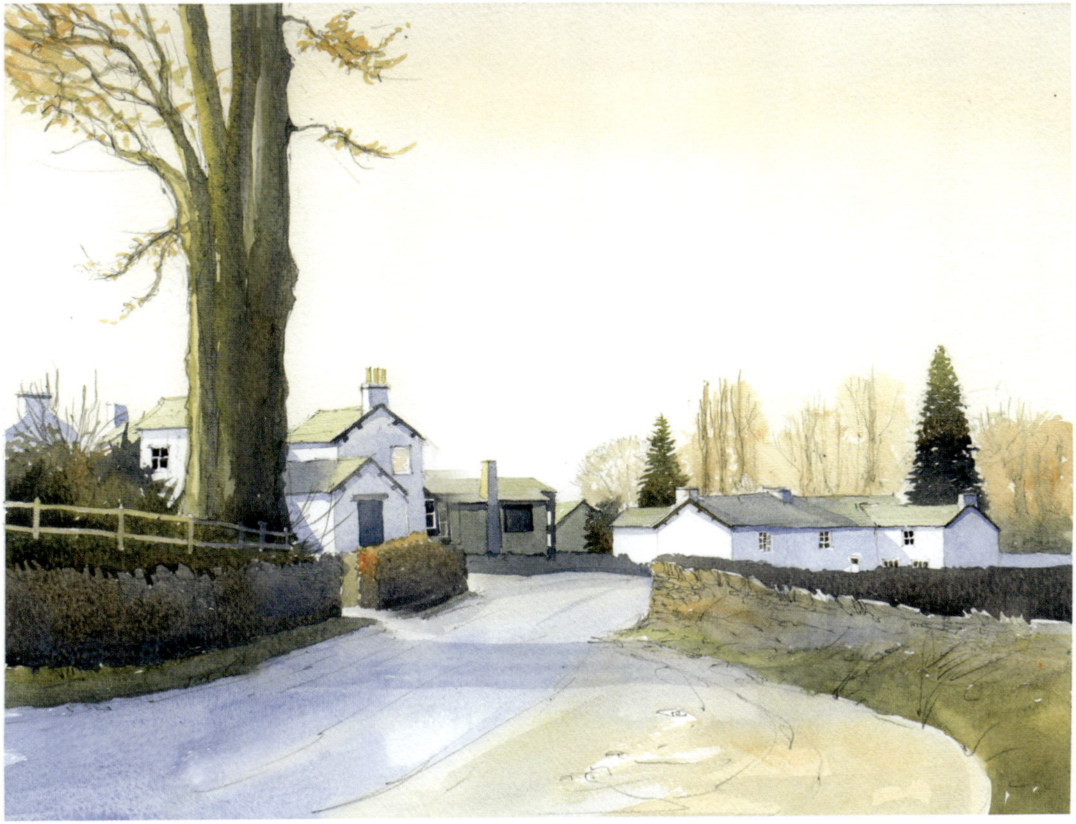

Autumn - Near Sawrey

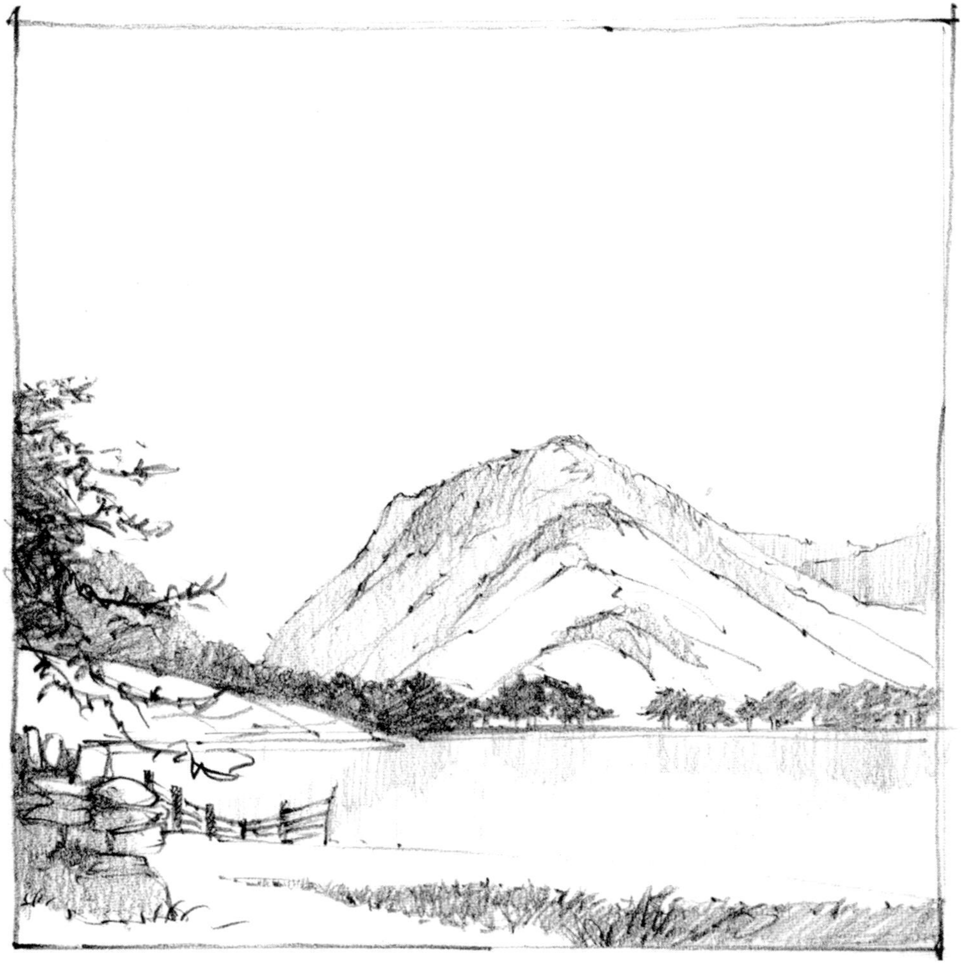

Seeds have set. Eggs have hatched.
Life's frantic round slows down.
Nature puts on her slippers.

Winter

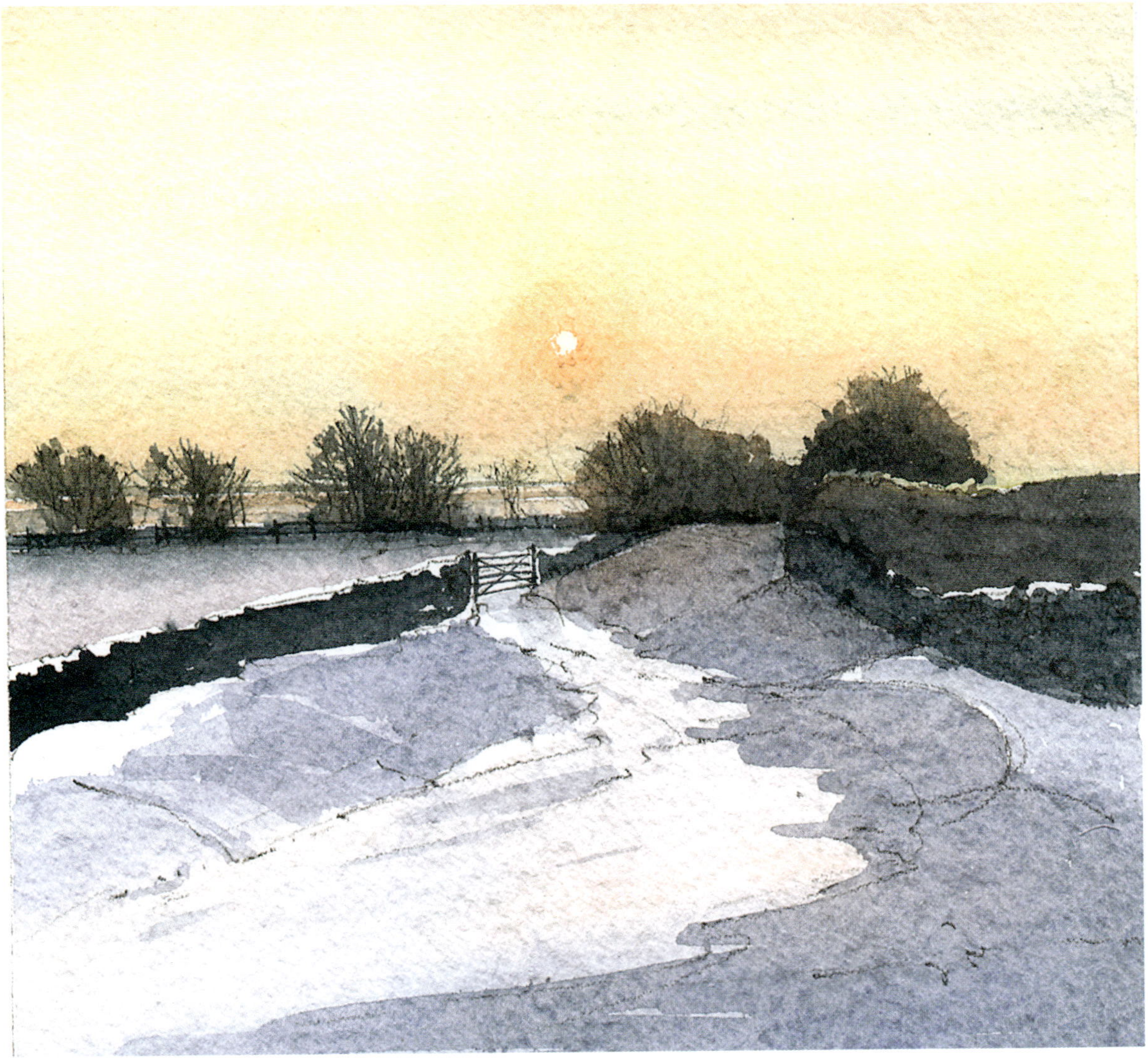

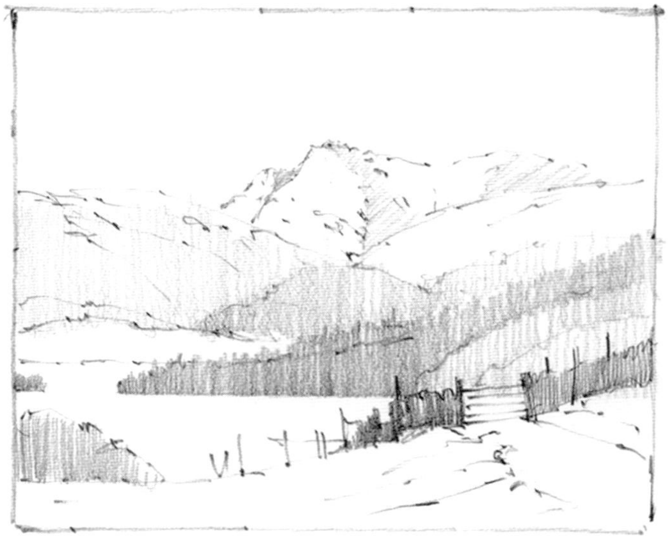

A cold winter's day and I was walking round Elterwater. As usual, the sketchbook was in my rucksack but it took determination to take it out, sit in the snow and make my drawing. Later in the studio, I took out the book and examined my sketch. Something was lacking. As a picture it just didn't work.
Placing another piece of paper on the drawing board, I began to re-work the drawing (all the time remembering that as I was *making* a painting, I was free to make any alterations the sketch needed). The painting was the important thing.
Eventually I added (purely from my imagination) a stone wall and a gate in the foreground.

Now it worked!

This painting became a Limited Edition print and sold extremely well. However, what really amused me, was the number of people who looked at it and said -

"I've walked through that gate many times.
I can't believe that you've actually painted it!"

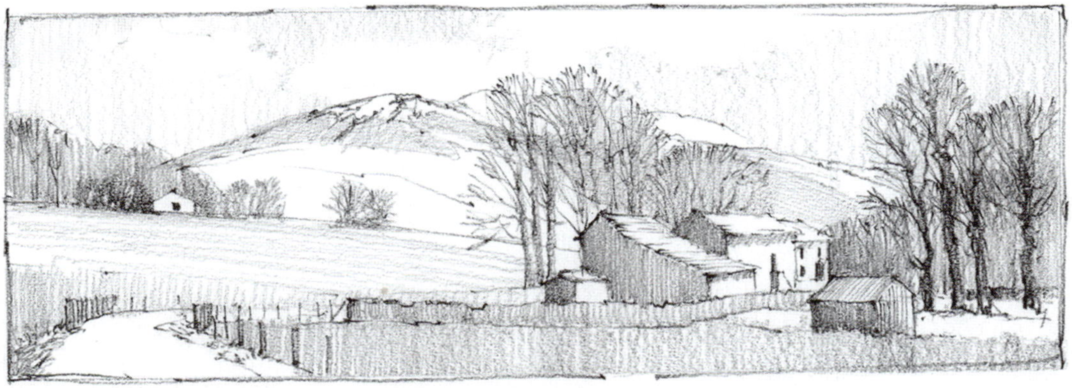

View Towards Blencathra

The drawing looked good but it was only when I started the painting that I decided to move things round a bit. I think it makes a better painting.

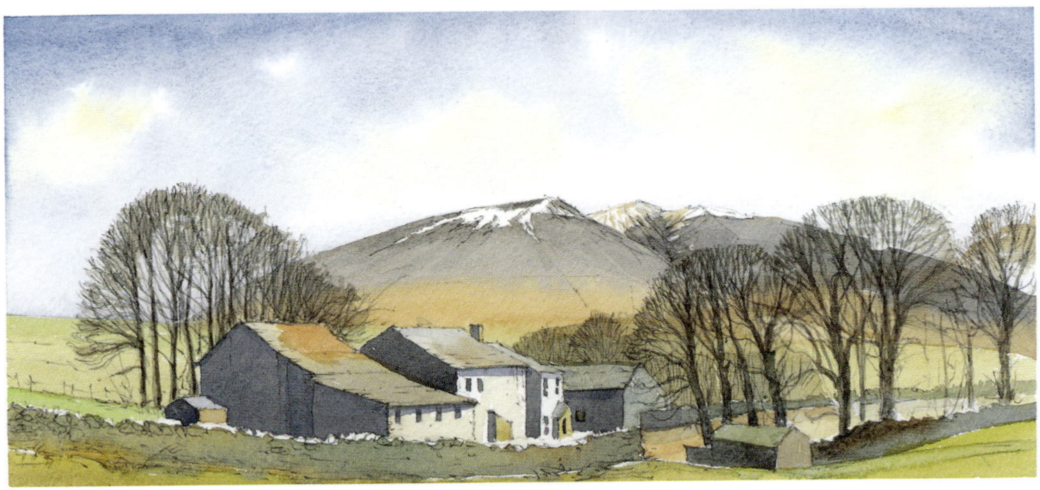

Snow on Blencathra

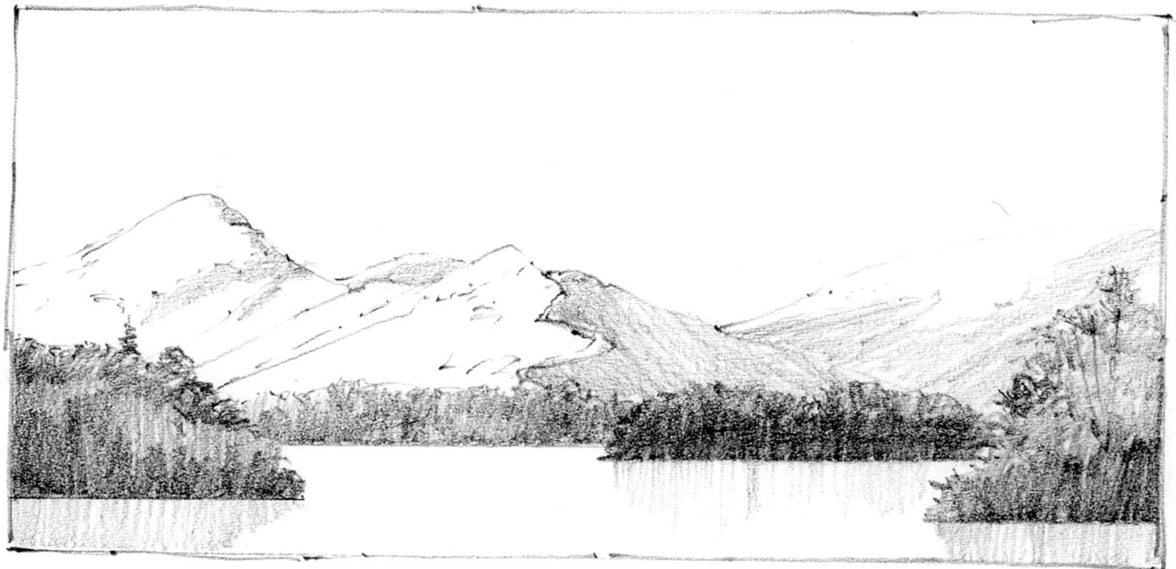

Catbells in winter.

Most people who stay in Keswick will visit Friars Crag on Derwentwater. It is one of the most well known beauty spots of the northern lakes. Standing under the Scots Pine at the end of the crag, there is a wonderful view across Derwentwater to Catbells. For some, this will be enough and following the usual photograph, they will turn away with scarcely a second thought.

Others however, will be tempted to cross the lake and make the ascent. It is not difficult. There are always many other people doing it so you cannot get lost. Age does not matter. From children riding in back packs carried by their fathers, to geriatrics with sticks making their slow way to the top, all will find it a most rewarding experience. The effort is sufficent to give people a sense of achievement and the views from the top are magnificent.

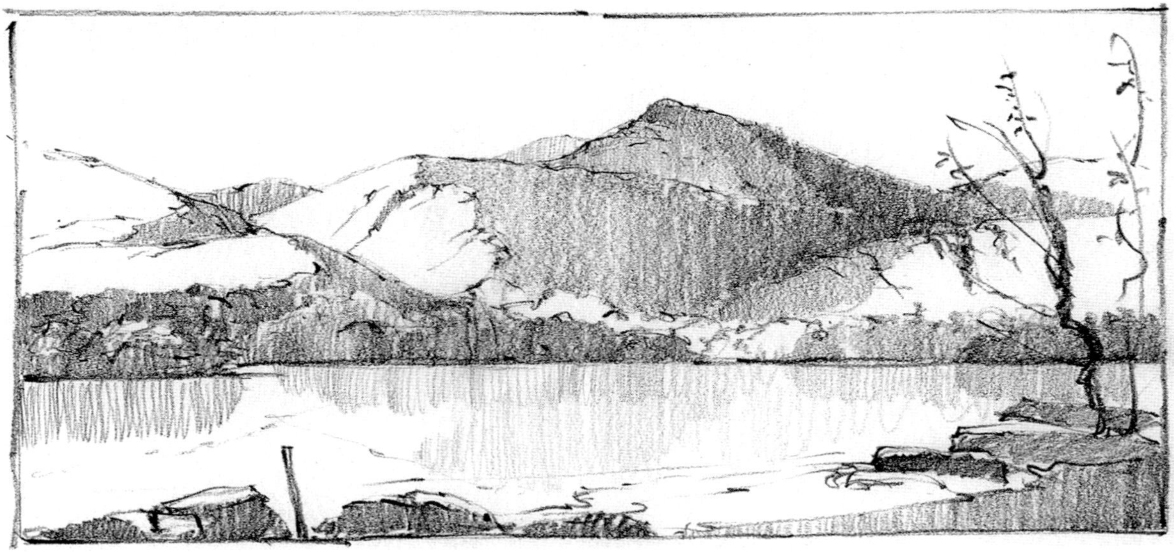

Causey Pike over Derwentwater

To the right of Catbells is the distinctive shape of Causey Pike. One fine winters day my son said *"What about doing Causey?"* The ascent was not difficult until the last twenty feet when the rock gets almost vertical. On this particular day it was coated with ice. Reaching the summit we stopped to have a drink and take photographs. The walk continued downhill across wonderful powder snow to the valley below Barrow and then back to the car. A remarkable day.
The following year we did it again and this time had the unforgettable experience of seeing something I had read about but never seen -

the *"Spectre of the Brocken"*.

My son tried to photograph it but unfortunately the results were not as spectacular as the original. Never-the-less another fantastic day on Causey Pike.

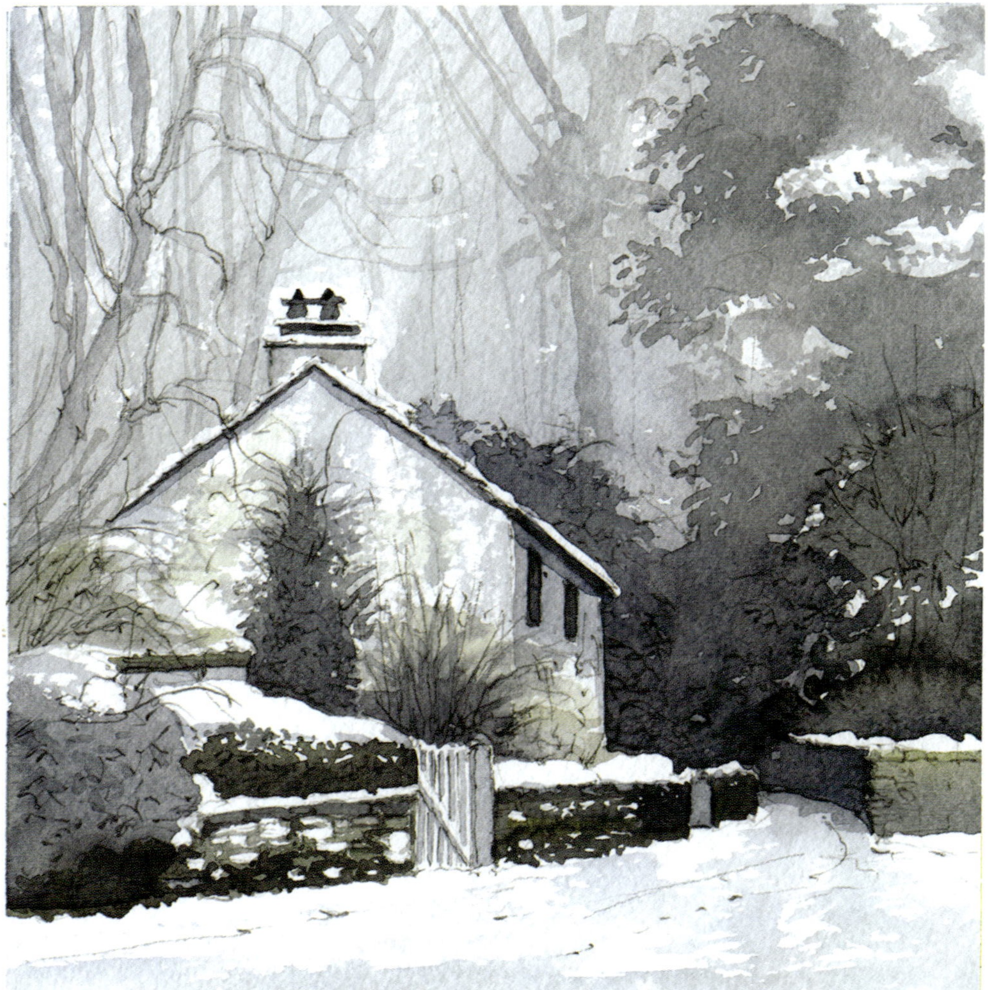

Dove Cottage in Winter.

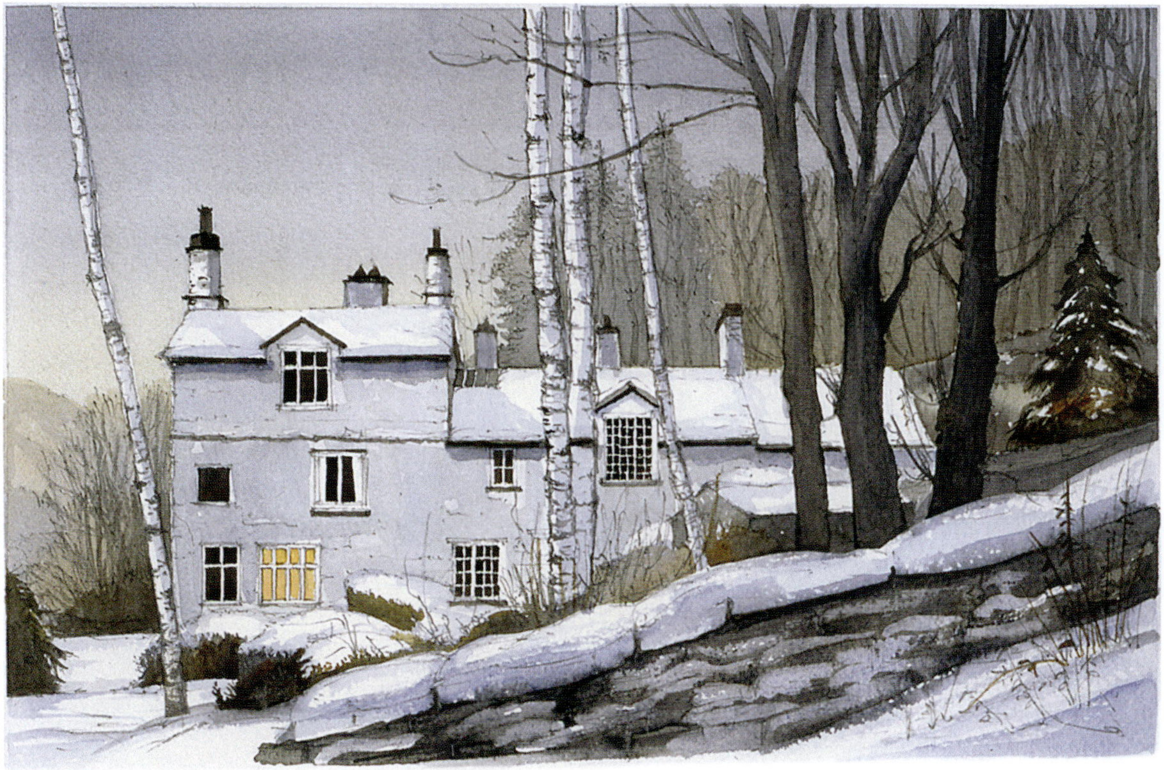

Snow on Rydal Mount.

During a winter break at the Red Lion in Grasmere, we awakened one morning to find a great stillness had settled upon the land. Pulling back the curtains, I discovered that in the middle of the night, six inches of snow had fallen. The moment breakfast was over I grabbed the camera and set out to take photographs before the snow melted (it was much too cold for a sketch book). Later, in the warmth of the studio, these photographs developed into paintings.

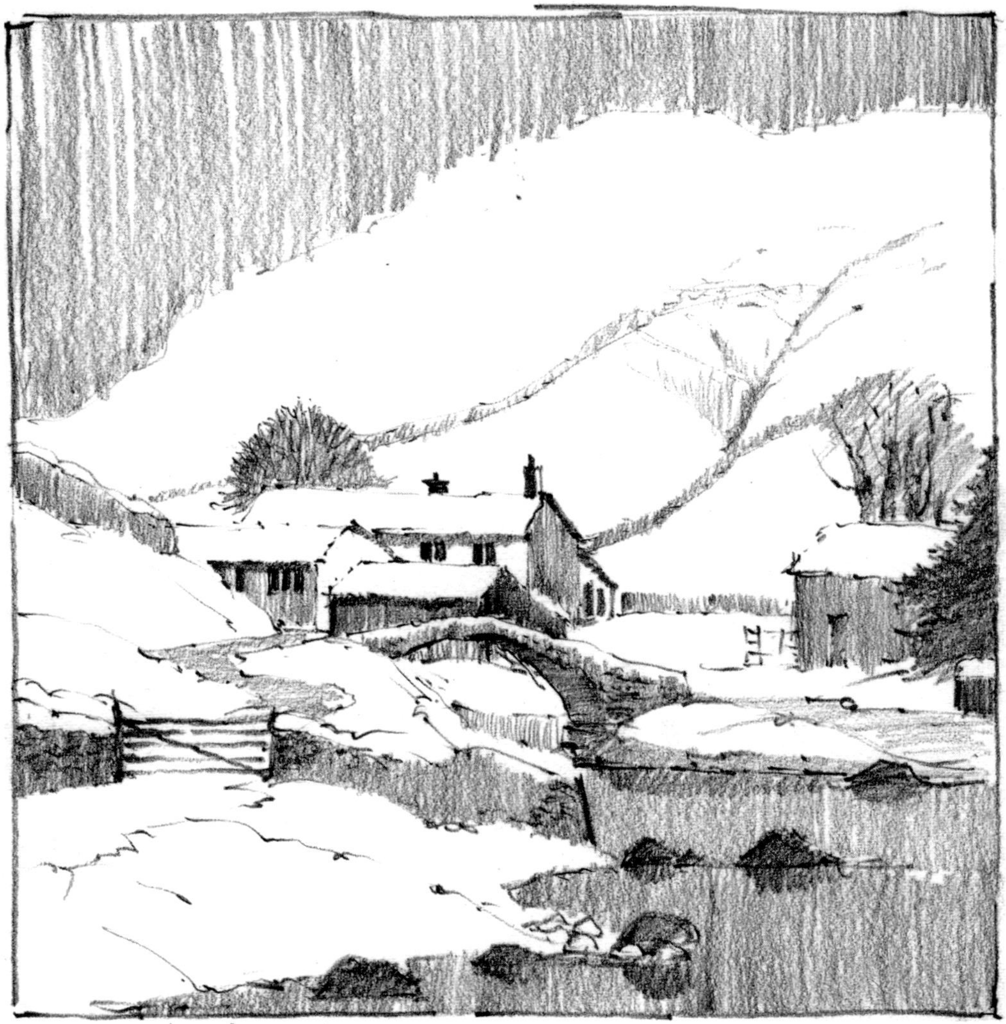

Watendlath in winter

It was the second week in January. My son and I decided to walk from Stonethwaite in Borrowdale to Watendlath. On the ground, the snow was deep with an icy crust on top. Leaving the car near Grange we passed a Lakes Warden who asked: *"Where are you going lads?"* When we answered he said *"Take care, it's minus five degrees up there!"*

A deep cushion of snow covered everything as we walked through the wood and started uphill. Not a sound could be heard. Even the birds were silent. It is not a long walk but in deep snow, hard work. There is often no indication of what is lying under the snow. We took it in turns to lead.

Eventually we reached the top and could look down on the tiny hamlet of Watendlath, crouching in a hollow in the hills. The nearby tarn was frozen over, all but for one small patch, which the ducks seemed to have kept free of ice. No sound could be heard. Not one person could be seen. Even the chimneys did not appear to have smoke coming from them. The whole scene looked deserted.

Sitting down in the snow behind a wall to shelter from the wind, we stopped for a snack and a warm drink. However deserted the scene appeared, it did not take long for the Chaffinches to find us. Soon they were almost eating out of our hands. No place to sketch! Grab the camera; take the photo and head back to the car.

Going downhill we met another man plodding up. We stopped to pass the time of day, as walkers do. *"I have been following your footprints."* he said *"I knew I'd be alright as two silly beggars had been up here before me!!"*

Downhill. Into the car. A quick cup of hot coffee and away home.

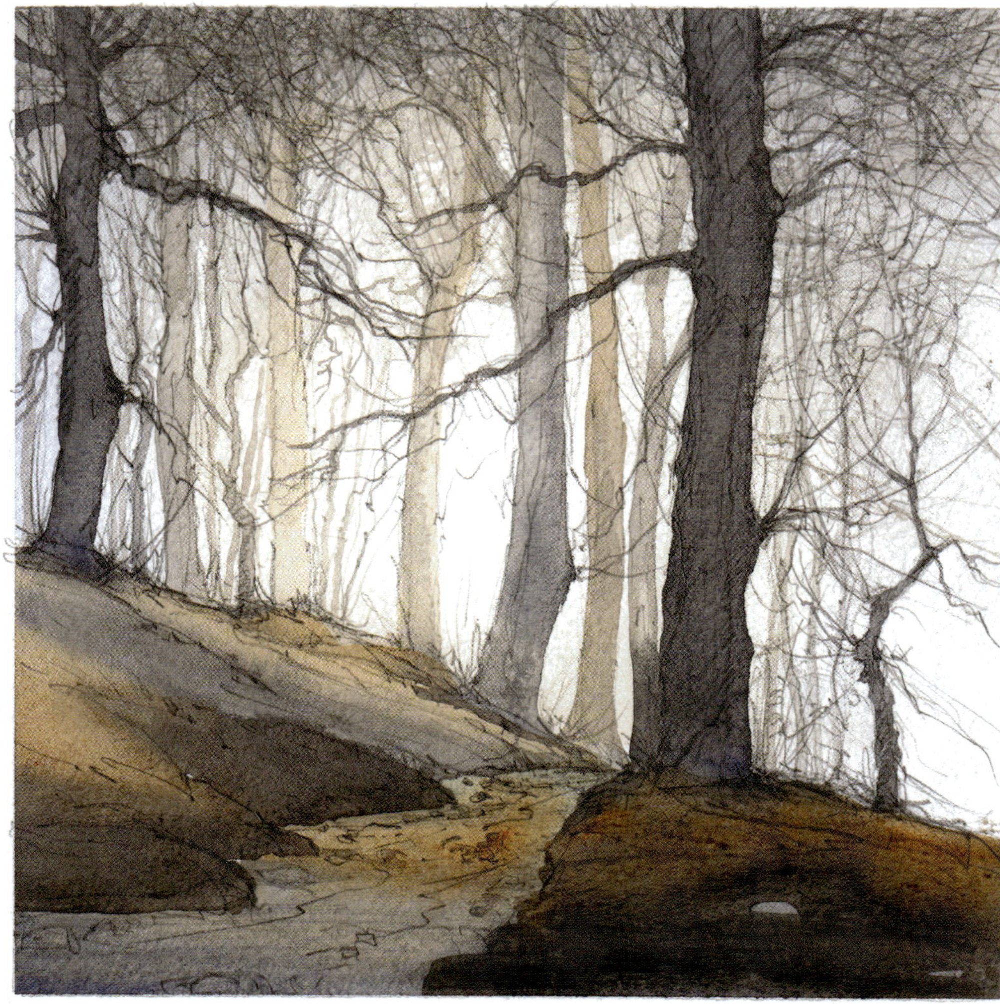

Winter

Trees In Winter

Do they know me?
Are they aware of me?
They stand there, tall and silent,
Two hundred years of history locked within their gnarled trunks.
Are they aware of me?

The path threads silently between them.
Do my footsteps fall upon deaf ears
Or are they listening?
Marking my presence.
Are they aware of me?

Do they know the pleasure they have given me?
The sight of their silent presence in Autumn
Standing knee deep in leaves of glorious burnt sienna.
Then the explosion of green in Spring.
Their flowers small, shy, insignificant.
Are they aware of me?

The world without them would be unthinkable
Like a song unfinished
Or an uncompleted poem of love.
A portrait without a face.
Are they aware of how much they mean to me?
Are they aware of me?

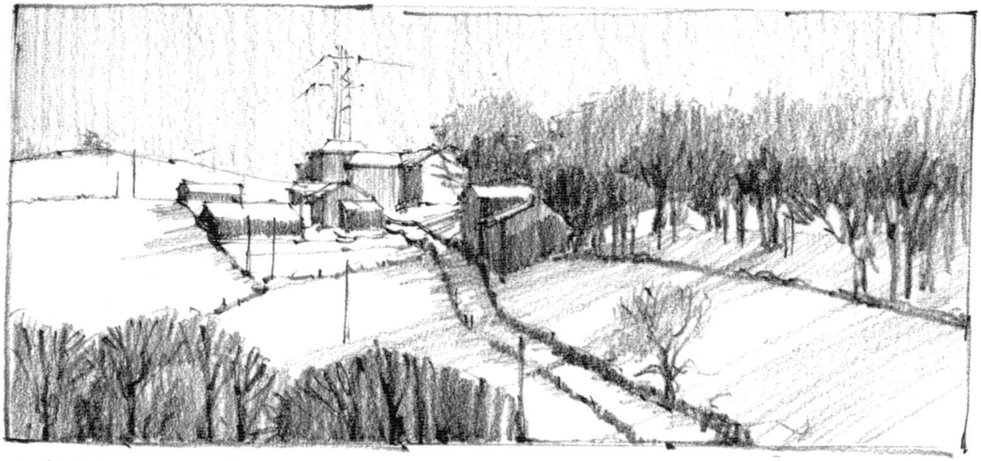

Winter Landscape - Ripponden

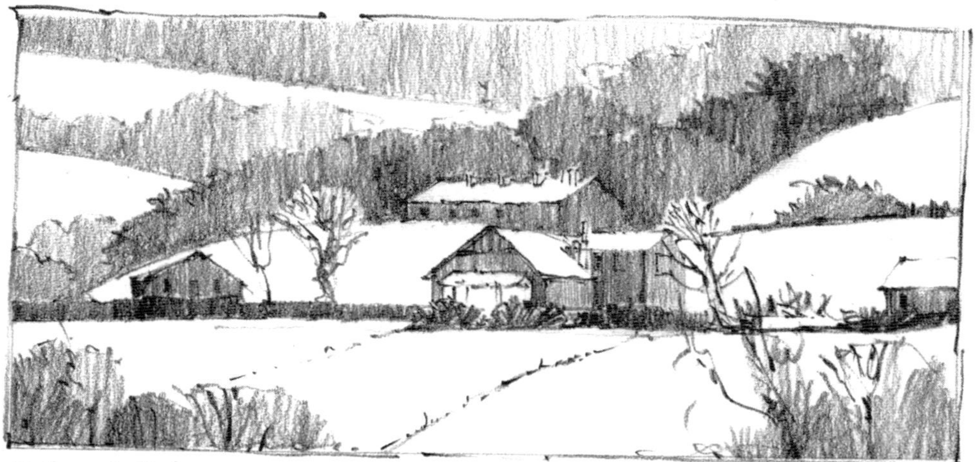

Winter in Ripponden - View from my window.

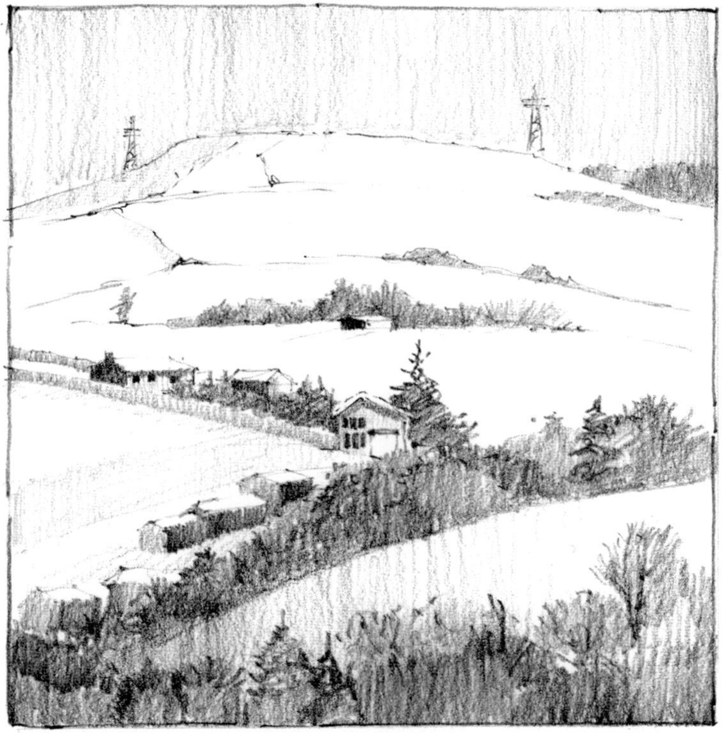

Sunshine, Snow + Shadows, Ripponden

It was the worst winter for years. The gritters had forgotten the street outside my cottage. Getting the car out over the ice was impossible, so I decided to stay at home. Looking out of the bedroom window was like looking at an alpine scene. Blue sky, white snow and bright sunshine over everything. There was only one thing to do - grab the sketch book, sharpen a couple of pencils and draw. It made a pleasant change to sit in a nice warm room and sketch the view whilst listening to Classic FM. To back up the drawing I also took three photographs. A successful morning. Three drawings which later became three paintings. That does not often happen.

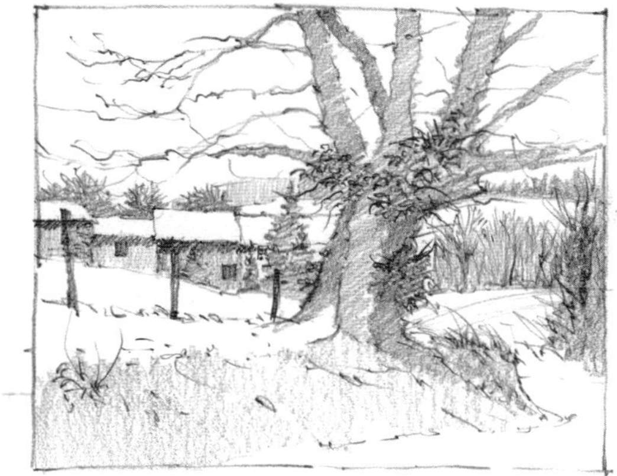

Winters Day at High Wray

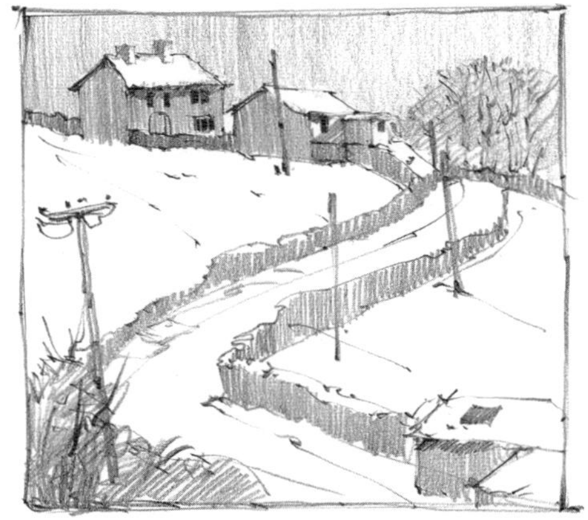

Snow in Lothersdale

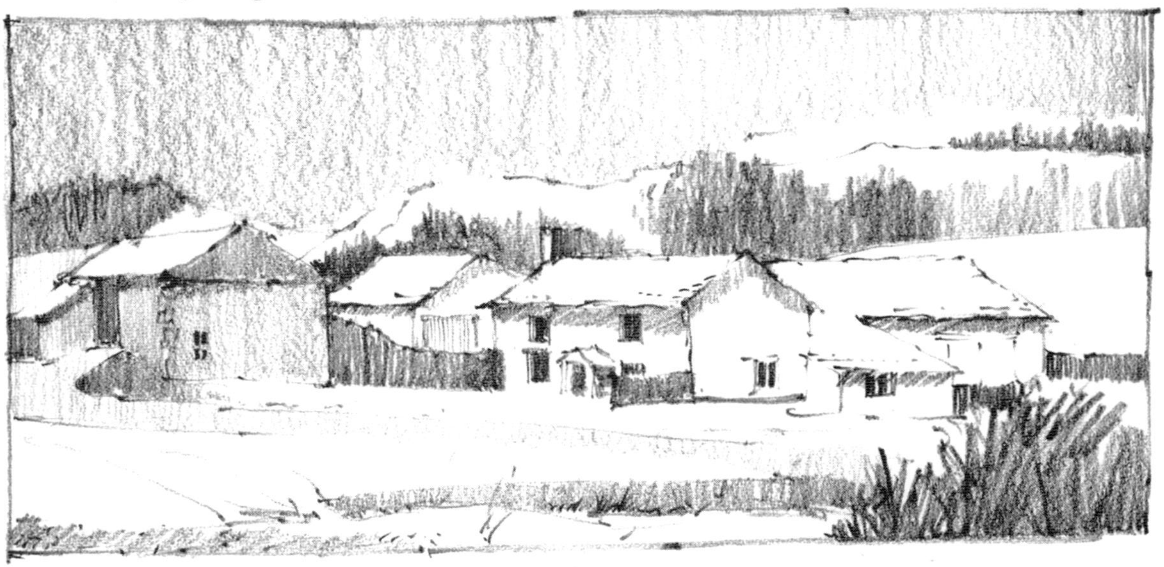

Winter Above Grasmere

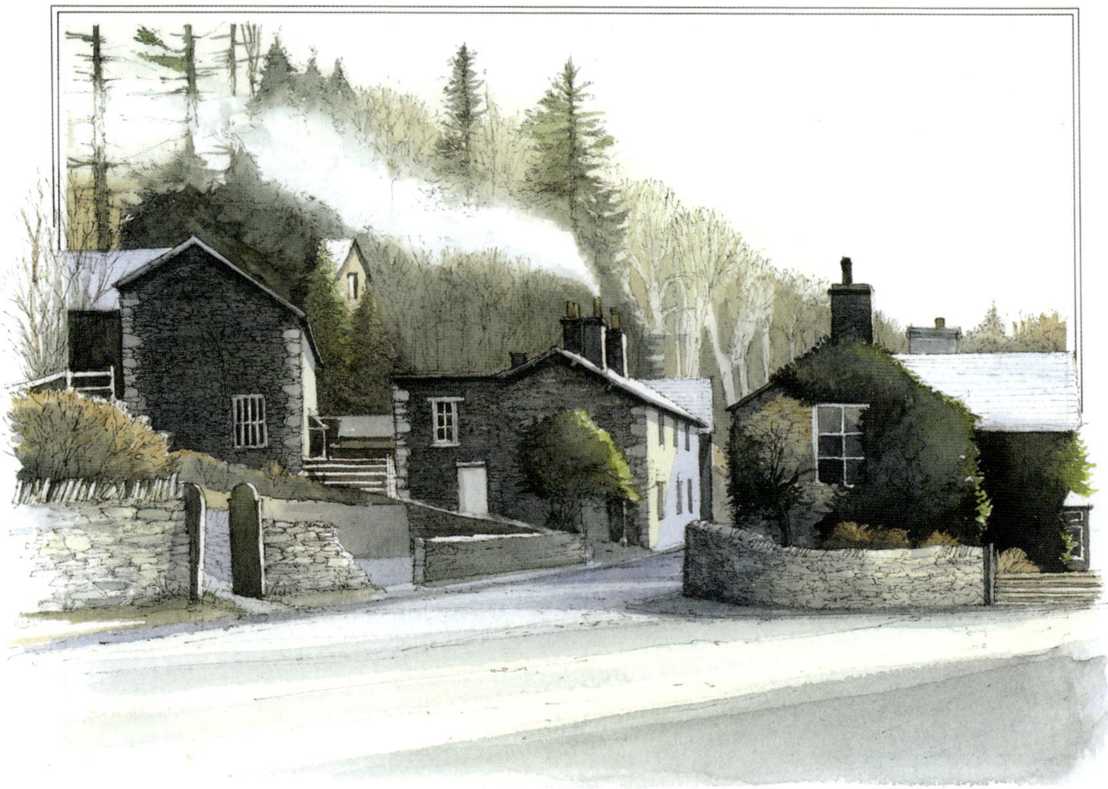

Winter Morning (Townend Grasmere)

Some time ago, before the building of the impressive Wordsworth Museum, we were motoring down Dunmail Raise from Keswick, when I saw this view. Quickly stopping the car I grabbed the camera and took a photograph. Later in the studio I worked the photograph up into a drawing, which eventually became this painting and one of our more successful prints.

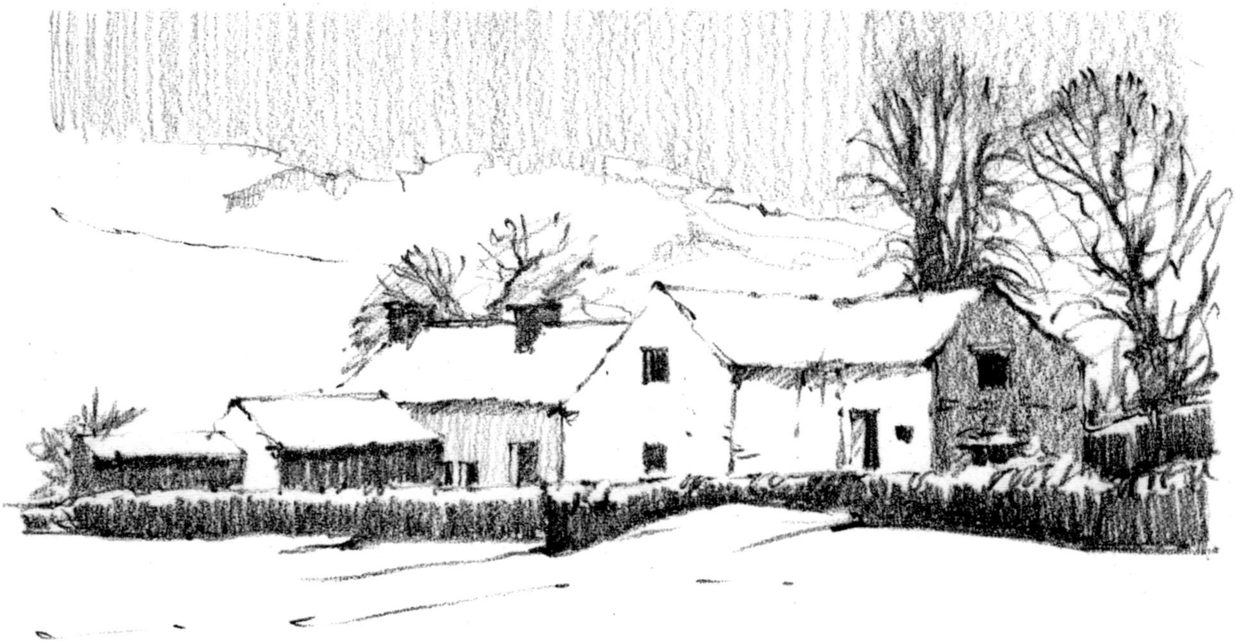

A Winter's Day - Dockray.

Spending a winter break at "The Royal" in Dockray, we had been blessed with good weather. Clear blue skies with a crisp cold wind, making drawing from the car a good idea. On our third day we wakened to that strange silence which could only mean one thing - SNOW. As it was not possible to get the car out, I left Pauline in the warmth of the hotel and went out to make a sketch. This was the result and it actually made a good painting.

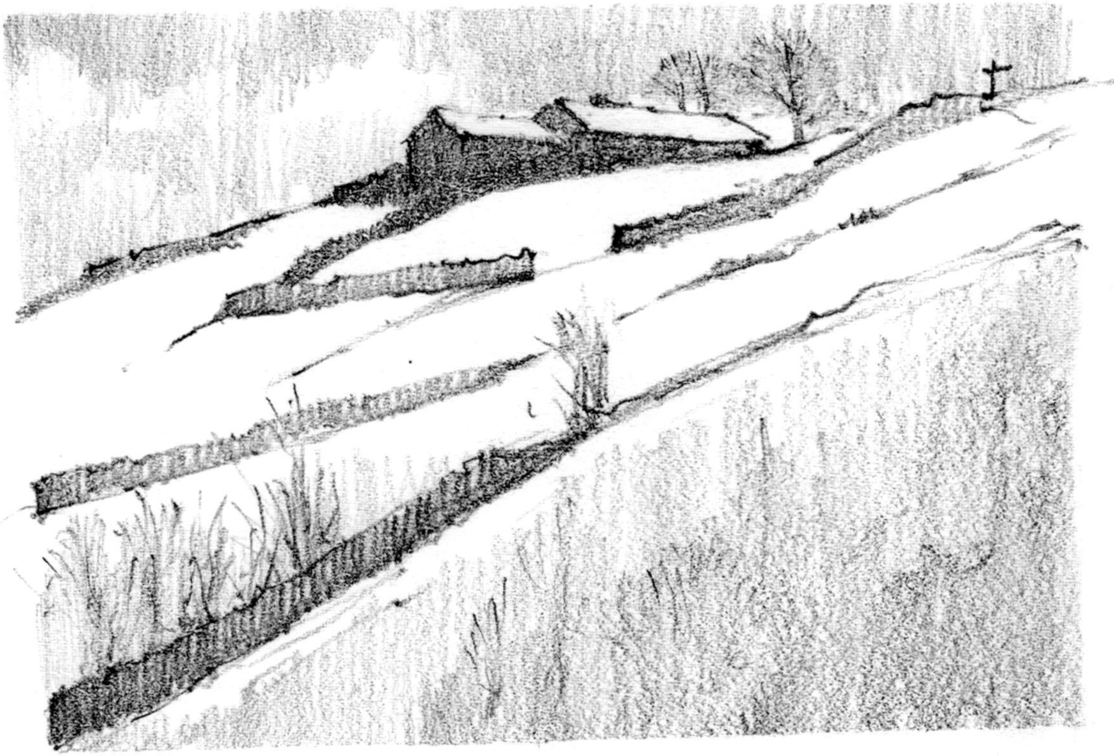

Up Hill to Moorend Farm in the snow.

One of my favourite places. Most visits had been in summer, but it was in winter that I realised just how difficult it would be to farm these limestone uplands. The old farm seemed to crouch for shelter, hugging the ground to escape from the freezing wind. Impossible to sketch in these conditions, so out with the trusty camera and then quickly uphill to generate some body heat.

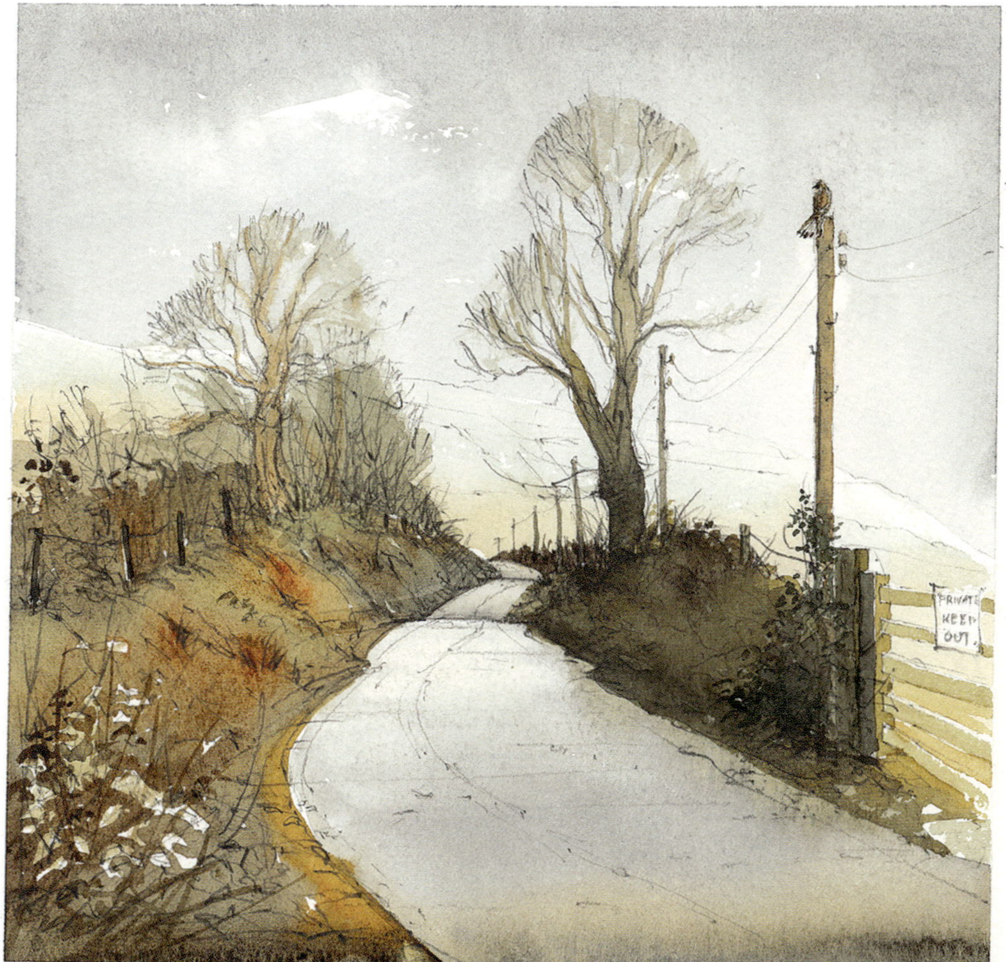

Brief encounter.

A Brief Encounter

The sun had tried - but not really succeeded.
All day it's anaemic light
Had filtered through a pale sky,
Scarcely lifting the temperature.
Now evening was approaching.

My pace quickened as I thought of the car and coffee.
For the greater part of the day,
Only movement had kept me warm.
Sketching had been something of a penance,
To be hurriedly completed before fingers became numb.

By the church, I chose the road to the left as being the most interesting.
It twisted into the distance
Between marching ranks of telephone poles.
As I walked, I felt the watchers eyes upon me,
Following my each and every movement.

On the top of the pole sat the Kestrel.
Its back towards me.
Its head turned so that the beautiful eyes could see me better.
It watched my approach.
I felt compelled to offer a greeting - *"Hello there"*!

And so we progressed, the Kestrel and I,
Pole by pole, he waiting until the last minute
Before launching himself in a downward trajectory.
Then, lifting with scarcely a wing beat,
To settle on the next pole.

All the time aware of me - those beautiful watching eyes,
Until, after the sixth pole,
At the lowest point of his dive, with hardly a movement of his wings,
He lifted over the wall and disappeared - forever,
Leaving behind a memory that would last - forever.

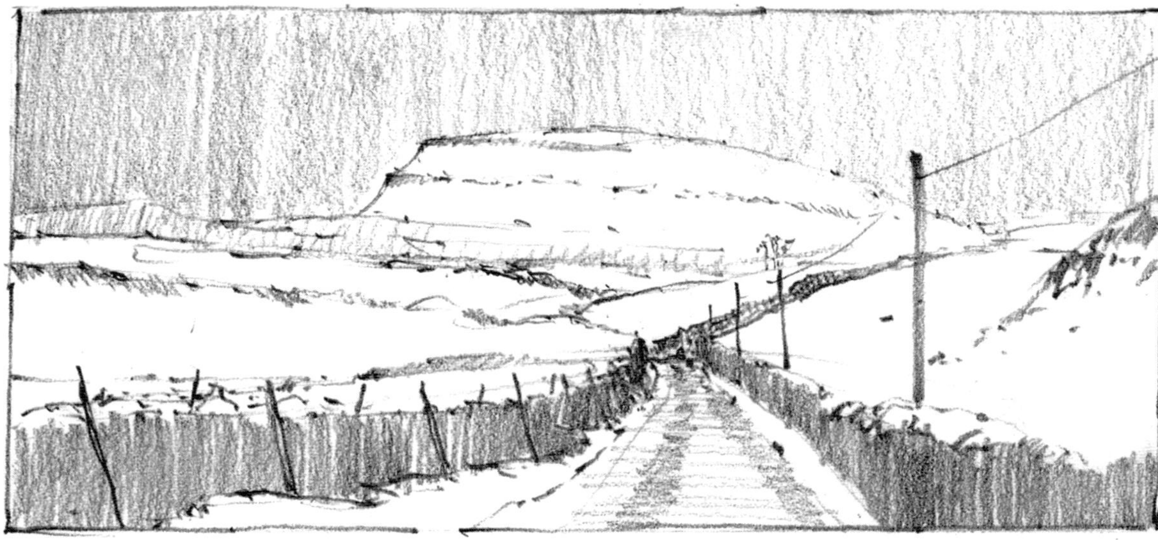

Penyghent Under Snow.

Penyghent is my favourite hill in the Yorkshire Dales. To reach the summit there are two good ways and one very boring way. My preferred routes are either from Dale Head and the keepers cottage or Horton-in-Ribblesdale to Brackenbottom joining the Dale Head route at the double stile. They way I would never recommend is up the long lane passing Hull Pot and Hunt Pot, best to keep this for coming down. The drawing opposite was done on a winters day when it was obvious that the weather was deteriorating. Above Brackenbottom the wind became gale force. Overhead the sky was getting darker still. Sheltering behind the wall before the last climb, I stopped to make this sketch. I then made the sensible decision and turned back!

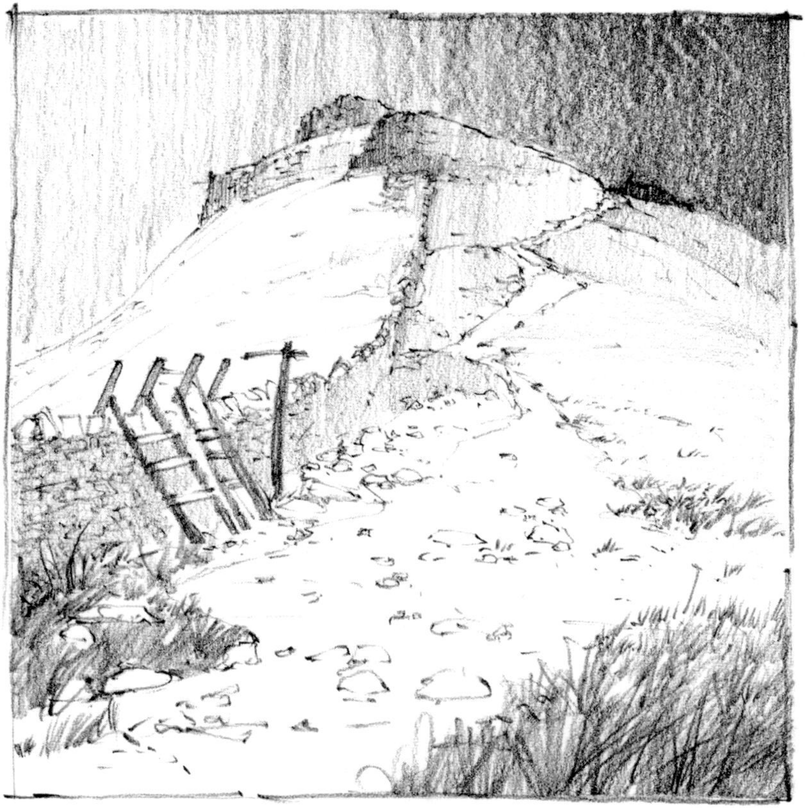

Penyghent at the junction of the paths from Brackenbottom and Dalehead. This time I walked up from Horton via Brackenbottom. Rest here to make a sketch and have a drink before bad weather made me retreat.

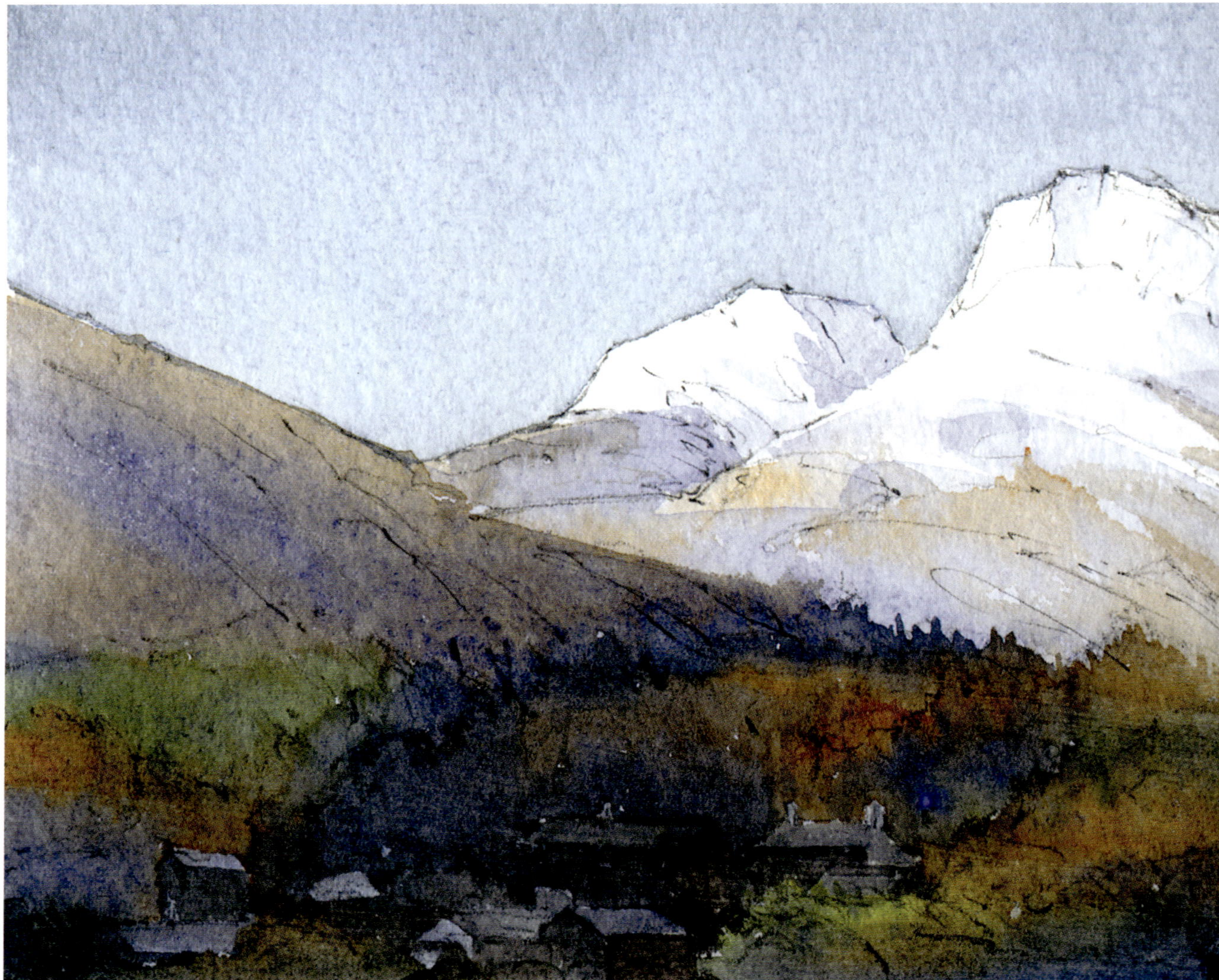

The Langdale P

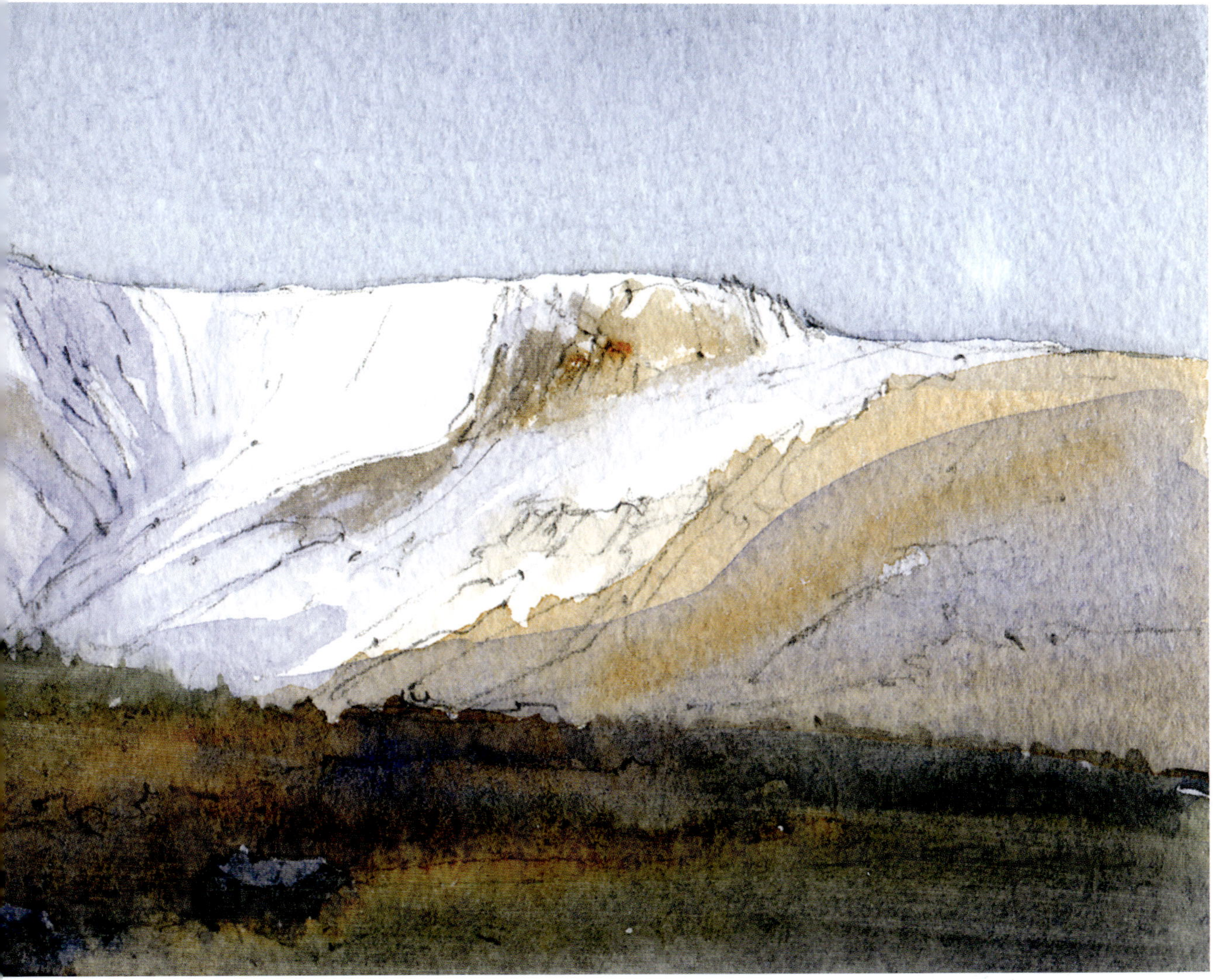

i Winter.

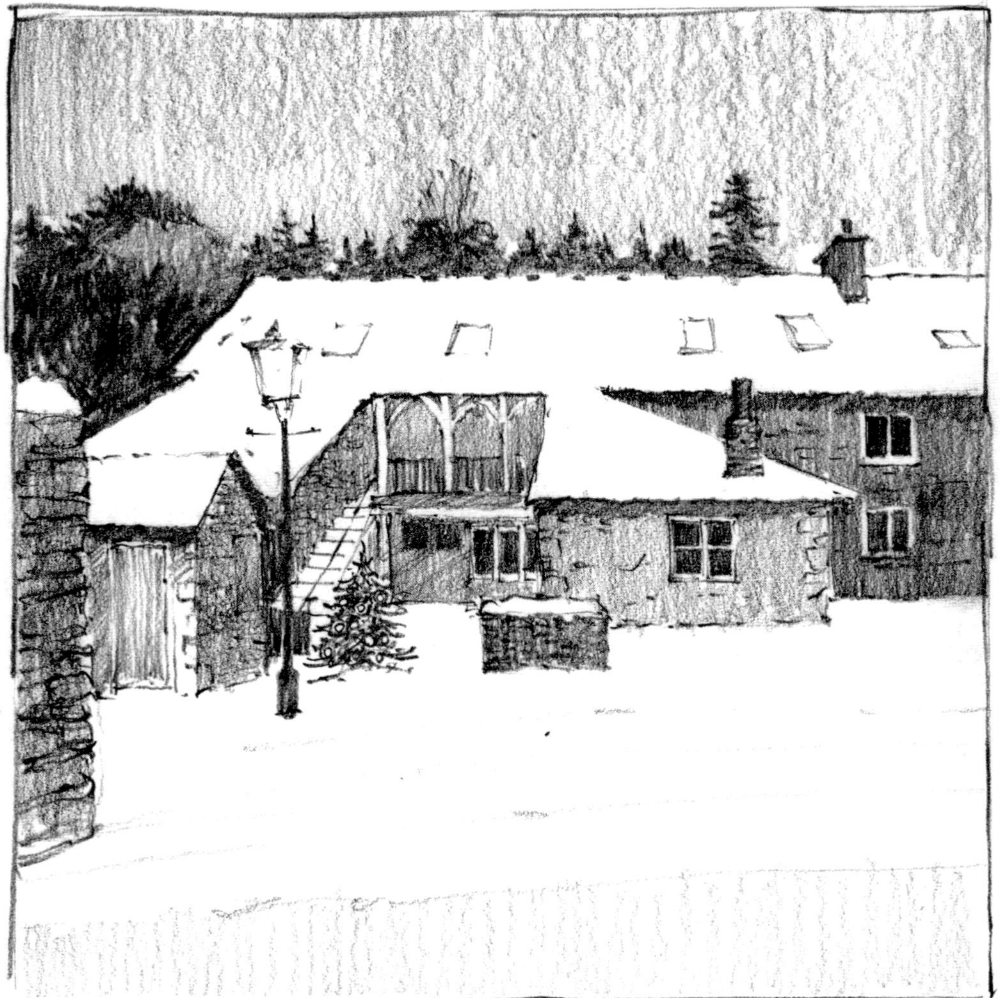

Heavy Snow in Lakeland.

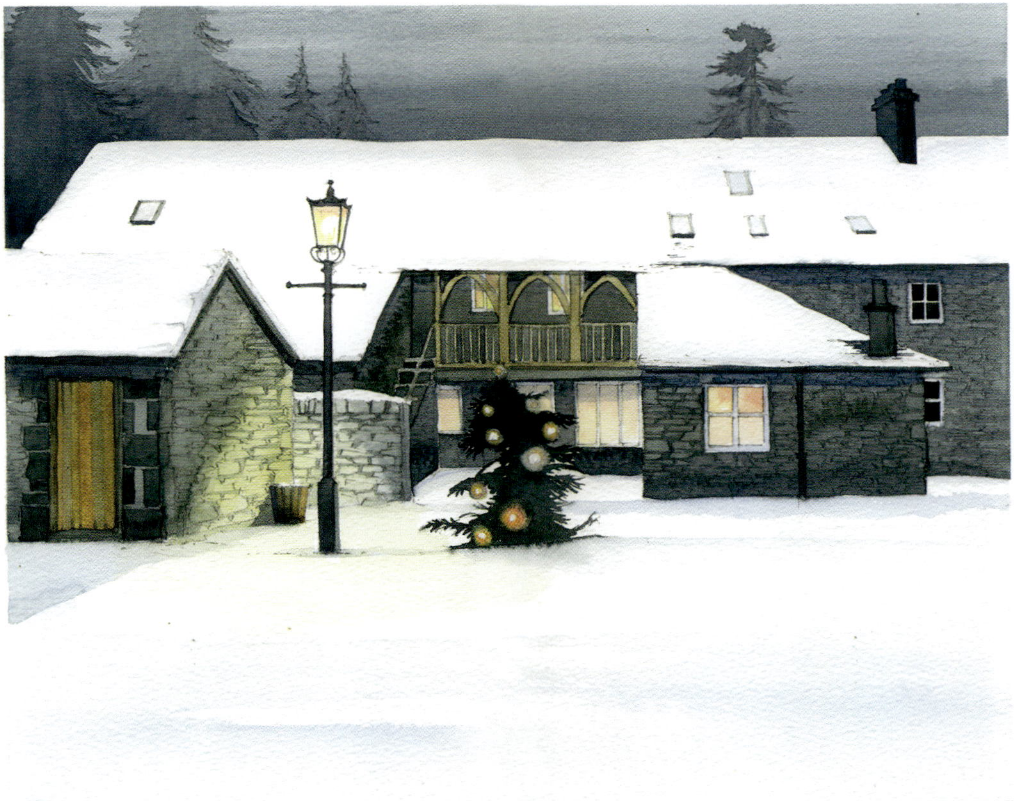

Christmas at Graythwaite

Darkness falls and the lights outside the cottages come on, adding to the feeling of what a real Christmas should look like. Quickly picking up the camera, I went outside and took several photographs. Later in the warmth of the studio, they would be worked up into the drawing opposite and the painting above.

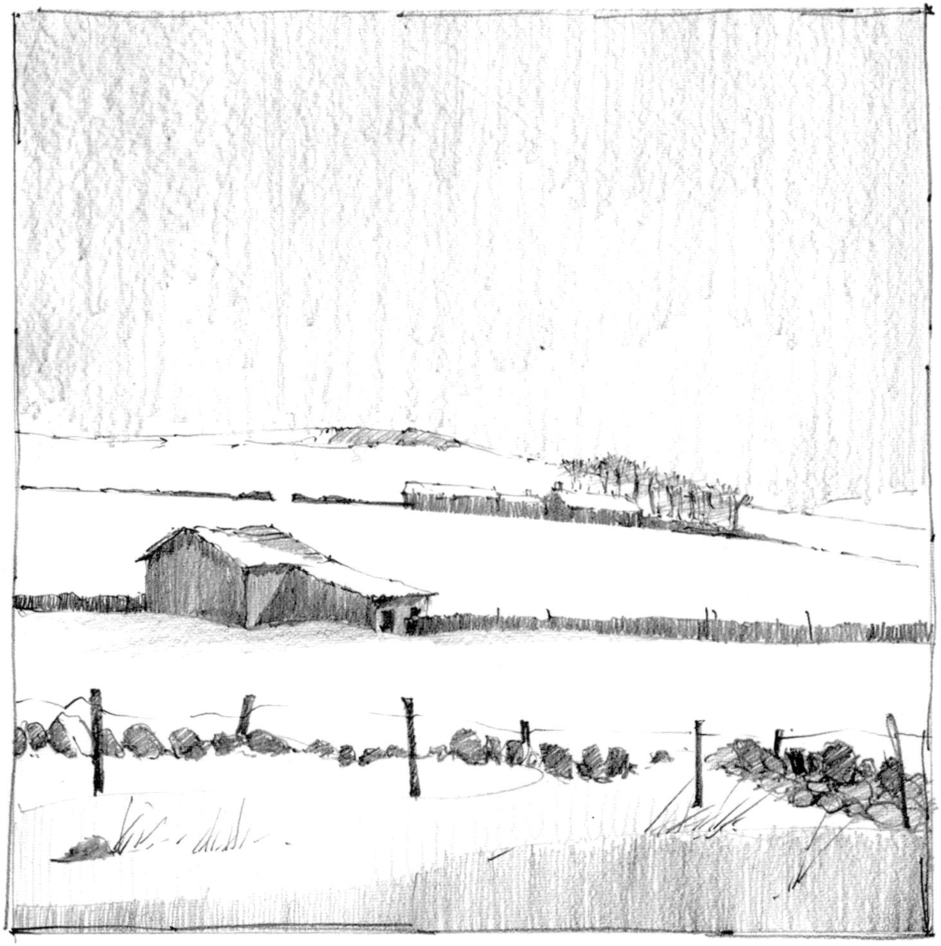

Ground hard, frozen,
Breath smoking on the still, cold air.
Nature silent, waiting.

Once again I have come to the end of, what for me, has been another mammoth undertaking. However, through all the difficulties, it has been a process of great nostalgia. Looking back through almost thirty years of sketch books has been a rewarding experience. The drawings I did all those years ago, have brought back memories of the events described as if they had happened last week. Wonderful memories of walks in the Yorkshire Dales, the Lake District and Scotland. Of walking with friends and the conversations we had. The jokes we told and the laughter which often took over and made the walking so much more fun. The end of many days on the hills when healthily tired, I returned to the car with my mind bursting with ideas for more paintings.

My sketch books contain more than just drawings. They have taken on the nature of a journal describing my walks; the wild life; the state of the weather and the way I was feeling at the time. Once again I have realised how important is the sketch book to an artist. Often, when sitting at the drawing board desperately searching for an idea, I have only to look through my sketch books to find all the inspiration I need. I have never been a great believer in the philosophy of *"doing it out of my head"*. This only works if you have put something there in the first place. Sitting with the sketch book - examining the landscape - making your drawing - this is putting information into your brain which, sometime in the future, may make a painting.

If you have read through this book, you will realise that I often repeat my favourite walks. I make no excuse for this. Each time I complete a walk, I see something new. Something remarkable which often makes me think *"Why didn't I see this before?"*

This book records what, for me, became many *"glorious hours"* which have made my life so happy and satisfying. Working my way through all those sketch books and selecting my favourite images has been very difficult (I would really like to have included many more.) However the task has been made much easier by the help I have received from my son Andrew. As one who is "computer illiterate" I have watched in amazement the skill with which he has taken my scribblings and often very old and dog-eared drawings and made from them something which is so professional.

Without him, this book would not have been written.

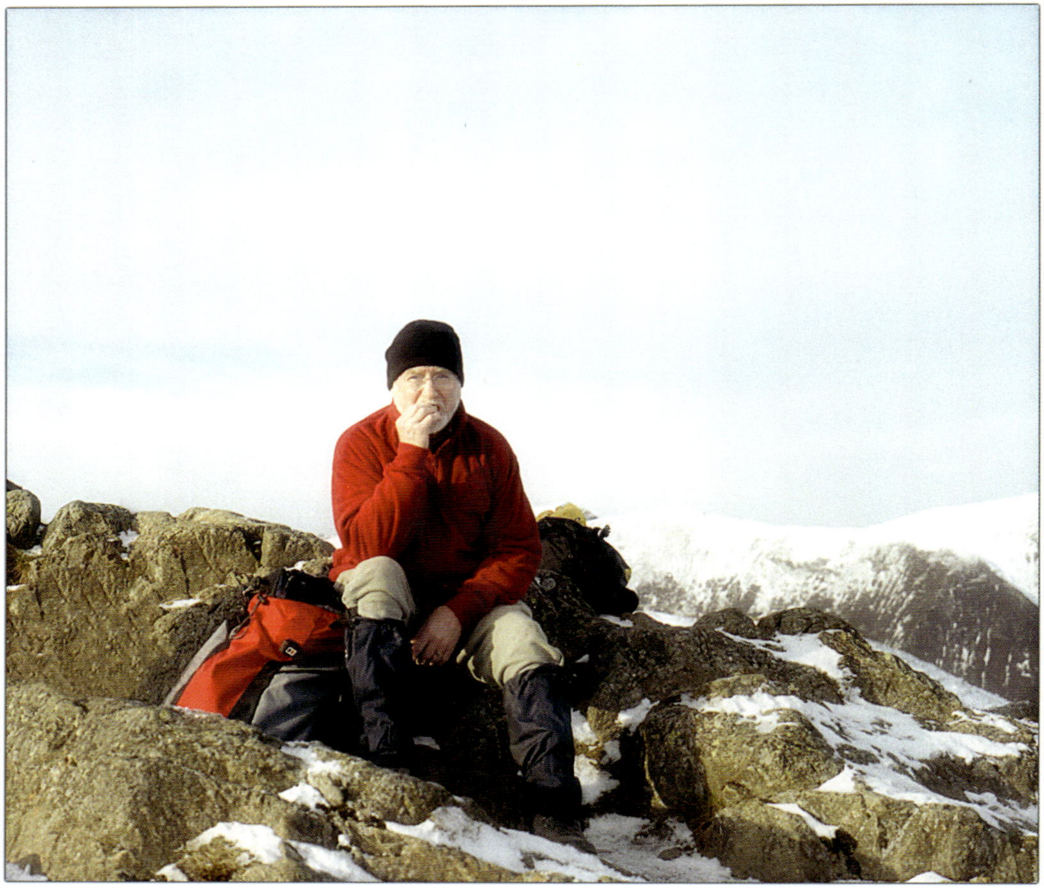

Winter on Causey Pike

"One crowded hour of glorious life
Is worth an age without a name."

Thomas Osbert Mordaunt
1730 - 1809

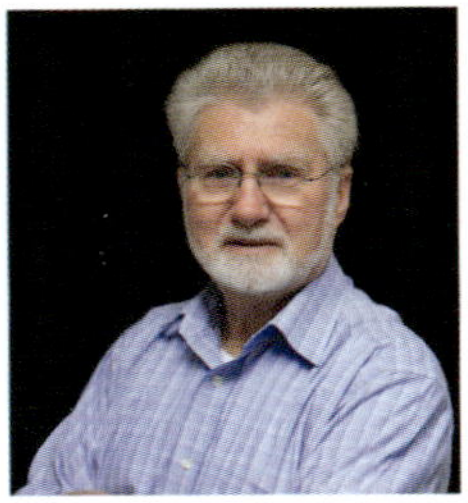

Geoffrey Cowton was born and educated in Bradford. From his first day at school he showed an interest in drawing and painting. Any day in which art and craft appeared on the timetable was a good day.

School was followed by two years in the Royal Air Force, where his artistic ability was once more put to good use. He was given the job of providing many squadrons in Bomber Command with painted crests to hang in their respective head quarters. His training continued at St John's College, York, which led to teaching art in schools in Bradford and Halifax.

A further year was taken learning print making at Leeds College of Art and it was this that provided the impetus to set up Glendale Studio with his wife Pauline. Here he was able to specialise in etching and painting in water colours.

Now digital printing has arrived and this allows his son Andrew to produce all Glendale's prints and also print for other artists.

Discovering the Yorkshire Dales, at the age of fourteen,was an important event in Geoffrey Cowton's life. From that time on he became an ardent fell walker, spending many happy days walking the hills of Yorkshire and the Lake District. His training as a teacher of Art saw him always equipped with sketch book and camera, to record the scenes which he loved so much.

This book contains many drawings and paintings selected from an output extending over sixty years. Each double page spread is complete in itself. This enables you to open the book at any page and begin to read.

Unlike his first book *"Over The Hills And Far Away"* which was geographical in style, this book follows the seasons of the year. Lovers of the Dales and Lakes will find much to interest them in one painter's response to the beauty of the North Country.